VALUE PRICING

VALUE PRICING

How to Maximise Profits Through Effective Pricing Policies

Tony Fletcher and Neil Russell-Jones

KOGAN PAGE

First published in 1997

Kogan Page Limited
120 Pentonville Road
London N1 9JN

British Library Cataloguing in Publication Data
A CIP record for this book is available from the British Library.
ISBN 0 7494 2043 X

Typeset by Saxon Graphics Ltd, Derby
Printed and Bound in Great Britain by Biddles Ltd, Guildford and King's Lynn

CONTENTS

ACKNOWLEDGEMENTS

The authors would like to acknowledge the following for allowing the use of the case studies:

Andrew Cresswell, Cresswell and Co.
Tony Ferrari, Innsite
John Higham, William Levene
Graham Howe, Orange

Other examples are taken from information in the public domain, and where known, all sources are acknowledged.

In addition we are grateful for advice and suggestions from Emma Scott and Gerry Brannan.

We have used the convention of using the expression he to stand for both male and female persons. All trade marks, copyrights and brand names are acknowledged.

ABOUT THE AUTHORS

Dr Anthony Fletcher

Tony is a management consultant, has a PhD and is a member of the Chartered Institute of Marketing. He co-wrote *Marketing for Success* (Kogan Page) and *The Marketing Pocketbook* (Management Pocketbooks) with Neil Russell-Jones. He has worked as a marketing manager in both industrial markets and in consumer goods, and as a management consultant in nearly 50 countries.

He specialises in marketing, selling, pricing and other commercial issues and has worked extensively with the public sector on commercial issues, and with the United Nations on economic and strategic planning issues.

Neil Russell-Jones

Neil is a management consultant and a Chartered Banker; a member of the Strategic Planning Society and is an MBA. He has written many articles and several books including *Marketing for Success* (Kogan Page) and *The Marketing Pocketbook* (Management Pocketbooks) – both with Dr Fletcher: *The Managing Change Pocketbook* (Management Pocketbooks); and *Financial Services – 1992* (Eurostudy).

He has worked with many organisations in the UK, Europe, the Asia Pacific Region, and the Americas; particularly in the areas of distribution and channel strategy; corporate strategy; business transformation; risk; change management; and market entry studies. He is a guest lecturer on the City University Business School's Evening MBA programme, and has lectured and spoken in many countries to many organisations.

PART ONE

A BACKGROUND TO PRICING

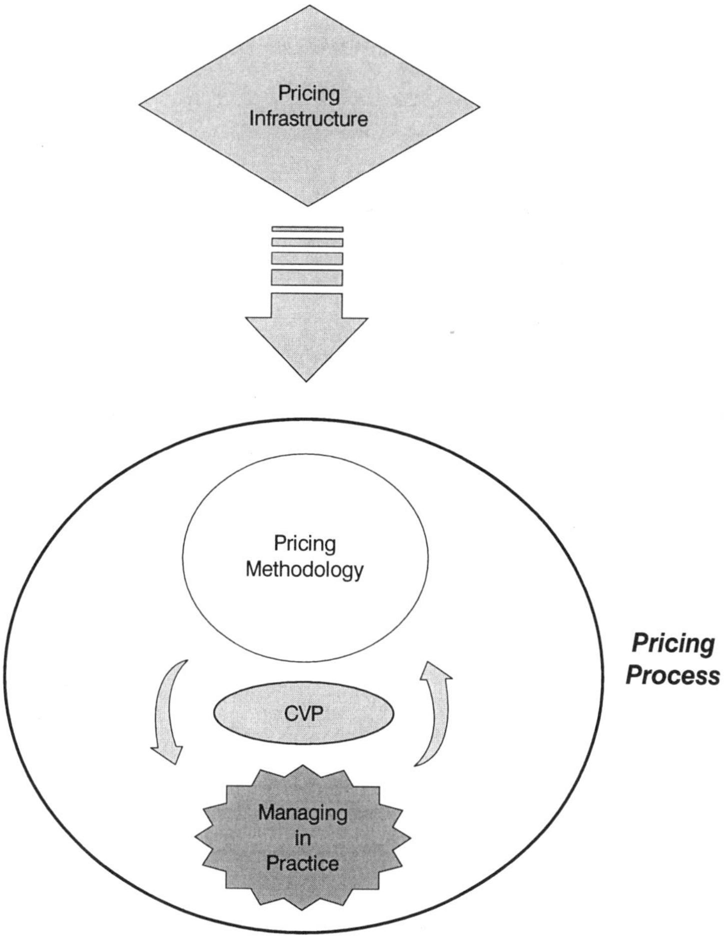

1

INTRODUCTION
What this book is about

OVERVIEW

This book is about pricing — that is the setting of a price for goods and services to be supplied to a third party. The types of organisation that set prices include:

- manufacturers;
- service providers;
- intermediaries (eg wholesalers);
- the public sector;
- retailers;

Transfer pricing also occurs between parts of an organisation and in its simplest form is merely an agreement between two individuals. Whatever the type of transaction the need to set the right price exists.

The directors of Camelot (the UK lottery), the directors of Guy's Hospital, managers at Coca-Cola and your local greengrocer all share the same thing in common: they all offer something to third parties, and they have to price their offer accordingly. Where they differ is how they go about it and what their ultimate objectives are.

This book provides a grounding in the theories that relate to pricing. This will then enable the reader to determine which method(s) or principles will be applicable to his organisation, whether he is involved in the pricing decisions or not. It lays out a pricing methodology which will enable him to establish a pricing framework and subsequently manage pricing in practice.

Structure

This book falls broadly into three sections:

- The first (Chapters 1 to 2) sets out the *introduction and background to pricing* by introducing the concepts which underpin the book and exploring pricing theory.
- The second (Chapters 3 to 5) looks at the theory of *value pricing* and includes the inputs to the pricing infrastructure and the *pricing method-*

ology. This part looks at policies and strategies as well as classic approaches to pricing
- The final section (Chapters 6 to 7) looks at *practical pricing*, including how to manage pricing on a day to day basis and contains useful tips and techniques to help.

This book is based on the authors' experience both from line management 'in the field' and from consulting in most industries and in many countries, backed up by extensive research. We use an approach known as *value pricing* to underpin the whole book.

This concept is discussed in detail in subsequent pages but is essentially the idea that a buyer's view of 'the right price' is based on his perception of the value of the offering. (Another way of looking at it is that the buyer will only assume that the price is right if it encapsulates all the benefits he wants from a product.)

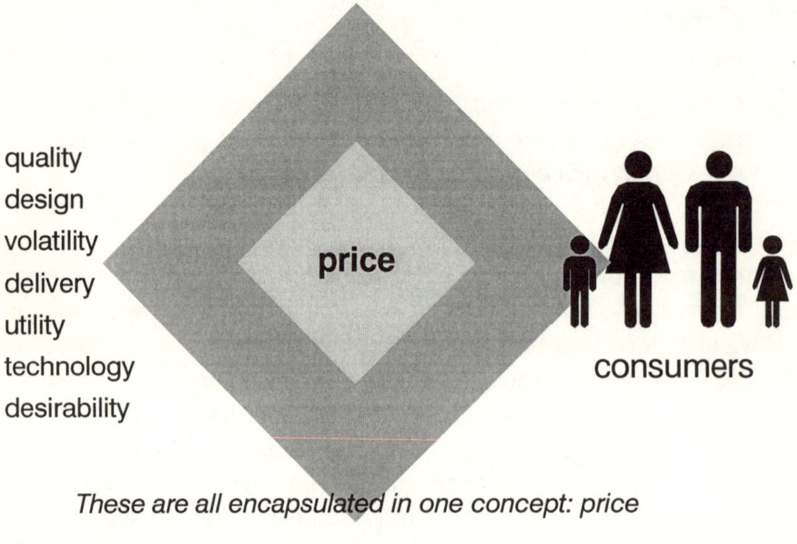

Figure 1.1 *Is the price right?*

The structure of the book reflects this approach to pricing and examines the fundamental issues, in particular:

- you must understand the *market*. This means analysing the dynamics of the markets within which you intend to operate (suppliers, buyers, competition, substitute goods etc) and how you will respond to them;

- understanding the nature of the *products or services* you intend to offer;
- the *strategy* of the organisation/enterprise must be clear, particularly with respect to the type of offerings and the positioning within the market.

Having understood the relative dynamics you will then be able to analyse the various *pricing techniques* (and there are many) to decide which will be appropriate to your organisation.

This enables you to arrive at what is known as the *customer value proposition(s)* (CVP). This is explained in greater detail subsequently in this chapter but is essentially the idea that all the benefits of your offer are embodied in a price that exactly matches the perception of the customer.

When an organisation understands the market, its own offer and consumer needs and has set a CVP then it also needs two further things to put its strategy into action: *a framework* and *good management*.

We discuss *pricing frameworks* in the middle section of this book, and we devote the last chapters to *management in practice*.

Some definitions

A variety of terms are used in this book:

- *Market* — a group of buyers and potential buyers with broadly similar characteristics, often sharing similar interests, eg everyone buys food and at that level there is a food market. Within that market there may be several sub sets, eg vegetarian, kosher, French, Chinese, fast food, food for home consumption, restaurants etc. A market may exist in physical goods, services, money or concepts and ideas; in fact for anything of value that can be traded.
- *Buyers* — those who purchase or use the offerings of a supplier in a market, to satisfy a need or want. We sometimes call these people consumers, but it is worth noting that not all buyers are the end consumers of a product, for example a newsagent buys confectionery from a wholesaler, but he does not eat his own stock!
- *Seller* — those entities that offer a product or service for consumption (purchase) in a market to meet needs or wants. Again, some sellers are also producers of the goods (think of companies like Boots or BT who produce products and services from raw materials), others simply act as agents in the marketplace and pass products or even services along.

It should be noted that without both buyers and sellers there is not a market. Markets are characterised by deals, that is to say by bargains where people swap goods and services for money (or occasionally for other goods and services).

The book refers to products, services and brands. By these is meant:

- *Product* — a manufactured item (eg a car, washing-up liquid, baked beans).
- *Service* — the supply of (usually) people-based services (eg architecture, consultancy, tax advice, travel agents, banking, flights) but also including, for example, outsourced facilities management, payroll and IT services;
- *Brands* — the actual name that an item (or group of items) is sold under (eg in the UK Coke, Pepsi and Virgin are all brands of cola; and Daz, Persil and Surf are all brands of washing powder).

Accountants and marketing people use a variety of terms to define some key financial ratios, particularly:

- The difference between the cost to deliver goods and services and the price obtained is called by several names including *margin* and *contribution*.
- There is also often confusion over the idea of *profit* and *margin*. By and large profit is what is left after all operating costs are accounted for and is less than the margin.
- The money received when goods are sold is sometimes called *revenue*, and sometimes simply *sales*. Revenue is used here.
- Similarly, people often use the terms *cost* and *price* interchangeably, depending on whether you are buying or selling. Thus they might say either 'this newspaper cost me 50p to buy' or 'the price I paid for this car was £3000'. Look for the context of the sentence for this.

In his book *Marketing Management*, Philip Kotler defines a *product* as: '*anything that can be offered to a market for attention, acquisition, use or consumption that might satisfy a want or need*' and thus includes services. Similarly where the term 'product' is used in this book it can be read to include services, for ease.

WHO SHOULD READ THIS BOOK?

This is a hard question to answer, as this book is designed for any manager that has input into the pricing process. As organisations differ in their objectives, so they differ in the way they are set up and managed and thus the extent to which pricing input permeates the organisation differs.

From the owner of a corner shop or sole trader, to the world's largest companies (eg General Motors, NTT or ICI), there is a world of difference in decision-making processes and management.

For example, in the case of very small companies, the pricing decision is normally made by one or two people, often in an informal, unstructured manner. In large firms, pricing committees often meet to determine prices, they have formal inputs, timed plans and many of the organisational overheads that typify big organisations.

However, whilst the method may be different, the basic processes are really very similar and the decision trees are identical.

This book is aimed at two types of people in the widest sense:

- those who participate in the pricing/marketing decision-making process whether directly or indirectly; and
- students of marketing and pricing.

If you are a sole trader then all of the book will be relevant to you, as you must understand all the processes and act on them.

If, however, you work in a large firm it is probable that input to the pricing process will come from many sources and decisions may subsequently be taken at higher levels in the organisation, but this does not exclude you from the need to understand what is going on.

The typical people who should read this book are those engaged at the sharp end, commercial managers, marketing people, brand managers and, of course, those in the sales force. This list is neither exhaustive nor exclusive, as people working in production, finance or operations will be expected to provide good input to marketing and pricing decisions.

Clearly students of marketing will also be particularly interested in the contents but so will anyone studying business or general management studies. This book accordingly aims to give them insight into the practical world of pricing to complement their studies.

Case studies

Illustrative case studies and examples are used to support the text, underlining key points. These are drawn from real life wherever possible to enable the reader to relate to them.

Case studies

We have asked our clients and colleagues who have been successful in pricing to help us by telling us what went on in their organisations. From a small company like Cresswell and Co. (page 141) where the pricing decisions are essentially made by one man, to Orange, (page 133) arguably the UK's most successful mobile telephone company, targeted and clear pricing strategies have helped them to achieve their success. These companies have thought long and hard about what they wanted to achieve and have been successful. The case studies have been written and authorised by the companies themselves.

Examples

These are based on the experiences of a range of real organisations, from a small IT consultancy to one of the largest suppliers to the UK National Health Service. We have used figures that are as realistic as possible and we hope that they demonstrate the kind of thought processes that managers have to consider.

SPECIFIC EXAMPLES

Examples are provided to enable readers to price products and services themselves. These take the form of worked examples based on two central themes:

- pricing a manufactured product, the Gizmo (looked at from the point of view of the manufacturer, the wholesaler and the retailer)
- pricing a service, IT consultancy as supplied by the small firm of Raymond and Partners.

The exercises illustrate the following points:

Gizmo

- *Exercise A*: This shows how to maximise revenue by plotting the demand: selling price relationship.
- *Exercise B*: This shows how to maximise margin looking at the cost of production compared to selling prices and demand.
- *Exercise C*: A decision-making matrix is shown to illustrate how you might compare competitive prices.
- *Exercise D*: This illustrates the decision-making process with a trade intermediary, and how it might arrive at a price based on supply channel considerations.
- *Exercise E*: This example illustrates target profit pricing, as applied by a retailer.

Raymond and Partners

- *Exercise A*: Illustrates cost-plus pricing as applied in a small service organisation.
- *Exercise B*: This shows market-related pricing in the context of competitive tendering.
- *Exercise C*: This example uses a market sector focus to show the development of pricing strategies for dissimilar areas.

All the examples, and the answers are be found in the final section of the book. Work through them when you have finished reading the book!

VALUE PRICING

A cynic is someone who knows the price of everything but the value of nothing.

Oscar Wilde

What Wilde meant was that there is a difference between the price at which something can be bought and the real value that people attach to it. Thus a painting by, say Goya, Van Gogh or Dali may be priced in millions of pounds and, whereas some people would buy it because they see it as an investment, others would buy it because they actually like the picture. Still others would see it as just another picture which could have been painted by anyone and therefore regard it as overpriced. *They thus perceive the 'value' differently.*

Were it not for this difference then not only would the world be a less interesting place but pricing would be much easier.

This book is so titled because it takes a specific approach to pricing. By following a robust process and taking a rigorous approach to setting and managing prices that reflect the value you are offering to your customers you should be able to beat the competition. An example of this is provided by Orange, the telecoms company, which by its imaginative use of advertising, branding and, above all, the innovative use of pricing to deliver value to customers, came from nowhere to its present position.

CUSTOMER VALUE PROPOSITION (CVP)

This term was coined in the early 1980s by Michael Lanning and Dr Lynn Phillips. The thrust of their analysis is that a customer chooses a firm over others because it offers the *greatest positive combination of end-result benefits and price* (ie the greatest '*value*') in the perception of that customer.

All organisations offer one or more CVPs. Many firms, however, are unclear as to exactly which CVP(s) they are purporting to offer to whom, and often they are successful by accident rather than design. Those firms which are consistently successful, however, have usually proactively decided on their CVPs and acted accordingly.

Where the customer chooses a firm, this is because it offers a better combination of benefits and price to that offered by competitors. Lanning and Phillips argue that successful firms are integrated around these CVPs, which drive their thinking. *This concept is fundamental to pricing.*

Getting the CVP right is the difference between success and failure. It is a truism to say that the organisation with a superior CVP will be the most successful in that field/market. In order to make them part with their money the firm must make the customer believe that there is a good reason for buying its goods/services and not another's. That is the 'value' that the customer places on your offering.

What is value?

The OED defines value as '*worth, desirability, utility*' and this is worth remembering; however, in considering the CVP there is a precise definition as follows:

- *Price* — total 'costs' to the customer — as perceived by the customer (which may not be solely in monetary terms).
- *Benefits* — the result of doing business with your organisation (ie what the customer gains).
- *Value — benefits minus price* (must be positive).

If it helps, you can think of this as an equation, which must be positive for the consumer, or you can think of it in terms of scales and balances:

Benefits v price — the trade-off

There is hardly anything in the world that some man cannot make a little worse and sell a little cheaper, and the people who consider price only are this man's lawful prey.

John Ruskin

Within this definition of what the customer perceives there is always a benefits/price trade-off to arrive at the *value*, otherwise the only successful marketing ploy would be to offer at the cheapest price. Essentially customers will either:

1) Pay you more than the competition because they believe they are getting better benefits and therefore more value from you; or
2) Take an option which offers less benefit but is at a cheaper price (therefore equalising the *benefit – price = value* equation).

The key for an organisation is to ensure that it can deliver that combination of benefits at that price which the customer is prepared to pay *profitably.*

A simple example will illustrate this. A keen gardener has the choice of two spades: a normal steel one (£20), or one made from stainless steel (£40). The latter lasts longer, stays sharper and doesn't rust (all features), so it is easier to use (benefit). The customer will choose the stainless model if 'easier to use' is perceived to be worth £20 or more. If not, he will buy the cheaper spade.

The price : value relationship

Our contention is that by concentrating on the *customer value proposition* (CVP), within which pricing is just one factor (although an important one), and using this approach to guide pricing, you can apply a different dimension to pricing decisions, and reapply traditional theories which should enable you to deliver radically better pricing decisions and thus maximise profit.

It is necessary to understand the relationship between *cost* and *benefit* (or *value*) in order to set the right *price.* Figure 1.2 compares benefit levels against the cost of delivering that level of benefit. Ideally, you should be positioned where you can deliver high benefit at a low cost. In the real world, of course, this is not always possible and, therefore, the price set must reflect the cost/benefit dynamics and strategies must be decided that reposition your offer into the right sector.

Because of the broad spread of needs and requirements there will always be a place for a whole gamut of offers, from the pile it high, sell it cheap, to opulent luxury (from a gold necklace bought from a street vendor to one from Garrards). The only real criteria for the vendor, is 'can I do this at a profit', and that question is answered by 'have I got the CVP right?'

A company consistently selling its offering at £12 when costs to deliver it are £13 will go out of business in the long term. Understanding your CVP is therefore critical when price setting.

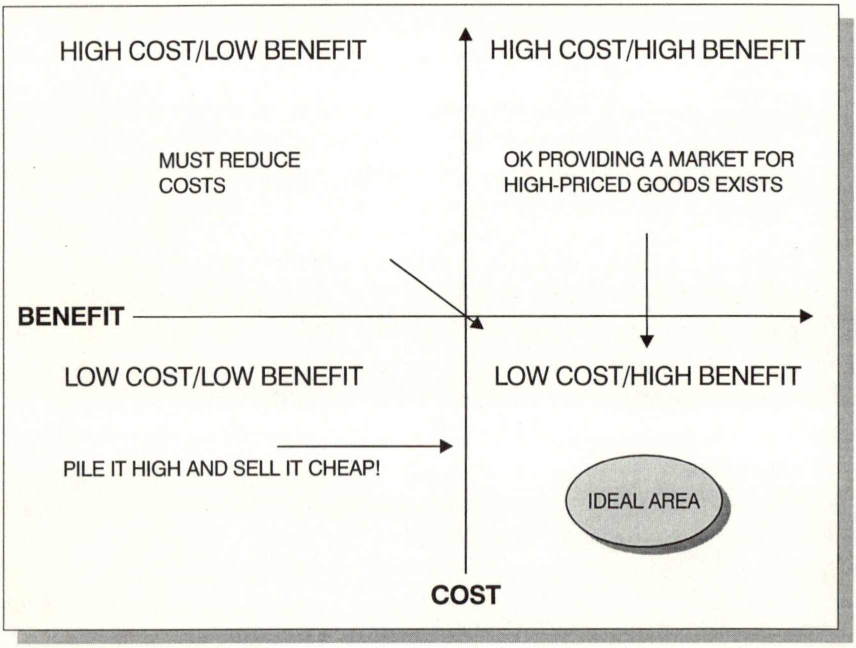

Figure 1.2 *Understanding the relationship between the costs and value of products/services enables us to categorise them*

The offer

It is necessary, therefore, to decide which CVPs you are going to offer *prior* to setting a price and also to choose to whom this CVP will be offered and, arguably more importantly, to whom it will *not* be offered (the market focus). This concept will be explored in detail in Chapter 4, but it is necessary to bear this in mind when considering what price to set and which mechanism to use, as price is only one factor in persuading the customer to buy.

A good example of the effect of different offers in the market was when General Motors (and other car manufacturers) in the USA took market share from the then dominant company, Ford, by offering many different features on cars that Ford did not offer; most famously colours apart from black!

Customers wanted these other features and therefore bought the other offerings.

WHAT IS A PRICE?

In order to further set the framework for the book it is useful to consider exactly what a price is.

A price is defined as:

- '*an amount, usually in money, for which a thing is sold or offered*'; or
- '*that which one foregoes for the sake of or in gaining something*'.

The 'thing' referred to could be a product or a service and indeed can be money itself (an interest rate is the price you pay for money). A price then is something paid for some product or service which, in the perception of the buyer (consumer), is of value. The price paid is a measure of that value and by understanding the value that consumers place on your offering you will know how to price it.

One of the key issues, however, is that not all buyers place the same value on the same offering. That is why the targeting of buyers for your offering is extremely important to ensure that the price reflects the value your targeted buyers place on the offering and therefore are willing to pay.

Why is pricing important?

Pricing is important as one of the key elements of marketing. Although it is only a part of the marketing mix it is critical in achieving desired outcomes and specific marketing objectives. Most organisations do not handle pricing at all well:

- Typically too much emphasis is placed on the cost inputs and the price set then fails to capitalise on actual demand and understanding of the real value that the purchaser places on the offering. This is demonstrated very clearly where a 'grey' market springs up in goods where the prices are much higher than producer output prices.
- Another common mistake is to look at pricing in isolation and forget that it is just one part of the marketing mix and, as such, an essential component in achieving your strategy. You might have priced your offer correctly but if you do not let customers know what the price is, or fail to make it available you will have missed the opportunity.
- Many companies do not think through their tactics and fail to vary prices to reflect different market segments. Your product may sell at its existing price in specialist boutiques/outlets but it is unlikely so to do in national distribution chains without varying (say) the packaging or indeed the price.

In some organisations there is a separate pricing department to set the prices or to 'approve' prices set by others. Typically it will report into the marketing department or sometimes directly into the board. This may be a reflection of the importance that those organisations place on pricing but can affect flexibility in changing prices to reflect special situations or special deals.

Many others will also influence prices, including sales personnel, production, accounts etc. Here are a few examples:

- In Life Assurance companies, for example, pricing is usually in the hands of a very specialised set of people known as actuaries who investigate the probabilities of life expectancy and produce and price products accordingly.
- In chemical companies, production people and accountants will be the main determiners of price.
- In financial companies products may be priced by sales and marketing or by the treasury depending on their precise nature and the funding required.
- In a multinational FMCG company it will probably be the brand or product managers.
- In retail chains and supermarkets it will be the buyers in conjunction with the marketing people.

Pricing can be very complex and it is therefore difficult to get it right. Not only do many managers have to contend with the vagaries of the market, they also have to contend with internal decision-making structures and even organisational politics!

It is very hard to give examples where organisations have used the wrong price and suffered as a result, partly because pricing is only one element in the marketing mix; and partly because badly priced items aren't normally around in the market long enough to register on the public consciousness. If wrong prices aren't adjusted rapidly the company goes out of business.

Note also that prices can be wrong in two respects: too cheap or too dear. If prices are too cheap, sales may not suffer, but the profit accrued by the producer certainly will. If they are too dear, sales will almost certainly suffer, and profits will fall as well.

Whilst some would say that setting the price right first time is crucial; in practice, as long as you are in the right ballpark, you have a chance to correct errors providing you are monitoring your pricing performance.

Price visibility

The price of a product or service is usually very visible in the market. Therefore both your competitors and, more importantly, your customers can see it and can make comparisons with others very easily. Often they will not have all the information to make correct comparisons and may draw conclusions that you would rather they did not. For example, a low price may be interpreted as representing lower quality rather than the real reason which could be greater efficiency.

Whilst a trip round Tesco's followed by a trip round Sainsbury's would help you gauge their prices for baked beans (assuming you had the time and inclination), to compare the prices of two pension plans might be harder. The prices are not so visible, and the product offers are much more complex than a simple tin of beans, and may not appear to be directly comparable.

Pricing is, therefore, an important weapon in setting the image of your offering and in getting across your message to the customers.

The following situation is a good example of different uses of price:

At Christmas most people (except the Scrooges amongst us) buy decorative paper to wrap presents. There are, however, many different types and grades of paper available, and different places to buy it.

Here are four scenarios:

A A market trader sells very low quality paper in quite large rolls, cheaply.
B A corner shop sells low quality paper in large rolls but at a higher price than the market trader.
C A general retailer sells medium quality paper in small rolls at a medium price.
D An up-market retailer sells high quality paper in single sheets at a premium price.

This can be shown in Table 1.1 as follows:

Table 1.1 *Positioning strategies*

	Quality	**Volume**	**Price**
A	low	high	low
B	low	medium	medium
C	medium	low	medium
D	high	low	high

and can be graphed to show the strategic emphasis (Figure 1.3):

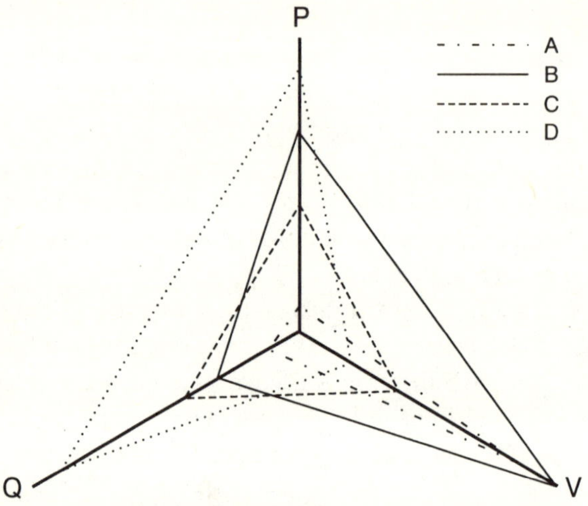

Figure 1.3 *Pricing strategies – Price v. Quantity v. Volume*

This graph shows where each of the outlets is positioning itself on the axes of quantity, price and quality. The trader is concentrated on one axis, that of quantity, whilst the positions of the others represent their emphasis on price or quality as appropriate.

There is a direct relationship between price and demand although the relationship varies between different products and different markets. You can, therefore, use price to affect demand. However, whilst it is easy to measure effect at each end (eg lemonade at £100 a bottle will have zero demand) in the middle ground it is much harder. A robust process is therefore necessary to price correctly.

WHERE PRICING FITS IN WITH MARKET

Marketing is about getting customers to buy from you rather than your competition. It is, therefore, about making your customers feel that by buying from you they are getting a better benefit than from anybody else. The higher the benefit that they receive, however, the higher the cost to deliver it to them (usually). The key elements in marketing are often categorised as the four Ps (and known as the marketing mix):

- price;
- promotion;
- place;
- product.

It should be noted that the only one of these elements that brings in revenue is the price. The rest involve costs!

For each product/service, therefore, you must:

- decide whether to *satisfy* or to *delight* your customers;
- determine not only the *cost* of that level of service delivery;
- but also the *price* customers are prepared to pay for it.

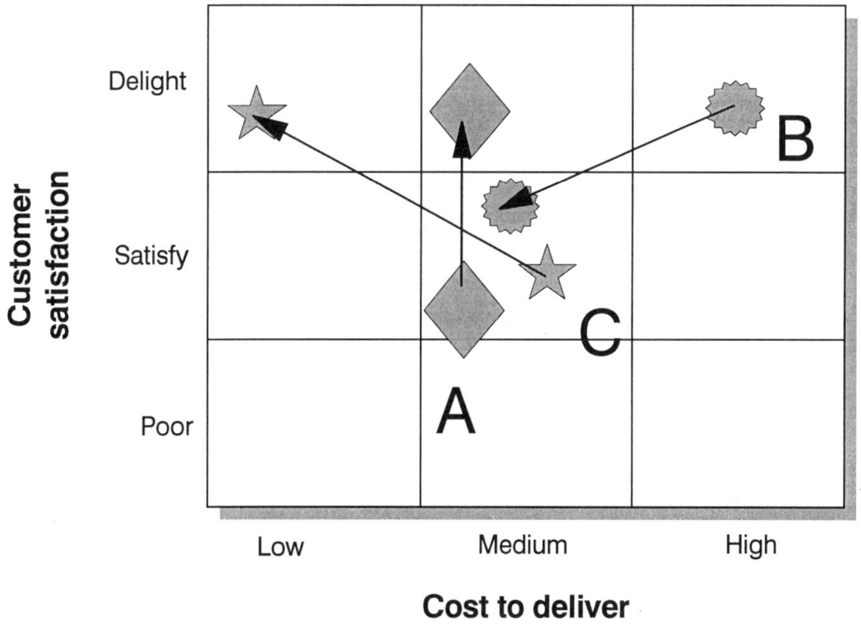

Figure 1.4 *Customer satisfaction versus cost*

This will represent your chosen CVP(s) which you will offer in the market. Figure 1.4 represents the changing strategy of a company as it repositions its product offerings.

The changes to the product strategies are:

A Moving up-market by offering more benefits, without affecting the cost too much, thereby allowing a better price to be asked.

B Reducing the benefits to the customer and, therefore, reducing the cost of delivery. This might expand the range of potential buyers.

C Using new technology to improve the benefits to the customer and at the same time substantially reducing the cost of that delivery.

Examples for a microwave oven:

A The insertion of a new 'controlling chip', which is inexpensive to put in, would allow several different types of heating and cooking programmes — thus more benefits at a similar cost of production but for which a higher price can be charged.

B Using a lower power element (called a klystron) is substantially cheaper but cooking operations take longer. Probably most users would not notice and, therefore, it might be possible to reduce costs and at the same time deliver only marginally less benefits.

C Integrating a grill element and a microwave into a single unit but charging less than the price of the two as separate items.

If you decide to offer higher quality it usually involves greater cost. The key question is whether this can be passed on by way of price rises and what impact this will have on sales. Price is, therefore, an integral part of the marketing process as you can only obtain a higher price by convincing the customer of the extra benefits and therefore value he is receiving — *ie equalising the price/benefits/value equation*.

WHY SET PRICES?

There is an implicit assumption in economics/marketing that demand tends towards infinity whilst supply is finite.

A petroleum cracking plant is very expensive, takes a long time to build and involves many variables. If demand for its output rises it can be met only up to the capacity of the plant. When that capacity is reached, and if demand is still as yet unfulfilled, something must give; either a new supply must be found or the available output must be divided between those demanding it. In the latter case, and assuming no competition, the refinery would simply raise its prices to reflect the huge demand for its products until people stopped using petroleum products and moved to something else (eg electricity).

In practice competition renders this unlikely; however, some mechanism is needed to regulate unfettered demand and to equalise it with available supplies. In a free market this mechanism is price. In a controlled market it may be rationing or artificial demand constraint.

Prior to the introduction of money: trade (demand and supply) was by barter which has inherent difficulties (how many deer equal two doves and a pig; or how much salt equals a tractor and, anyway, I wanted a sewing machine etc?). Money provided an easy means of facilitating exchange between these two forces acting as a means of buying and selling without barter.

Because the value of money is (relatively) stable and it is ubiquitous (ie not related to any particular product or service) it can regulate demand by acting as a rationing agent.

There is only so much money available in the world (responsible governments cannot just print money willy-nilly or they would soon go broke). It is consumers who decide how this money is spent. With only so much money available to satisfy demands/needs it must somehow be allocated across all the goods/services a person requires.

The trick is then for a supplier to ensure that his offerings allow him to gain the most from transactions. Prices must not be set too high or his offerings will not be taken up in the right quantity and not set too low such that he loses revenue (in effect, loses profit).

Common pricing problems

In setting a price there are many problems which beset those responsible:

- How will other goods affect demand for mine?
- What prices should I charge?
- When should I introduce a new price?
- How to price consistently, when I base this on many inputs which change their price (cost) at different times?
- When and by how much should I discount?

By finding the answer to these types of question and others relating to your business you will be able to price your products or services successfully.

This is the key to pricing: to find that goal of the exact price.

The rest of this book will focus on that goal: how to set prices to maximise utility to the organisation or enterprise.

2

PRICING THEORY

INTRODUCTION

The last chapter indicated the need to focus on the goal of setting prices to maximise utility. To do this it is necessary to look in some detail at three key areas: *economics*, *marketing* and *finance*.

- *Economics* is basically the study of production, consumption, distribution and exchange of goods and services.
- *Marketing theory* largely grew out of economics and was an attempt to probe beneath the more usual economic analysis of demand and supply etc. and look at areas in more detail.
- *Finance* provides inputs to the pricing process (cost information) and also monitors the financial results of action (profit, sales volumes etc).

To understand pricing the reader must have a basic grasp of the principles of these three areas and this chapter will give a basic grounding in these. A reference and further reading list is included on page 220 for those who wish to explore these concepts in more detail. The key ideas that must be understood in the areas are:

- in economics — markets, demand, utility and cycles;
- in marketing — research techniques, buyer psychology and promotional techniques;
- in finance — costing methodologies, profit and loss, margin and cashflow.

In addition, an understanding of basic management techniques is required including cash management, forecasting, information use, planning and strategy. These will be explored during the course of the book.

Supply chains are a good example of these elements in action as they often involve a whole host of interactions and transactions between many parties from raw material producers, manufacturers, assemblers, intermediaries, distributors, storage agents, wholesalers and retailers as well as others such as financiers. This chain includes several levels of supply and demand and very complex dynamics in different and often overlapping markets (see Figure 2.1).

The final price of a product at the end of the chain reflects the complex interchange of these parties which is frequently very different from the, often simplified, economic analysis models.

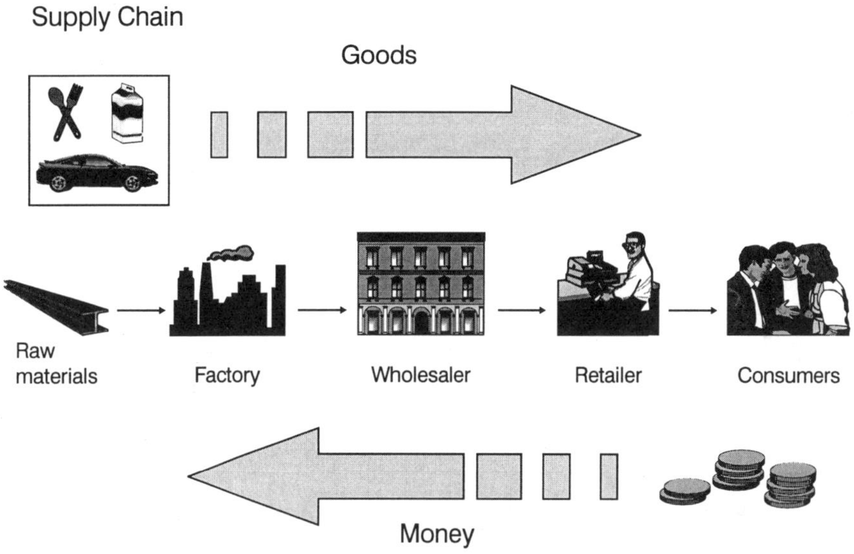

Figure 2.1 *Supply chain*

Each party has to understand the fundamental economics of its processes, has to market its goods to the buyers and, of course, money has a significant role in making it all work.

The problems with theory

Unfortunately economics (usually classed as a *social* science — and often known irreverently as the *dismal* science) is not quite as scientific as economists would have us believe. This is because it is not possible to conduct repeated experiments in controlled environments and analyse the results until a consistent theory emerges as it is in, say, physics or chemistry. Economics is an attempt to rationalise an irrational world and as such requires assumptions to be made, sometimes requiring quite breathtaking leaps of faith as well as involving some subjective decision making.

These assumptions about behaviour of people and markets, however, do allow the construction of both frameworks for analysis and models against which hypotheses can be tested. Unlike the true (natural) sciences, however, an economic experiment is less likely to deliver the same result every time and, therefore, there is always a margin for error and the unknown.

Many economic theories rely on assumptions which over time are challenged and ultimately disproved (or fall out of favour) as new understandings are gained. It is often the case, therefore, that economic thinking changes as new theories and ideas come into fashion and then again as they are discredited or fall into disuse. (The move in the 1980s from neo-Keynesian thinking (government-led demand management) back to monetarism (government control of the money supply) under the influence of the Chicago School in the USA, led by Milton Friedman, is a very good example of this.)

It is also extremely difficult to test and quantify these theories (for example, elasticity of demand), particularly at the micro level, but nonetheless they provide some rational framework for assessing markets and buying behavioural patterns. This means, however, that in putting theories into practice you can be surprised if there is a too slavish adherence to them.

Similar problems are found in the study of the theory of marketing. Whilst academics might suggest that marketing theory is a science, in practice it is very difficult to predict the effect of specific actions and to rationalise these to an intellectual framework. As a famous adman once said, half of the money you spend on advertising is wasted, you just don't know which half.

This is generally true when applied to marketing: the complexity of marketing tools available means that plans are constructed using basic principles, but are then honed in practice using feedback from the market — not a pinpoint approach, but an effective one, providing you only alter one or two variables at a time. Sadly, most firms don't have the resources, money and particularly the time to do this, so marketing activities are often altered wholesale, thus leading to problems in isolating cause and effect.

With regard to finance, the main principles are cast in stone, governed by a set of professional statute-based rules. That said, however, even fixed rules are capable of interpretation and as we move away from the principles used to cover statutory audit and reporting requirements and into the area of money management, things become more subjective.

General principles hold good, but when the area gets complex, you will not be surprised that the approach of one accountant differs from that of another, so you have to look deeply not only at the answer, but also the method used to achieve it.

The key to understanding theory in these areas, therefore, is an inquiring mind (if you don't understand, look it up!), healthy pragmatism (why are the professionals telling me this? is there any other way?) and a huge dose of common sense. Be the man on the Clapham omnibus (or the business equivalent thereof) and always ask yourself 'does this make sense?'.

GENERAL ECONOMIC THEORY

This book is not intended to be an economics textbook and if some of the concepts referred to seem complex or require further exploration then you should get hold of a basic economics textbook such as one recommended in the references and further reading list on page 220.

The difficulty of setting prices

Pricing is only easy (in theory) in what is known as a *price-taking market* — that is a market which is approaching perfect competition.

The conditions for this are:

- transparency of transactions;
- homogeneity of goods;
- many buyers and sellers (perfect competition);
- knowledge universally available; and
- highly mobile resources.

Where these conditions are met then all suppliers have to charge the same price.

Unfortunately, for all the reasons discussed below in 'market distortions', this only rarely (if ever) exists although sometimes stock markets are considered to display these characteristics.

Stock market — in an ideal stock market

- Everyone knows (instantly thanks to computers and information feeds) what everyone else is buying and selling. This is called *transparency*.
- The goods (stocks and shares) are all valued based on the same principles (accounting rules, stock exchange regulations) — *homogeneity*.
- There are thousands of firms quoted and millions of buyers and sellers — *perfect competition*.
- The extent of information that companies publish on their business activities is covered by statute (no insider trading) and must be made available in the public domain — *knowledge universally available*.
- Anyone can participate, from the man in the street with £100 to pension funds with billions of pounds under management — *mobile resources*.

Because markets are usually distorted in some way it is usually necessary to set prices proactively to allow for, and sometimes take advantage of, distortions and to have a method of so doing which brings in all the necessary factors, allows them to be weighed up properly and then enables the execution mechanism. This is done by applying general principles or theories to the real world and acting on the outputs.

These theories and principles are considered below. Prior to this, however, it is necessary to examine briefly the process used by businesses to produce and set prices — the *pricing process*.

The pricing process

Figure 2.2 below shows the steps to be followed in setting prices. Like all good processes it includes feedback for subsequent revision. During the course of this book this methodology will progressively be explained and analysed.

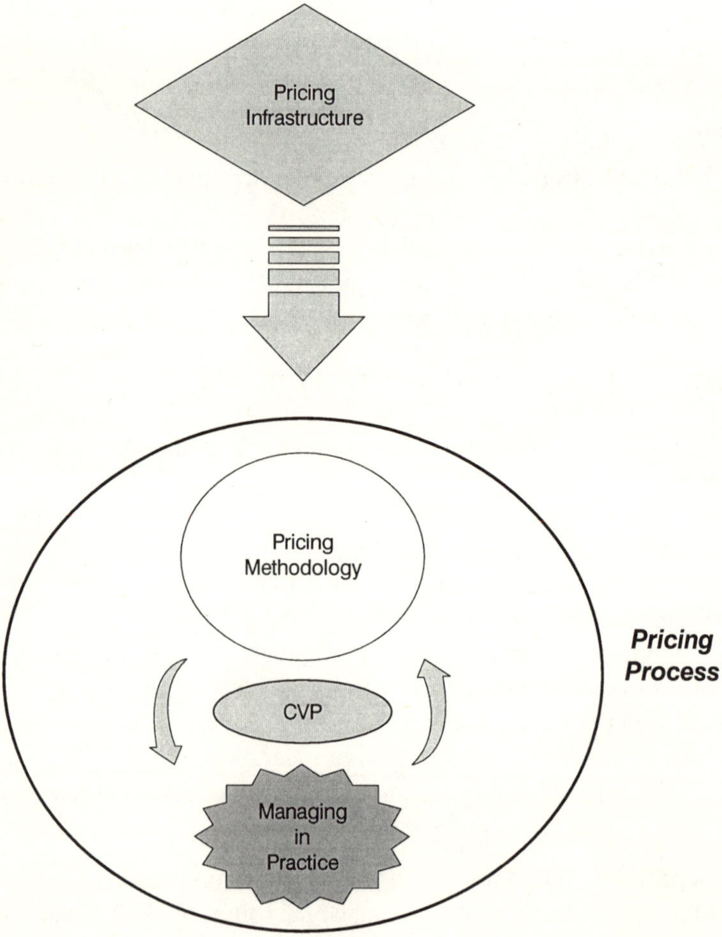

Figure 2.2

There are three basic components of the process:

- pricing infrastructure;
- pricing methodology; and
- managing pricing in practice.

Looking at this as a sequential flow we can see that information is received into the infrastructure and processed there. Response is managed through the methodology and managing in practice helps to see that plans are turned into action.

By following this process a number of advantages accrue:

- The process is sequential and can, therefore, be followed in a logical and rational manner.
- It is a complete process in itself, although extensive inputs are required from other parts of the business and the market.
- The process allows for feedback to ensure that signals received from the market can be interpreted and acted on.

Keep this simple process in mind as you read on through the book.

Market distortions

The ability of an organisation to set whatever price it wishes exists in most countries to a greater or lesser extent *in theory*; however, in practice this freedom is limited by many factors. If there were no restrictions then prices would almost always be very much higher than they usually are. This tends to happen where monopolies or oligopolies (a single or a small group of suppliers controlling or dominating the market) exist or where there are cartels (a group of suppliers getting together and agreeing to charge the same price for goods to maintain their profit levels).

In these situations the supplier merely charges what he feels like as there is no other option for consumers. In a remote village, for example, there may only be one shop and therefore prices will usually be much higher than in, say, the nearest branch of a national chain of supermarkets which might be many miles away.

In practice, there is usually legislation in place to stop this sort of distortion, although evidence of cartels is usually difficult to obtain.

There are many other things, however, which distort the prices that an organisation can set (see Figure 2.3). Some are *internal* and within the ability of management to influence or control and some are *external* and, therefore, largely outside the control of the enterprise.

The major factors are:

External

- competition;
- legislation;
- customers' demands;
- changing markets
- technology.

Internal

- costs;
- profit targets;
- growth.

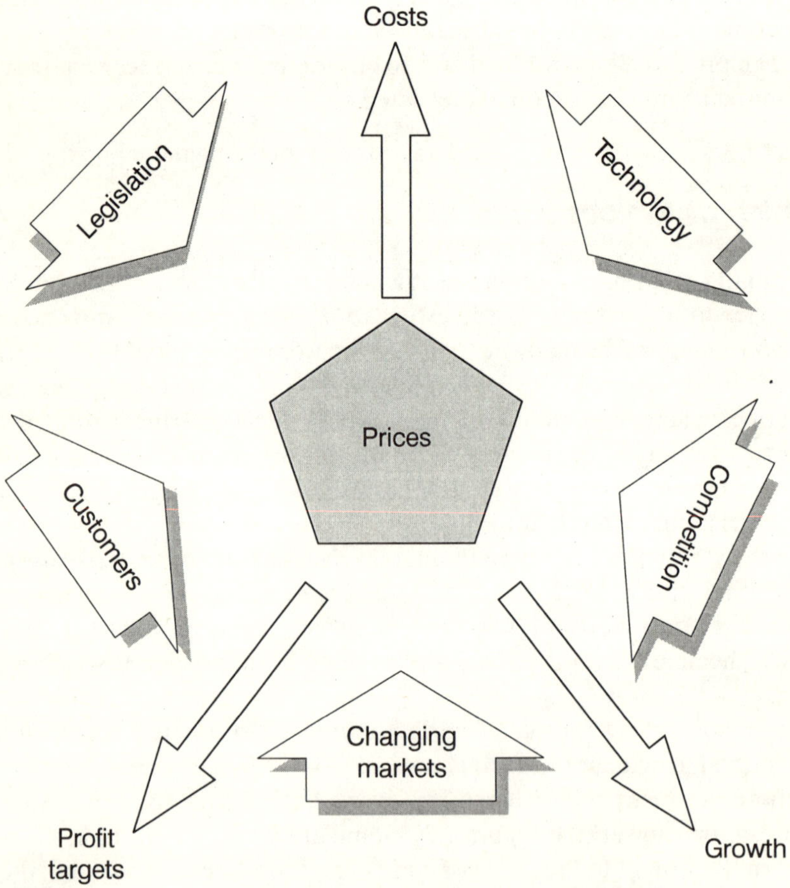

Figure 2.3 *Factors distorting price*

Each of these is briefly considered in the following sections:

External

These distortions are caused by another entity doing something which impacts on you as an enterprise. They are usually out of your direct control but may be subject to indirect influences — lobbying; press campaigns etc. They usually act to force prices down, but not always.

Competition represents the other players in your markets. This can be direct competition where the product/service is an exact substitute for yours (eg bookmakers where there are usually many concentrated in a small area or plastic buckets which are produced by many firms); or it can be indirect competition from something which competes for the same expenditure but is not the same, eg the Football Pools or a National Lottery which competes directly for those who would bet (and also with many other forms of expenditure). (The National Lottery was introduced in the UK in 1994 and was subsequently used as an excuse by some executives for poor performance in betting organisations and others — including, unbelievably, the book trade.)

It can also be a totally different type of product which impacts on the demand for and, therefore, on the price of your product. As the price of petrol rises so demand for large uneconomical cars falls, and so do the prices.

Generally, the higher the margin (the amount a firm makes on its operations) the more likely a market is to attract other suppliers which in turn usually leads to depressing of prices, as supply and demand equalise. On the other hand a shortage of supply can cause prices to rise quite quickly. The effect of a competitor withdrawing from a market would cause this until other suppliers 'geared up' production to meet surplus demand, and could attract new suppliers.

A competitive market is usually characterised by price wars in the mature phase of its cycle. The consumer has plenty of scope to 'shop around' and, therefore, suppliers have to fight for custom.

Legislation is, by and large, passed to protect customers from being taken advantage of and tends to reduce the potential price charged (eg monopolies' commissions, official regulators in some markets (eg OFWAT, OFTEL in the UK) or anti-trust bodies). It can also, however, push prices of your offering up where it requires changes to the way you produce or sell it, thereby increasing costs.

Health and safety is a very good example where legislation requires that safe practices be introduced and that goods are safe to sell. In financial services very high regulatory requirements were introduced throughout the EU in response to the feeling that clients were being sold inappropriate products/services. The cost of complying with this is very high for organisations in this market. This is virtually the opposite situation from the typical nineteenth-century philosophy that prevailed which was *caveat emptor* — let the buyer beware — and reflects the increasing power of the consumer.

Some governments try to control prices directly through price and income controls. This distorts the market very quickly and in the long term tends to have very harmful effects on economies; usually resulting in an explosion of inflation when the lid comes off (or breaks) and high wage demands are put in leading to higher prices etc.

Legislation can also put prices up by imposing tax on the offerings. Cars, spirits, tobacco and petrol are good examples of this. In most countries there is also some form of sales tax levied on goods and services. In the EU it is called value added tax (VAT) and is levied on each stage of the value chain, being reclaimable back, usually, from the next step and netted off. It is a very complex tax and unwieldy as well as being very unpopular. (It also flies in the face of most of Adam Smith's canons about tax — which is not surprising as it was conceived as a compromise between differing countries' bureaucracies.) In many countries there are extra taxes over and above this sales tax, eg car tax, luxury goods tax and there may also be import duties.

Customer demand affects prices in both directions. Where there is increasing demand for the offering, then unless the supply expands quickly to meet the demand, the price will rise as it is rationed by price, eg in the USA in the late 1980s where consumers literally besieged shops to buy Cabbage Patch dolls forcing the price up. Similarly where customers' perceptions change the demand may fall thus causing prices to fall until demand and supply are back in equilibrium. In Europe this happened at the end of 1995 to beef prices caused by the BSE scare.

Customers can also cause change by demanding more value from products/services (usually at no extra cost) particularly where there are lots of substitute offerings or their perception of what is a fair value changes.

Changing markets will affect prices in several ways. A new product or service may render your existing offering obsolete (the move to increasingly powerful desktop PCs in the early 1990s dealt a severe blow to mainframe manufacturers, and where are black and white TVs now?) thereby forcing prices down; or it can result in the price rising as suddenly the offering becomes the flavour of the month, eg mobile phones took off in the 1980s in many countries but these markets are now almost saturated and prices have fallen.

A good example is the *foreign exchange* (F/X) market where prices for currencies bounce all over the place in response to fears (real or imagined) about US inflation, Bundesbank rates, UK or French unemployment figures, trouble in the Middle East, fears about the Japanese banking system etc, rendering long-term planning extremely difficult without hedging.

Technology has the ability to enable more efficient production but, of course, can push costs up in the short term as the capital/operating costs are incurred usually prior to receipt of the benefits. Technology can also distort the market place significantly by introducing new working or operating practices. Expert knowledge systems can now make decisions very much quicker than people and at less cost, similarly with telesales operations which can render vast branch networks almost redundant. The success of Direct Line (the UK telesales insurer) is a clear example of this where turnaround times were reduced substantially as well as prices. Many companies now have substantially less support staff due to the use of voicemail, faxes, e-mail and networked PCs.

Internal

These factors are those which are usually within your control and over which direct influence can be exercised. They usually act to force prices up, but not always.

Costs fall into two kinds — those incurred within your organisation and those which come in from outside as the product/service passes up the value chain. Those within can be contained by management action whereas the external costs must be controlled in different ways such as supplier negotiation, shopping around and exercising purchasing power. The impact depends on the relative weighting of the cost type that is rising — in financial services historically staff costs have been one of the biggest (if not the biggest) proportion of costs and therefore a rise in this affects final prices much more than, say, the rise in the cost of paper. In the UK newspaper industry, however, raw newsprint costs rose by some 50 per cent during 1995 which was enough to put several papers out of print, including a national tabloid.

In an effort to avoid this type of situation, however, customer/supplier partnerships are becoming more of the norm, thus helping to control costs. Where a newspaper goes out of production it is not only the owners of the paper that suffer but the suppliers lose a customer and this is often an incentive to spur suppliers to partnerships.

Profit targets/return may have the effect of forcing prices up as organisations strive to maximise the return on their capital investment. In many cases this is driven by the aspirations of shareholders, particularly where new investors are present or the rest of the market is achieving higher returns.

Raising prices, however, does not always have the desired effect as it can drive customers away. The effective development of a long-term strategy is the only way to ensure that all aspirations are met. The capital markets in some countries are reputed to allow management greater freedom from 'interference' by shareholders (Germany and Japan are often cited as examples of this); however, this has not really been tested in very difficult times.

Growth affects organisations as, in order to grow, higher expenditure is required in terms of investment in assets and capital as well as cash to fund the business. This clearly pushes up the cost base until the benefits from this investment come on stream. Cashflow control is vital in this situation.

In the short term prices may be forced down in an effort to take market share (and thereby hope to achieve economies of scale). Extra orders may push up marginal costs as the current resources reach capacity requiring further investment. The cashflow cycle diagram (Figure 2.11) at the end of the chapter, shows the importance of this. Where outflows exceed inflows over a sustained period then the cycle breaks, often with disastrous results.

Summary

Distortions in the market, whether they are within the control of a company or outside have a significant effect on the pricing process. To be successful management needs to have understood these distortions with respect to its markets and have factored them into the decision-making process. This will enable informed pricing decisions to be made.

Basic economic concepts

Four ways in which money is spent:

- *your money on yourself;*
- *your money on another person;*
- *another person's money on yourself;*
- *another person's money on another person.*

Milton and Rose Friedman (1980) *Free to Choose* (a classic text on economic liberty)

Some basic economic concepts need to be understood in order to set prices properly. In this section the following key items are examined:

- demand;
- size and elasticity of demand;
- product utility;
- life cycles.

Demand

Assessment of demand is a crucial area in pricing. For example, shortage of supply (excess demand) nearly always leads to rationing by price (which in turn can lead to supra-profits to manufacturers and intermediaries — known as speculation or price gouging), whilst oversupply or heavy competition will drive prices down.

Economists assess demand as being a function of the following:

- price of the product;
- disposable or discretionary spend;
- price of other competing products;
- consumer taste;
- advertising or marketing effort;
- market size;
- future expectations;
- other issues (eg seasonality).

These are considered below in more detail.

Price of the product

As prices go down, more people are able to buy and demand will tend to rise. Pricing experts talk in terms of price points — areas where a small change in

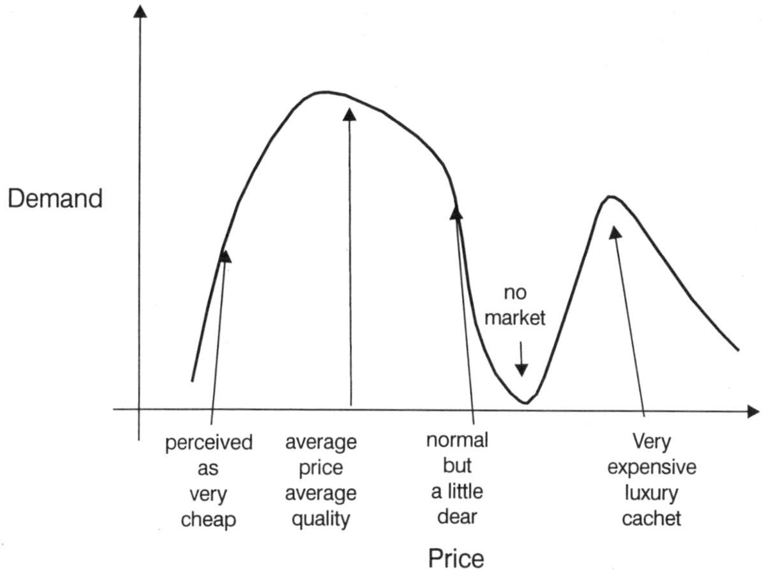

Figure 2.4 *Price points – hypothetical example (exaggerated for clarity)*

price causes a huge change in demand. Usually demand moves in an inverse relationship with price, but there are exceptions. Some price rises cause huge increases in demand as perception of the product changes (eg 'if it is expensive then it must be good'). Psychology comes into play in assessing this. The diagram below is a hypothetical example of this type of occurrence.

Disposable or discretionary spend

When budgeting, most people subconsciously differentiate between required spending (on basics such as housing, food, warmth etc, sometimes called 'necessaries') and discretionary spending (entertainment, luxuries such as cut glass, holidays etc). Where their income changes for the better, the relative amount in these categories will change and thus more may be available to be spent in some areas.

The recent recessions in Europe saw the extent of spending on discretionary goods fall sharply. People concentrated more on what they regarded as essential items, and away from luxuries. The perception of goods can also change: telephones, refrigerators, vacuum cleaners and televisions have all moved from being considered as luxuries and into the necessity bracket in the last 20 years.

Price of other competing products

Consumers do not generally earmark their disposable income for any one particular item or group of items (except in the case of relatively large items, which for consumers could be a car or a good holiday). A consumer, therefore, may have £100 'to spare' and will have to decide whether to spend it on clothes, eating out, an interest or hobby etc. As the relative prices of these apparently non-competitive things change, the idea of spending money on them will also become more or less attractive, and therefore the market will change.

Consumer taste

Many believe that this is a function of popular demand but in practice it is as likely to have been manipulated as not. Manufacturers have a vested interest in predictable taste so that they do not need to respond to it, which can be expensive, but rather anticipate it. Many large clothing retailers order their raw materials up to three years in advance in order to secure good prices and therefore would not wish to see purple as the '1996 colour' if they had purchased khaki. If it is generally predicted that the 'colour' for the year 1999 will be orange, then this will have been settled in 1997.

Much marketing and advertising is aimed at persuading people to buy a 'new product' to replace their current (often perfectly adequate) model/line to keep up with fashion. Some hi-fi manufacturers bring out two or three new models just for this purpose. In many areas the latest model is obsolete, in terms of new features and enhancements, before it is sold. Increased automation has also allowed the time-to-market to be reduced dramatically thus facilitating this. New product enhancements may also be a good opportunity to put the price up to 'skim' the market — see Chapter 6.

Marketing and advertising effort

If a company invests enough money (or skill) in an area, markets can be 'manufactured' overnight. The recent introduction of isotonic or sports drinks is a good example of this. Demand was developed from nil simply by sophisticated manipulation of marketing communications' activities. It should be noted that often huge expenditure has to be made to get and keep new products into the public eye whilst demand is solidified, so this activity is only open to organisations with a large financial resource. This often allows smaller firms to get into the market on the back of the first firm's efforts.

It should not be undertaken, therefore, without a very good idea of the rewards that can be garnered in a short time. The windows of opportunity are becoming much shorter as the ability not only to innovate but also to copy becomes easier.

In other cases new markets are developed on the back of others (for example by development of the brand). Because consumers feel easy and comfortable with a particular brand then its characteristics can often be used to stimulate demand in another area. In recent years Harley Davidson has been rumoured to make more money out of its clothes ranges than its motorbikes: consumers perceive the clothes as rugged, hard-wearing and macho like the bikes. Lotus recently introduced a very high technology push-bike in just the same vein. Marlboro (the US cigarette manufacturer) sells clothing and accessories to complement its cigarette brand image (rugged outdoor) whilst Dunhill has a large share of the luxury accessory market. The range of sports accessories with the Jaguar logo has been around for some time as has that of BMW and Porsche (sun-glasses). This does not always work, however, and a set of golf clubs branded with the name of a well-known toothpaste was a failure a few years ago.

Market size

Market sizes can grow or decline with little or no effort from manufacturers. For example, in the developed world improved health care has lead to many more (relatively) healthy elderly, a rapidly growing market that was once ignored. Similarly, a declining birth rate leads to reduced demand for baby clothes. Technological innovations can also lead to huge increases in market size. The fax was originally developed for a limited market (Japanese domestic use) but in the 1980s global demand took off in such a way that everyone now has one at work and increasingly at home. The normal product cycle will also result in market growth as the product moves from a select few to mass awareness and demand.

Future expectations

The consumers' view of the future is very important. If a consumer perceives that the economy is weak and he believes that he might lose his job, then he is likely to put his money into somewhere or something safe (eg a building society, or gold or maybe just under the bed). If he perceives that things are booming, however, he is more inclined to spend his money on holidays, new cars and other discretionary goods. He is also much more likely to use credit to buy things in anticipation of future prosperity using the 'buy now, pay later' philosophy.

Other issues (eg seasonality)

Some markets react to the weather or time of year. Sales of candles obviously shoot up in winter and shorts sell well in spring, as people plan for their holidays. For many ice-cream manufacturers the whole profitability of the year can be based on how good summer is, and for most specialist chocolate shops over 70 per cent of their income comes in just two short periods: before Easter and before Christmas! Companies operating in these types of market must understand the implications and plan accordingly. This may mean arranging appropriately timed marketing campaigns, special financial deals or attempting out of season promotions to change the dependence on seasonality, eg summer skiing linked with Alpine walking holidays.

Size and elasticity of demand

In pricing it is critical to know two key characteristics of the market:

- the size (total spend available now and in the future); and
- how the market reacts to changes in price (elasticity).

Size

The first step in understanding these characteristics is to assume that any discrete market has boundaries: that is to say that the amount of money being spent is known and that the types of product sold are fixed.

Whilst we would like to believe that people earmark money for specific uses, in practice this is not normally the case and markets therefore 'leak' into one another. In business-to-business markets, the size of demand may be fairly well delineated, primarily because the goods and services themselves are well defined, and with no real competition. If an engine builder requires a new piston, he has to buy one, and can't replace this with, say, an air conditioner. However, the marketing people promoting these new engines could choose either advertising or direct mail to promote the product, interchangeably, so the market for the provision of these services will definitely overlap.

A simple example will illustrate this:

A baker in a village could define his market as consisting of his output (supply — no-one else bakes bread) and the people that live in the village (demand — no passing trade). He then further divides his offerings into two: loaves and rolls. Within these definitions then the amount of money available can be ascertained. (If he sells 100 loaves per day at 75p and 400 rolls at 25p then his market is worth £175 per day.)

He could then calculate revenue and set prices to match expected demand. For example, he could put prices of loaves up to £1 and expect to sell only 75 and drop the price of rolls to 20p and thereby sell 500 (total market value remains the same). In practice, however, customers might swap from one product to another depending on how they perceived the value.

Elasticity

Whilst markets may be bounded by the availability of competing products, they are also characterised by the amount of money to be spent in them. This is called elasticity and the way demand changes in accordance with price changes (elasticity) is determined by four key factors:

- *How good the substitutes are*. In the case of bread there is no substitute if one wants to make toast, but as a component part of one's diet it is easy to replace with potatoes, rice or pasta.
- *The importance of the product to one and one's budget*. For some people the price of bread is very important (eg those on low or fixed incomes or where it is a large part of their diet). For others it is largely irrelevant: just look at the recent rise in demand (in the UK) for speciality products like ciabatta and focaccia, priced at over a £1 a loaf!
- *How quickly one can adjust to the price change*. If one buys bread for oneself then there is no problem, one can easily swap to potatoes for tomorrow's lunch, but if one ran a sandwich shop one would probably have to develop a new product to stay in business;
- *Whether the good is a necessity or a luxury.* For some bread is a staple item in their diet, and they would suffer if it wasn't available. For others it might be an extra luxury, eg a farmer growing rice and potatoes.

The amount of revenue available in a market can expand or decrease by the stimulus of macro-economic factors (inflation, recession etc) or micro-economic ones (eg by aggressive pricing, which takes away share from other products or markets or by advertising, which can be used to expand markets).

Markets are said to be elastic if they change with respect to internal or external stimuli. If, therefore, the baker drops the price of his loaves and rolls, people might buy more of them (perhaps replacing potatoes or rice or other carbohydrates in their diet). Similarly, if prices were to be raised they might buy less bread and more of the other goods. In this case the market is said to be *elastic* — it responds to the stimulus of price changes.

If, however, there is no reaction to the alteration of prices and demand remains the same then it is said to be *inelastic* — there is no response to the stimulus of price changes.

This concept only applies over a given range of price. If prices were dropped to say 1p a loaf then people would probably buy bread to feed the ducks resulting in an increase in demand. Similarly, if the price were to be raised to, say, £10 a loaf then demand would probably fall to zero. Neither of these scenarios would particularly help the baker, of course.

For the baker, therefore, the second characteristic (elasticity) must be considered. This measures the likelihood and the speed of a market changing in size if subject to a stimulus (eg price changes) and how fast it returns to the previous state if the stimulus is removed (prices revert to the previous level).

A reduction in price of rolls to 20p might make them twice as attractive to customers and they might buy 800 a day. If the price of loaves remained the same demand for them might only be affected a little (say falling to 80) and thus a price reduction would have increased the total size of the market (£220).

The application of micro-economic theory is not, however, very useful to managers in a practical sense as it is almost impossible to understand the link between price and elasticity. Thus, pricing decisions are generally made on an iterative (trial and error) basis, and are thus subject to constant review.

Product utility

Utility is defined as the satisfaction or value derived by a consumer arising from the purchase of the product in question. As consumers (including businesses) have a limited amount of money to spend on goods, they seek to get the best value from purchases (in economic terms this is known as maximising the utility) and accordingly they tend to pay proportionately more for products that they perceive have this better value (greater utility). Consumers often compare this utility by using social and cultural values, even where these are inappropriate and so for suppliers a very good view of the particular market is required.

We can illustrate the idea of utility by considering what buyers might look for in a refrigerator. Effective marketing of such products relies on persuading the consumer of the increased utility or benefits offered by a particular product, not by listing technical features. Thus the consumer would tend to rate the items on the left of Table 2.1 below (benefits), rather than those of the right (features), even though it is the features that confer the benefits:

Table 2.1

Benefit	**Feature**
environmentally friendly	CFC free
quiet	low noise compressor
less defrosting	air recirculation system
cheap to run	high-quality insulation
keeps the lettuce fresh	temperature gradient controls
etc	

The more features that manufacturers can add to their products, the more they increase the utility and the more they make the product appeal to consumers (who are, therefore, likely to spend more money). The trick is to increase the utility at a faster rate than the price!

Japanese consumers are very sensitive to brand names, especially Western ones, which lend an air of sophistication to the product. Similarly in the West, Japanese products used to be derided as being synonymous with poor quality. This situation has changed enormously over the last 20 years where now many Japanese companies (eg JVC and Honda) are a byword for quality.

Often the image that a product has is based on ignorance of true facts, prejudice or on a past reputation which now no longer pertains. The campaign at the end of 1995 by Volkswagen (VW) to tell people that it is now producing Skodas, is a good example of an attempt to change low image of products by linking the name of Skoda (synonymous with poor Czech engineering and shoddy workmanship) with that of VW renowned for excellence in engineering (Golf, Porsche) and German precision.

This concept, when used by a firm to position its offering in the marketplace, is an integral part of the *customer value proposition* (CVP). This means that manufacturers can charge higher prices for those products that are perceived as having a greater utility as purchasers will not object to paying more for a product which they perceive has greater worth.

The most obvious example of this is what is known as 'badging'. Where a label brings with it some perception of quality or value then simply attaching that label to an ordinary product will raise the value of the product enormously. Marketers call this process *brand extension*. Of course, if the product is not up to standard then this will also diminish the value of the up-market product and ultimately lead to the demise of the label.

Harley Davidson allows its label to be applied to a huge range of items, some apparently inappropriate, although all highly priced. It was also applied to cigarettes. It is impossible to be definitive in this area as it is about opinions, but whilst applying a brand to a packet of cigarettes might help short-term revenue, it will probably be of no help to the longevity of a brand given the social disfavour of cigarettes. (The cigarette product was produced under licence and has now been withdrawn from sale.)

Companies go to great lengths to protect the value and integrity of their brands, and rightly so, they are a huge asset to the firm. Rowntree Mackintosh (a UK confectioner/food firm) was bought by Nestlé (a Swiss confectioner/food firm) primarily for its brands which Nestlé felt were underexploited. Marks & Spencer, the UK retailer, only sells its own products all of which are perceived as at the quality end of the market. It recognises the need for the brand to maintain its quality image and enforces this rigorously. Generally, you will not find poor quality goods at Marks & Spencer, but if you do it will refund you immediately or change them for something else, with no question, such is the value it places on its reputation.

Product life cycles

As products are developed and moved into the market place, the pricing tends to vary according to well defined bands, as follows

- After an initial high price, low prices (or discounting) to achieve initial market penetration and gain acceptance by consumers.
- Higher prices to capitalise on growing market demand and ensure that profits are maximised. This also takes account of (initially) limited competition.
- Reducing prices as more competition enters the marketplace.
- Low prices as the market becomes a commodity market. Products are often phased out in this area as the cost of supply often increases beyond the achievable price.

Note that Figure 2.5 ignores the costs of production, which vary across the life of the product, and fall as, for example, capital costs are gradually written down.

This idea of life cycles is a very important as it provides a basis for targeted pricing.

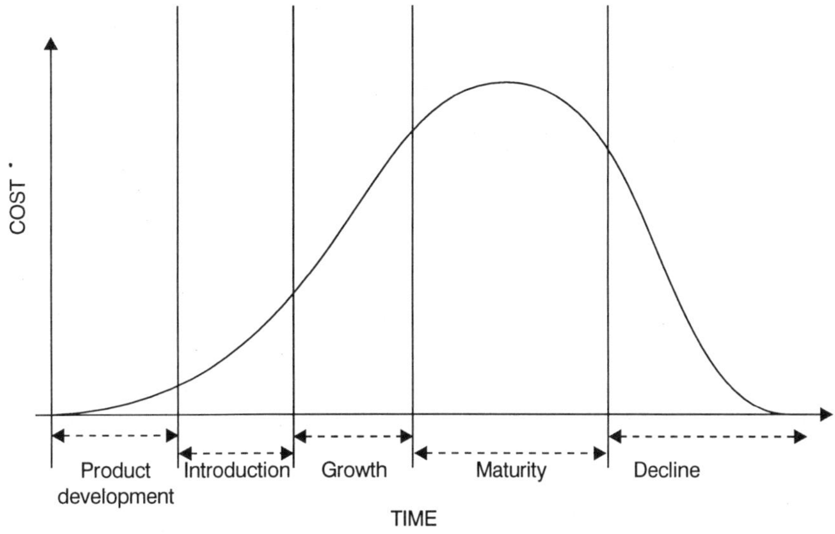

Figure 2.5 *Typical product life-cycle*

The development of markets

Like many areas, markets develop over time, and economists place great store by the stage of development of the market.

Broadly speaking markets have four main stages of development, which we will discuss with the use of an example, the instant camera.

Nascent: This is where the market is brand new. In this case a firm brings out a new and evolutionary product that enables you to take a photo and watch it develop on the spot. Because the firm needs to recoup its investment, advertising is at an early stage and production is still quite low, the products are expensive and only the most adventurous of consumers buy one.

Growing: By this stage many people have heard of the product, the price is falling and many people just have to have one. Sales will be rocketing upwards and other firms, anxious not to be left behind, will be introducing their instant camera to the market.

Mature: There will now be a wide choice of cameras to buy, but as the big players have built up a significant position they will be reaping the rewards, production costs will be as low as they can be, and all their selling activities will be optimised. They will be raking in the money. By this stage most consumers who are going to buy an instant camera will have one, and maybe some of them will trade up to a better model. They will have many different makes to choose from, including some very cheap products introduced by firms competing on price.

Declining: The advent of new products has now caused sales of instant cameras to decline. Some firms have started to offer throw-away conventional cameras for no more than the price of a roll of instant film, and really high entrants start to offer digital cameras that take a picture on a floppy disk that you can view and edit on your PC at home. The sales of instant cameras are falling fast and unless the manufacturers can develop ideas to rejuvenate consumers. The market may all but disappear.

In general prices tend to start off quite high, especially as manufacturers will have had high start-up costs and will not have any economies of scale in production. There may also be an opportunity for price skimming, taking advantage of no competition. The time of the life cycle varies widely; with fashion lines, it might be as short as a year, but with more established items it may be measured in tens of years. Mature markets tend to develop an equilibrium price in absence of external influences. Towards the end of the life cycle, products tend to metamorphose into new products which then have their own cycles.

The Ford Cortina was a prime example of this. Introduced into the UK in the 1960s, five separate and different versions of the car were produced, all called Cortina (after a skiing resort in Italy). When Ford felt that the Cortina had run its course it was replaced by the Sierra (named after the Spanish word for 'hill' but keeping the same style of name — three syllables, ending in a vowel, foreign association) which was based on the same concepts and aimed largely at the same market (company fleet drivers). When that, too, had had its day it was replaced by the Mondeo — 'the world car'.

Summary: economics

This has only been a very brief look at economics theory as it applies to pricing. Economics is a very important topic, for both the individual and for the organisation, and further study is well-advised. Some topics and subjects you might like to consider reviewing in further depth include:

- Macro-economics looks at topics like inflation, money supply, government budgets etc. On a day-to-day basis it is not so important to the pricing manager, who is better advised to concentrate on micro-economic issues;

- the idea of marginal cost: when firms add extra business the costs of this can be accounted for in a number of ways and understanding of this can aid you in considering the consequences of decisions regarding new business;
- there is no real conflict between theory and practice, but the linkages are not always clear and economists cannot always fully explain why things happen. Treat theory with a healthy scepticism and continually ask yourself: why are these linked?;
- in the same vein remember that the two key logical fallacies of economics are: false cause, ie event 1 causes event 2, simply because they appear to be linked and the so-called *ceteris paribus* problem (all things being equal). Just because a thing is true for a whole, it may not be true for a part.

Finally, remember that economists tend to be good at post-rationalisation (ie explaining why something happened) but not so good at predicting what might happen.

GENERAL MARKETING THEORY

Introduction

Marketing is a complex subject, involving more than just a mastery of techniques; it can also be considered a culture within an organisation. Those firms that are oriented towards their customers tend to be far more successful than those that are production-driven. The body that represents marketing in the UK, the Chartered Institute of Marketing, defines marketing as:

> *...the management process responsible for identifying, anticipating and satisfying customer requirements profitably.*

and the average marketing professional would probably say: 'the process of matching the resources of the business with customer needs, profitably'. (Note the use of the word profitably!)

It is perhaps also worth noting that even 300 years ago marketing was acknowledged as a key tool by economists, even if it had not been named as such.

Adam Smith – the famous seventeenth-century Scots economist and author of *The Wealth of Nations* said: 'The sole intent and purpose of production is consumption' by which he meant that the only reason for producing something is for it to be used, ie by a consumer.

Finally, it is perhaps worth looking at the definition in the *Penguin Dictionary of Economics* (1978), which defines

> The function of sales, distribution, advertising and sales promotion, product planning and market research. That is those functions in a business that directly involve contact with the consumer and assessment of his needs, and the translation of this information into outputs for sale, consistent with the firm's objectives.

There are numerous textbooks on marketing, and if you are unfamiliar with the topics briefly covered here, further reading is recommended.

The basics of marketing

Marketing can be broken down into four main components:

- understanding your customers and the market: *market research*
- deciding what you will do, and setting goals: *strategy development*
- formulating the steps to achieve your goals: *planning*
- doing it: *implementation*

Above all else marketing is about understanding who will consume the goods and services you offer and what they want. In essence it is about understanding what people *need* (what they have to have) and what they *want* (what they might like to have) and there is a big difference. It is then about providing your offer in a form that is attractive to them (ie it meets their needs, and maybe even meets their wants!).

The key areas of marketing theory that the pricing manager needs to understand are research (ie finding our wants and needs) and the role of the price in the promotion of the product (that is to say the psychology of the consumer). The role of price in the marketing mix is also relevant and we discuss this separately.

These are complex areas and it is not appropriate to go into them in detail in this book; however, a few basic pointers are in order:

Research

Market research is undertaken to get consumers' (buyers') views of your product or service offering. Without structured feedback managers operate totally in the dark and thus any decisions they make are simply based on instinct or gut feeling. This is hardly an ideal state of affairs, and can be likened to driving a car in a strange place, in the dark, with no map.

Hard and factual data can only be got from buyers and thus market research has to be carried out by asking customers.

The major methods of research include:

- telephone research;
- written questionnaires;
- street interviewing;
- face-to-face interviewing;
- product tests;
- consumer panels;
- focus groups.

All these techniques have a role to play in finding out what price is appropriate for any given product or service. The pricing manager will often commission specialists to advise on the best techniques and even to analyse the results.

Whenever pricing research is undertaken, the following points should be borne in mind, as shown in the following checklist:

Who are you going to ask?	*The sample*
How are you going to ask them?	*The method*
What are you going to ask them?	*The questions*
What will you do with the information?	*The results*
How much do you want to pay for the answer?	*The cost*
By when do you need the information?	*The time-scale*

The best answers come from using a mix of several techniques.

Strategy

The right price can go a long way to helping achieve strategic objectives. For example, if you want to expand rapidly, have a good financial base and have patient, far-seeing shareholders then you may well choose to price aggressively to achieve market share, even in the knowledge that it will take you longer to become profitable. Where, however, cash is an issue then you may try to squeeze every last drop of profit (ultimately cash) out of the market at higher prices. Chapters 3 and 4 look at these aspects in relation to marketing and pricing respectively in much more detail.

Planning

This is one aspect which is often underrated or even ignored (often to the considerable detriment of long-term results). A price plan needs to be prepared that will give you the flexibility to respond to changes in the market as part of the overall strategy and policy and includes in particular:

- regular reviews of your prices vis-à-vis your competition;
- contingency plans to cope with changes that happen infrequently and/or irregularly;
- understanding the likely product life cycle so that you know what changes to make to the price at each stage.

The marketing mix

Before moving to implementation, it is appropriate to consider the concept of the marketing mix. Traditionally this is considered under four headings, and is often referred to as the four Ps of marketing:

What your offer consists of	*Product*
How to communicate with your buyers	*Promotion*
Where to distribute	*Place*
How much to charge	*Price*

Briefly, this means that the manager will be considering what the product (or service) should look like, how it is packaged, displayed etc (*product*). He will also consider what methods of communicating the product offer to the customer will be used (*promotion*). We cover this separately in the next section.

He will also look at distribution, how the customer sees the product, where it can be bought, how it is delivered (*place*). And finally, he will consider the *price*.

It is vital that pricing is used to reinforce the other activities in the marketing mix (or be reinforced by them!). To take an extreme example, you would not seek to sell designer watches by putting leaflets through doors (you would probably advertise in glossy magazines) and you would not set up a High Street retail shop to sell aerospace components.

Price is often seen as an indicator of quality by consumers, and many organisations who start off with a low price as the key element of their marketing mix often find it very hard to move up-market in the future as they are indelibly linked in the public eye as low-cost suppliers.

Implementation

Ways of promoting products are many and varied. They include:

- TV and radio advertising;

- print advertising (eg posters and newspapers);
- direct mail;
- leafleting;
- public relations;
- telephone selling;
- face-to-face selling.

In some of these techniques it is appropriate to tell the reader about the price of the product, in others it is not. For example, an advertisement on the TV for food or beverages rarely tells you the price, but a car advert nearly always does. Similarly, many company's adverts in the press are little more than glorified price lists (look at an example from a large DIY chain or an electrical retailer).

A typical example of a UK TV daytime advertising break is shown in Table 2.2 below:

Table 2.2 A typical UK TV daytime advertising break

Advertiser	Premise	Key Message
Food retailer	Cheapest, price shown	Price
Furniture	Interest free credit (ie cheap)	Price
Pensions	Easy to understand, no price shown	Benefit
Food manufacturer	Good for you (no price)	Benefit
Beverage manufacturer	Fun to drink (no price)	Benefit
Car manufacturer	Performance, price shown	Price

There are no hard and fast rules on this topic; however, where products are somehow undifferentiated or available from a wide variety of sources then the advertiser may perceive that the price is the key purchase determinant and choose to promote this aspect heavily. If they feel other aspects are more important (eg quality, life-style, health) and that the product is relatively price-insensitive, then they will concentrate on these.

The choice of promotion and communication method depends entirely on the target audience, the budget and resources available to the firm and the nature of the product. Feedback from the market is vital. Not only should you know if the communication of price is important, but also how you communicate the price and to whom.

Summary

Marketing is a complex subject: it is no good setting the right price if you do not communicate it to your potential buyers in the right way.

GENERAL FINANCIAL THEORY

Introduction

Whilst finance may be the purview of accountants, the good manager should have an understanding of the basics so that he can not only understand what accountants tell him but also to enable him both to ask questions and then use the information in practice.

Costs are clearly an important input into prices as in the long term if you do not cover your costs, you will go bust. It is important, therefore, to understand the nature of your costs, how their dynamics move and the influence they will have over your ability to set the right price. There are several mechanisms for assessing costs including:

- direct costing;
- absorption costing;
- activity-based costing;
- standard costing.

It is not intended to investigate the different types of cost in great detail as this is beyond the scope of this book and there are many others written in more detail on each subject. The basics will be examined, however, in order to give an understanding of their relative pros and cons in the context of assessing pricing mechanisms.

In addition to costing, there are three further financial concepts that are important:

- break-even analysis;
- transfer pricing;
- cashflow.

These are important as business is as much about investment and risks as it is about money. Break-even analysis in particular is an important concept as it allows the manager to calculate whether an idea is likely to be profitable, and how risky it is.

Transfer pricing is a specialised concept and is really a form of internal pricing used in large firms, or those with many subsidiaries or departments. In recent years modern management thinking has led to a huge growth in transfer pricing type mechanisms, most commonly in the form of internal profit centres, for example where the personnel department charges the marketing department for its help in the recruitment of a new manager, or the IT department charges other user departments for its help and advice! It is also used in its more traditional sense, where raw materials or part-finished goods are shipped from one factory to another.

Finally cashflow, which effectively measures how money comes in and out of the business, is a vital technique to understand. There is often a long wait between delivering a product and getting paid for it (30 days, 60 days or more sometimes). It is reputed that eight out of ten business failures are caused by poor cashflow, even if the firm is notionally profitable.

Costs

Costs are often one of the key drivers in setting prices, so understanding how they occur and how they are accounted for is crucial in pricing. Figure 2.6 shows a typical cost hierarchy adopted by many firms as the basis for setting a price.

In this model each step in the production process adds further incremental costs onto those already in existence until finally the total cost to produce is obtained. Then profit is added to arrive at the price. Whilst this model

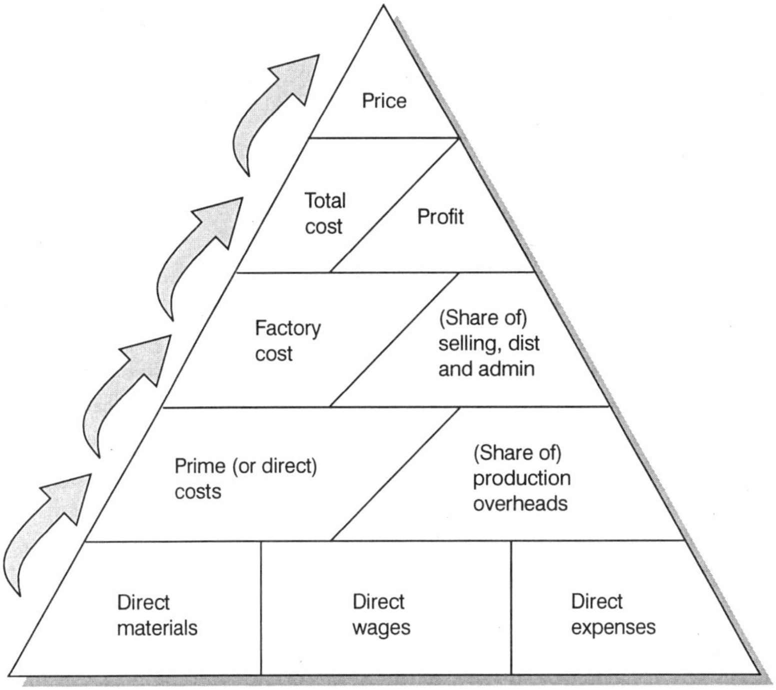

Figure 2.6 *Traditional cost-driven pricing*

looks at production the same model is applicable to services with slightly different terms.

There are many methods used by accountants to allocate costs:

Direct costing

This is probably the simplest method of all. Those costs which are considered to be directly attributable to the production of the product are allocated on the understanding that if the production was discontinued then the costs would not be incurred. The difficulty here is how to allocate general costs such as marketing, research and development, corporate overheads and others which disappear into the general melting pot of expenses. As both fixed and variable costs are included this can also distort the effects of changes in volume and thus affect pricing decisions. It does, however, have the advantage of being a simple method and providing the basis of cost allocation does not change and the business remains the same, it can be useful.

Absorption costing

With this method, all costs, whether direct or indirect, are allocated to products. The approach taken may be based on certain conventions but can often be inaccurate and arbitrary. Further, no allowance is taken for inherent inefficiencies in the organisation which should not affect the product. A good example would be the inclusion of 'head office expenses' which are often wholly inappropriate and disproportionate to production costs of goods offered for sale. Some products are much more price sensitive than others and increases from say, allocated costs of a new corporate building, could make specific products wholly uncompetitive when that is not really the case (although the costs will impact profits generally).

Activity-based costing

Activity-based costing (commonly known as ABC) was developed to correct the imperfections of the other types of costing analysis. The theory is that whereas most cost responsibility is allocated to functionally based cost centres (eg operations, sales, compliance, marketing, finance etc), costs are actually incurred by a series of activities which make up a process. Thus, the sales of a particular product may involve input from a whole host of departments and sections cutting right across functional boundaries, eg sales and marketing, internal audit, processing and many others.

By looking at the activities which incur the costs it is possible to ascertain the true cost of getting products/services to the market and realise the real profit potential. (This method also allows analysis of non-value added costs and therefore assists in cost control and reduction.)

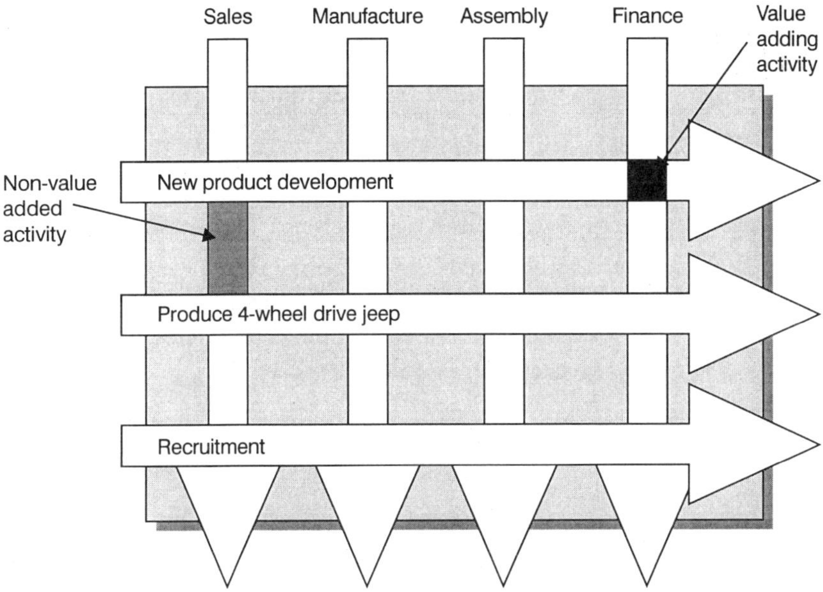

Figure 2.7 *ABC analysis – car manufacturer – traces process across functional divides and allocates activities thereto*

As each activity is allocated in proportion to the output and the value ascertained, what is known as 'white space' appears representing activities that add no value to the customer and, therefore, should be discontinued. Conversely 'holes' where activities which do not take place and should in order to add value also appear (known as 'black space'). By introducing these activities it is possible to increase the value to customers and, therefore, increase pricing accordingly, thereby improving profitability.

Standard costing

With this method cost calculations are undertaken on a theoretical basis which may be grounded in some real costs to arrive at standard (benchmark) figures, and subsequently used to provide costs input. Actual costs are then compared against this standard and the variances noted and analysed. (This is often the prime function of the management accounts department.) The key problems with this approach are the changing nature of costs and the usual time lag between the recalculation of the standard and the accuracy of assumptions.

Summary

There is no one right method of costing — all systems have their advantages and disadvantages, but the pricing manager needs to be aware that the simple existence of a 'costing system' can introduce pressures and distortions into the pricing process.

The pricing manager (and his colleagues in the accounting department) need to be able to work well together to understand and explain their own systems so that due allowance can be made.

There are usually standard cost conventions in operation in most firms and it can be difficult and unproductive to challenge these or deviate in many instances. A good understanding of the costs base of your products, however, allows real flexibility in pricing to ensure:

- that costs are covered;
- the relationship between contribution and discounts is understood very well;
- that decisions can be made which are accurate and allow true competitive advantage to be gained;
- that cost inefficiencies are isolated, and better still eradicated, and do not distort the price of the products;
- cost differentials between you and competitors can be understood and used in strategic pricing.

Other financial concepts

As indicated earlier, there are three further important concepts to understand:

- break-even analysis;
- transfer pricing;
- cashflow.

Break-even analysis

Break-even analysis is a method of analysing costs linked into sales volumes. Essentially it attempts to ascertain the level of sales needed to cover all fixed costs and thence the likely margin (contribution) achievable on subsequent sales after this point.

This type of analysis is often used to estimate the likely relationships between costs, profit and volume over time. The analysis tries to compute the volume of products that must be sold to cover the fixed costs. To do this it requires certain assumptions:

- that fixed and variable costs can be separated out;
- that variable costs change with volume;

- that price does not change over the period considered and at the volume levels taken.

The diagrams show the effects of high fixed costs or high variable costs, and how these affect profit opportunities.

The analysis is often graphed to show the point at which all fixed costs are covered (known as the break-even point) after which contribution is earned. Contribution after this point will be (for each unit) the price *less* the variable costs of production.

The higher the fixed costs the greater the volume needed before break-even is achieved and the more sensitive the profit calculation will be to volume variations.

In the longer term, however, all costs become variable as the limits of production are hit. Costs tend, therefore, to be stepped — as each limit of production is hit, further investment is required (eg in plant, machinery or people) which pushes the break-even up.

There is also an element of subjectivity in how costs are allocated. Electricity for lighting may be regarded as fixed whereas operating electricity could be regarded as variable in one firm (or even division of a firm) but viewed as wholly fixed elsewhere.

The impact of this is clear particularly at the margin of production. Where break-even has been reached the contribution could be, say, £2 per unit and salesmen might be tempted to accept an order at a discounted rate, eg £1.50. If this new volume takes production past the limit then the extra capital investment would destroy the break-even assumption and the levels of contribution. This could render the new order wholly unprofitable.

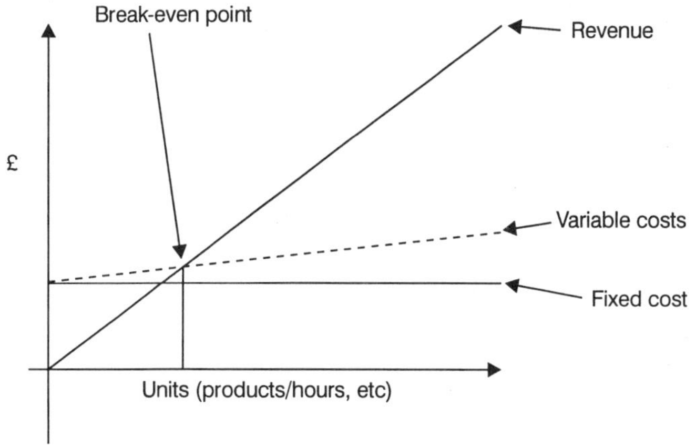

Figure 2.8 *Break-even chart*

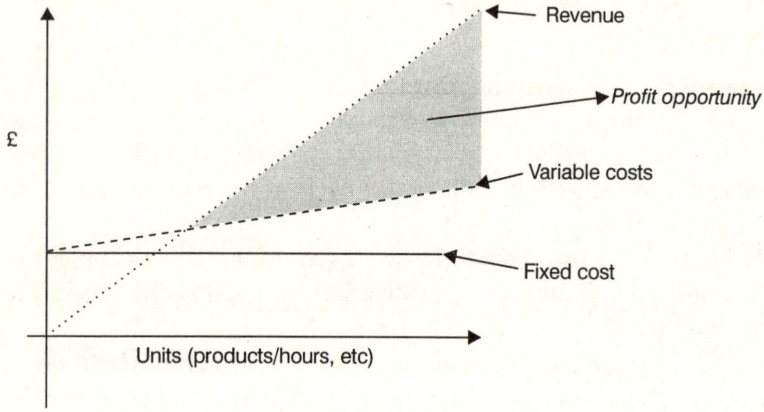

Figure 2.9 *High fixed costs in price*

Even variable costs can change if, for example, the extra labour required had to be paid a premium wage to attract them or if production took place in 'unsocial' hours requiring greater pay.

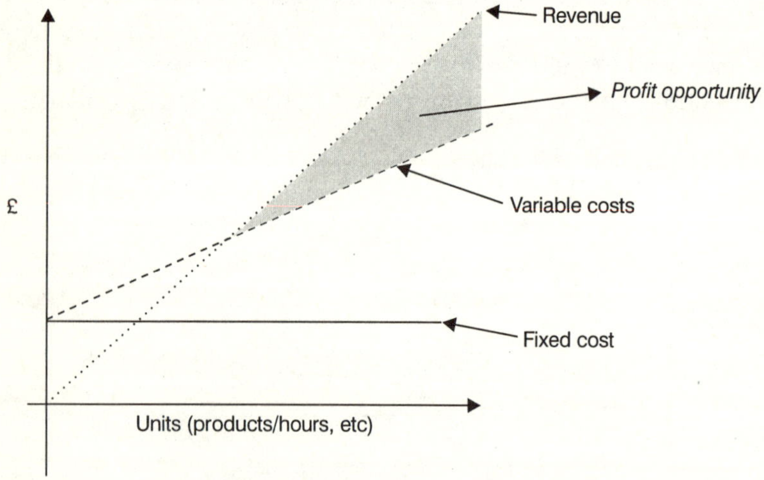

Figure 2.10 *High variable costs in price*

The basic equation for break-even analysis is:

$$\frac{\text{total fixed costs}}{(\text{net unit price} - \text{variable unit cost})}$$

This analysis allows you to see how many units you need to sell to cover your fixed costs, ie the minimum necessary to stop you making a loss.

The simple exercise below shows this:

Fixed costs	£24,000
Net unit price	£15
Variable unit cost	£9

The answer in this case is $\frac{£24{,}000}{(£15 - £9)} = \frac{£24{,}000}{£6} = 4000$ units

Clearly, the bigger the gap between the unit price and the unit cost, the less the break-even number will be. The break-even points can be graphed for different prices to track the numbers.

The real danger with this technique is that unless very accurate cost inputs are provided it can provide seriously wrong answers and secondly (and more importantly), the inherent lack of information on market-oriented factors can lead to unrealistic decisions.

Transfer pricing

These are the internal mechanisms within organisations for allocating costs across to other departments. A manufacturing division will use the Information Technology (IT) department, Accounts, Personnel etc and will be charged for their services accordingly. This charge will usually be based on some standard costs and methods of allocation, eg headcount for personnel costs, floor space for rent, time or units processed for IT etc. Some companies have very complex methods of recharging costs to other units involving multidimensional spreadsheets where services are recharged and then recharged out again (eg IT charge the cost of Human Resources (HR) systems to Personnel whose costs are then allocated to other units).

It can cause insuperable problems (as well as resentment) if it is not seen to be fair and accurate and may result in loss of business focus. One of the authors investigated the internal transfer pricing for a major UK company where all head office costs were charged out to business units and then subsequently allocated to products, and found that not only were the numbers wrong, due to old, inaccurate assumptions, but that it generated non-value added activities for staff who spent their whole time checking and challenging the allocated costs instead of selling products.

Transfer pricing is also used in other areas, such as tax avoidance (if you are a payer, collectors might see it as evasion). Where a company is operating across boundaries and tax regimes then by judicious use of pricing it can contrive to take costs in the most favourable regime (where, for example, they might be tax deductible) and make profits in low taxing regimes. Many large companies employ specialist tax experts for just this very reason who can often save them millions of pounds.

Transfer pricing is commonly found in financial institutions where, for example, the treasury will establish the internal cost of money which forms the basis for branches to make their lending decisions. It establishes the price that they will receive for money they place at HO (treasury) and also what they will be charged for borrowings from the HO.

This combines two very useful policies — all cash is monitored and managed internally as each branch is either in credit or in debit (net) from the treasury, which allows better rates to be obtained in the market due to the size of deals — but it also allows great flexibility to managers who are free to charge what they like in the knowledge that they will be making a profit or loss on the deal.

This enables them to underbid where relevant and to increase margins to reflect risks but also gives them a base rate against which to benchmark the opportunity cost of loans.

Cashflow

Whilst cashflow may seem on the face of it to have little to do with pricing, being related to internal controls rather than selling products and services, there is a link. The foregoing pages in this section have discussed the different types of cost analysis and allocation which form inputs to pricing. None of these will matter in the long run if costs are not controlled. It is not the sale of goods that raises cash; it is the actual physical payment by the purchaser. It is far more common for a sale to result in debtors rather than cash. Figure 2.11 (the cashflow cycle) illustrates this and the dynamics of cash.

Running a business takes cash — lots of it:

- you have to buy your raw materials and basic consumable items. Wherever possible you should try to get them on credit but there will inevitably be some payments;
- premises' costs must be met;
- staff have to be paid;
- transport and distribution costs;
- selling and marketing costs;
- fixed asset investment;
- basic utility costs;

- taxes must be paid at some stage.

Price plays an important part in ensuring that you can sell as many of your goods as possible in as short a time as possible to enable you to get as much of your cash in before you have to pay out.

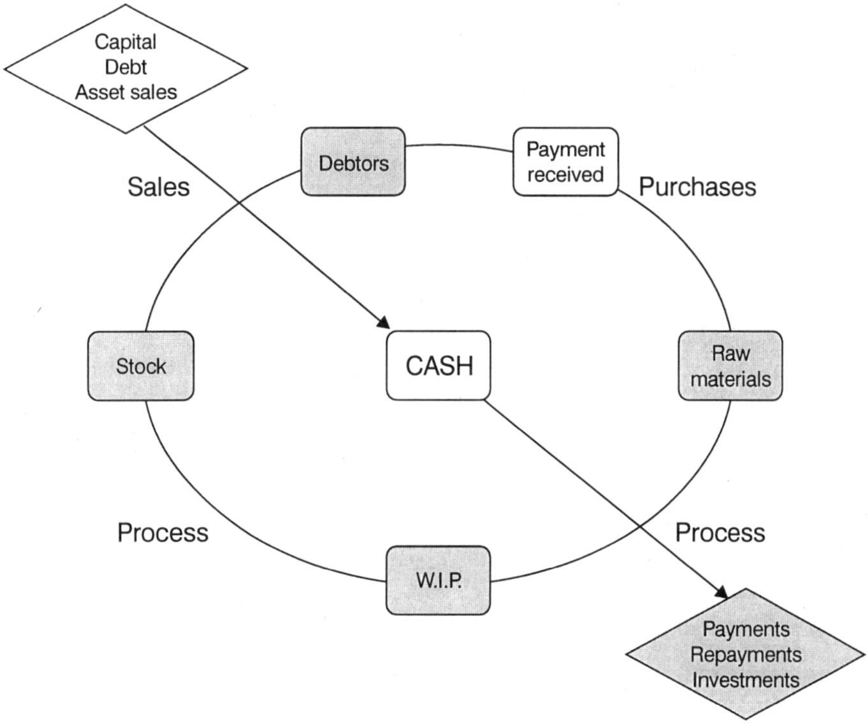

Figure 2.11 *Liquidity and cashflow cycle*

Whilst there is usually a correlation between long-term sources of funds (capital, debt) and long-term payments (investments) these never match up and it is the short term payments that must be made which usually lead to cashflow crises.

A company can last longer if it generates cash than if it generates huge paper profits although it must also make a profit to stay in business in the longer term. Life in business (and domestically) is a constant juggling act for most people; balancing cash in against cash out. By setting the right price you will go a long way to easing your cash management and therefore, where it is cost effective, discounts for prompt payment can provide the extra incentive for debtors to pay, thereby improving your own cashflow.

In practice, therefore, the pricing manager must pay attention to cash-flow. Because prices can be altered relatively quickly they can make a dramatic impact in a short space of time if reductions are linked with encouraging early payment, albeit with the possibility of causing damage to business in the longer term.

When small retailers close down, they put their remaining stock on sale, firstly with limited reductions, then latterly with enormous reductions, often selling below cost, simply to get cash in, before they close.

This is an end-game strategy, but even larger firms often discount or offer early payment reductions in slack times, just to ensure enough money is coming through the door that month — as they cannot wait for business to pick up in the longer term — they will just run out of cash!

Conclusion

This section has covered quite a lot of ground albeit at a high level; but none the less a rudimentary understanding of the key points of economics, marketing and finance, is vital for accurate and profitable pricing.

Without this understanding of customers' needs, market competitive forces and costing information, it is extremely difficult to produce a coherent strategy to enable pricing to take place. If you feel that you would like to understand a little more on these topics then there is a references and further reading list in the Appendices.

This section was an introductory section setting out the framework and background to pricing. The next section — *value pricing* — examines the pricing methodology and process in some detail and the methods that companies can use in practice.

PART TWO

VALUE PRICING

3

PRICING INFRASTRUCTURE INPUTS

INTRODUCTION

This chapter examines how organisations go about setting prices and the kind of management processes they use. The first stage is to look at the kind of information that comes into organisations and how people use this to set prices. Figure 3.1 shows information flows diagramatically, and how organisations manage this input is considered first.

The second stage is to consider how managers should take account of markets and competition in their thinking, and finally, how this should be factored into the strategy.

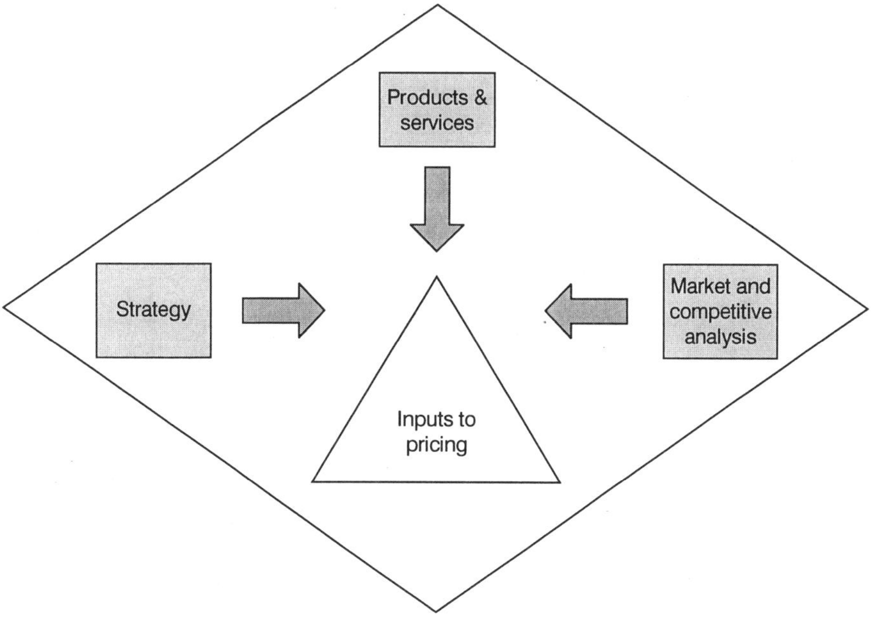

Figure 3.1 *Pricing Infrastructure*

Managing the inputs to decision making

In order to manage the pricing infrastructure a company will follow a procedure much like the following:

- analyse the *markets and competition* to ascertain the characteristics therein;
- examine its *product or service offering*; and then
- validate these against the *corporate strategy*.

Each of these areas is examined in detail in subsequent sections, but first it is relevant to take an overview of these processes.

Overview of the process

Unless they are a start-up operation, organisations and companies do not begin with a 'clean slate'. They will have information on markets, understand their own products (hopefully!) and will no doubt be trying to fit in with an existing strategy. The development of a new product or market, or a reappraisal of existing activities means that that the management process has to take detailed account of these three issues, which, of course, do not always fit neatly together.

This process is iterative, as each area does not stand alone, but inputs to and affects the others. Only when all aspects have been reviewed, compromises or decisions made and agreement reached, can a corporate framework for the pricing process be defined.

Typically, although not always correctly, the starting point will be from somewhere within the corporate strategy, which will typically set goals which are objectives and measures of attainment such as:

- to be ranked third or better by size;
- to be in the top quartile by profitability.

or more commonly and perhaps more usefully:

- set out a series of factors which provide a framework for action consisting of a number of weighted measures, some qualitative and some quantitative.

Where goals are expressed in sheer volume terms then different strategies will be required to achieve these than if they are expressed in pure profit terms. Combinations require more subtle matrix strategies to achieve these goals.

The statements within a corporate strategy, however, may not be detailed enough to be useful to management in setting detailed product, service or market strategies, and they must therefore be expanded to be in a format which states:

- the business segments served;

- the target customers within those segments;
- the products and services offered to those customers ;
- how the products will be delivered;
- the price.

It is only when the strategy has been defined at this level of detail that the *customer value proposition* (CVP) can be properly defined, and then used to drive the pricing strategy.

There should be at least one CVP for each product/market grouping. Each CVP will address different customers and set out the product offering thereto. This sets out the product pricing that is necessary to achieve the goals.

It makes no difference if markets are divided up by product type or by specific segment type; marketers use both types of segmentation. What matters is that the ultimate customer groups are homogenous and capable of being marketed to.

Managing segmentation

Some companies choose to manage themselves via product or brand groups – in a fast-moving consumer goods (fmcg) organisation you might find a 'personal deodorant manager', a 'washing products manager' or perhaps separate managers for tinned beer and for draught beer.

Equally, some choose to break it down by customer group. Thus you might find the 'home products' manager for a PC supplier, plus a 'corporate manager' and even a 'financial institutions' manager.

Normally a matrix is constructed with products and brands on one side and markets and customers on the other. Responsibility for each discrete section in the matrix is then allocated according to a variety of factors.

Having said that customer groups should be homogeneous, in the real world this is never the case and managers normally resort to analysing the spread of customers, to try to encompass the largest group, whilst still retaining homogeneity. This is often expressed as a Gaussian distribution (sometimes called a bell curve). Figure 3.2 shows a typical example of this.

Because the answers across a whole variety of sectors are often very similar this type of analysis gives an answer consistent with the so-called Pareto Law: that 80 per cent of your business comes from 20 per cent of your clients. Most firms will find that around 80 per cent of their customers group within the target range, with the other 20 per cent outside.

This approach is fine for well-defined target segments, but it does break down where the product offer or appeal is very wide. For example, an airline or a railway will have real trouble in selecting homogeneous groups to mar-

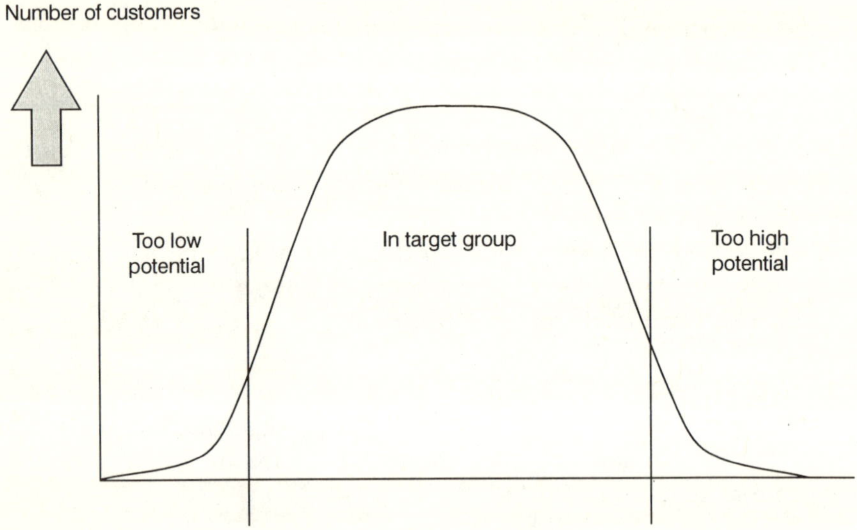

Figure 3.2 *Gaussian distribution*

ket to, and may well have to sub-segment extensively to achieve homogeneity, and thus arrive at a suitable CVP.

The CVP is thus targeted towards a core customer group and therefore, by definition, a number of CVPs may be required, depending on the business.

One of the features of a CVP is that it is targeted on a customer base that the organisation wishes to do business with. This means that those customers who do not fit in with this definition are not desired by the organisation as their requirements are not those that the firm is trying to meet. This will usually result in complaints from some customers who are not within the targeted segment but nevertheless do use the offerings. These must be ignored by the organisation or it will deviate from its CVP and almost certainly fail.

Examples of customers who can be alienated by targeted pricing and a defined CVP include:

- building society customers who wanted to keep passbooks when these were withdrawn from some building societies, and those still using cheque-books instead of cash cards/switch etc;
- banking clients with very small balances when minimum balances for banking products are introduced or increased;

- those travelling on airlines which offer a cheap 'no-frills' service and write in regularly asking for, eg meals to be served during flights; and
- people going to self-service garages when they were initially introduced and complaining that they wanted to be served by attendants.

Harsh as it may sound it makes good business sense to avoid these customers: they are ultimately not profitable. This said, the organisation has to be prepared for any bad publicity and ensure the overspill from this does not affect the targeted customer base.

UNDERSTANDING THE MARKET AND COMPETITION

A fundamental prerequisite for a company is to understand the market(s) in which it wishes to operate and the inherent dynamics therein, ie the customers and the competition (as well as regulations). Without this knowledge decisions will be made in a vacuum and may lead to disaster. These are critical inputs to pricing decisions as they represent areas which exercise great influence on your organisation. Examples of considerations include:

Is the market understood and predictable? This is to ensure that you respond to changes in a measured, planned manner and not reactively, running to catch up. If a seasonal price war takes place (eg January sales) you must have a plan in place to account for this.

Are you different? (What is your unique selling proposition (USP)?) It is usually very difficult to charge a lot more than the competition unless you can differentiate your offering. For example, what is the difference between most High Street bank offerings?; how do management consultancies differentiate themselves?; what is the difference between the 'branded' colas and own brands offered by many shops? These are all questions that need to be answered in terms of the customers' view.

Competitive reactions – If you take significant action (launch a new product, engage in a price war, or try to shift the price/quality fulcrum) what, if anything, will your competitors do and how will it affect you? Capturing this information requires that some level of research and subsequent analysis is undertaken. This can be in-house or by an external agency.

Generally speaking it is difficult to hold a price that is way out of line with your market competition. The only way to do this is by getting the message across that the product is worth the extra price due to the added value it represents (ie shifting the CVP).

Experience has shown that price wars typically result in a vicious downward spiral which can be to the short-term benefit of consumers but in the long term often benefits the suppliers as the overall level of competition is reduced as companies are forced out of the market. This then leaves the way open for significant price rises.

The market

As markets are somewhat amorphous, managers often find it hard to understand them and instead break them down into their characteristic components. Typically this includes:

- *Size* — measured both in terms of value and volume
- *Dynamics* — how the market has reacted and extrapolating those trends forward
- *Reactivity* — is the market stable or might it change rapidly?
- *Sensitivity* — do incremental changes affect the market as a whole or are they absorbed easily?
- *Maturity* — whereabouts in the life cycle is your market?
- *Attractiveness* — will others seek to enter?
- *Ease of entry* — what are the barriers to entry?
- *Profitability* — can we make money here?
- *Structure* — monopoly, oligopoly, open etc
- *Substitutes* — what are alternatives outside the market?

Table 3.1 gives examples of these characteristics for dissimilar markets:

Table 3.1

Product characteristic	Baked beans	Computer games	Book publishing	Independent radio
Size	big	small	medium	mainly small
Dynamics	static	erratic	slow	growing
Reactivity	stable	unstable	stable	unstable
Sensitivity	insensitive	very sensitive	variable	very
Maturity	mature	young	mature	adolescent
Attractiveness	not very	very	low	very
Ease of entry	high capital cost	medium	easy	difficult (licences)
Profitability	reasonable	high	variable low	high
Barriers	low, but distribution is key	high ad costs, 'credibility'	distribution is key	high to medium
Structure	oligopoly	open	fragmented	fragmented
Substitutes	many	few direct, many indirect	highly substitutable	few

The accepted way of breaking down complex markets is a technique called segmentation, whereby customers are broken into homogeneous buying groups. Thus, for example, in the book publishing market there are numerous types of sales outlets catering for different buyer needs (eg book clubs, up-market stores, specialists, antiquarian dealers, discount shops and many more), as well, of course, as the different types of books themselves (mass market paperbacks, 'bodice rippers', quality new fiction, hardbacks, paperbacks, coffee table books etc).

Competition

It is important to understand the nature of the competition in your chosen markets. In different markets there will be different structures including:

Monopoly where one firm controls the market (and therefore usually the price). This may mean that the market will be difficult to enter successfully but on the other hand may mean that it represents a good opportunity especially if you can demonstrate a differential from that firm, eg lower costs, better product etc.

Oligopoly where a small number of firms control the market and maybe an intensely competitive market or (often more likely) a degree of mutual cooperation exists to maintain prices. Again this can represent a good opportunity for attacking, via price, depending on the likely nature of the firms' responses.

Monopsony — although rarely found, this market is one where there are many suppliers but only one or very few customers (ie the opposite of monopoly). Examples of this would be the former Milk Marketing Board or the sole flour mill on an isolated large island.

Openly competitive where there are many firms operating in a market. This is also likely to be very competitive but at the same time open to variations in pricing strategies etc. Within this type of market the situation can vary dramatically; with one key supplier, with lots of smaller ones nibbling at the edges (eg the UK market for yacht paint); a market with two huge players and a number of smaller firms (cola with Coke and Pepsi is a good example of this); to markets where there are no dominant players. The petrol industry is a good example of this, where as well as the majors there are many independent firms. This usually makes price rises impossible to hold as the independents, with very much lower costs (ie no drilling/refining costs), can almost always undercut. There is virtually no brand loyalty in the petrol (gasoline) industry as it is the archetype commodity despite manufacturers' attempts to differentiate. Most people buy petrol because the station is located where they happen to be when they need to fill up, but they can be influenced by price.

As this book is being written an intense price war is being fought in the UK petrol market and seasoned observers believe many operators are now losing money on each litre sold. The end result is impossible to forecast, but one can confidently expect that the main protagonists will have charted likely outcomes (scenario planning) and seen a good chance that they will come out on top.

The petrol wars

A few years ago, the only place you could buy petrol in the UK was from a garage owned or operated under franchise by one of the oil majors (Shell, Esso, BP etc). Just a few discounters were on the scene (eg Jet) and the majors did not seem too concerned. By 1995, however, the situation had changed dramatically. The leading supermarket chains got in on the act and now account for nearly 20 per cent of all petrol sold in the UK. Some, like Tesco's, even run their own forecourts on the High Street and their own tanker fleets. These are not organisations buying small amounts on the Rotterdam spot market any more; they are major players, and they have built their positions through discounting and playing to their existing market, eg store visitors.

The traffic is not all one way, however, as petrol companies, eager to exploit the capital investment in their stations, have increased the range of goods available from car-related (oil, wiper blades, antifreeze) to almost anything. You can now buy groceries, gifts, fast food and many more items at 'oil company' service stations, a complete reversal of just 10 years ago. In this case price is not the determining factor: it is convenience of opening hours and location, therefore equalising the CVP.

Degree of foreign competition — competition may be domestic or may come from across borders. In the EU, free movement of goods, services and capital is one of the cornerstones of the common market. On the global scale, with GATT (*General Agreement on Trade and Tariffs*) and NAFTA (*North American Free Trade Area*) in place, barriers are disappearing. Foreign competitors in a market usually result in an increase in the diversity of both products and approaches and can often shake up complacent markets. Japanese cars were a very good example of this, as were Swatch watches.

Often firms and products can command a premium just by being foreign (French perfume is often accorded this status for no very obvious reason). Overseas firms will often have very different goals, eg trying to break into markets and following aggressive pricing strategies accordingly. For local firms, with poor external information, there may be little or no warning of their entry. Who can forget how the Japanese motorcycle firms virtually killed a complacent UK motorcycle industry in the 1960s and 1970s?

Competitive pricing

The competitive structure of your markets must be analysed and emerging trends noted to enable you to examine the likely responses to your own particular pricing strategy. Pricing strategies are very difficult to maintain where response is likely to be vigorous. In order to attack a major player or players on price you must have understood the pricing structure of the market and also the competition, in particular:

- How thin are margins?
- How long can they operate on low prices?
- How fast can they respond?
- Is the market one which they regard as a fundamental strategic necessity and therefore will respond until you are beaten, or will they be happy to get out if the going gets tough?
- In particular, would an aggressive pricing stance trigger a wholesale response that would lead to a vicious circle depressing profits to all players? This is frequently seen in large, highly competitive markets such as US airlines (where many have been driven into bankruptcy) or the UK retail food and clothing markets.

Customers

In understanding the market and competition, there is no more important person than the buyer or ultimate consumer of your product. The objectives, business outlook and forecasts of individuals or, in the case of business-to-business, the customers' own organisation are very relevant in formulating pricing policies.

Another critical factor which will be taken into account is whether the customers' need is 'must have' or merely 'nice to have'. With the latter selling will be harder and prices will be less firm. In the former case, however, the seller will often have the buyer 'over a barrel' and this will enable him to stick to prices and maybe charge premiums. One of the authors worked as a consultant on an assignment where if the work was not done very quickly the result for the client would have been loss of customers, poor cashflows and possibly closure. In this circumstance price becomes largely irrelevant and it is possible to obtain very high premiums over normal rates.

Another way of looking at this is to consider that when dealing with prestigious organisations or those that are growing or doing well in their own market you can often charge a premium price. This is not a general rule of course.

PRODUCT/SERVICE OFFERING

Customer perceptions of value for money (which are directly related to the price that can be charged) are primarily related to factors about the product or service being offered (although, of course, general perceptions of the supplier are important as well).

Marketers tend to use a technique know as 'gap analysis'. to look at their offer. This involves critically appraising products in the context of your customers and market, and deciding what, if any, differences there are between what you think you are offering and how they view it.

This is especially relevant as most firms will not be launching a brand new product into a brand new market, but will instead be seeking to reprice existing offerings or to attempt a relaunch.

Gap analysis is carried out by charting the characteristics and desires of the market (for which read consumers) and plotting these against the current offer. An example (for a hypothetical product, a photo frame made from recycled soft drink cans) is shown in Table 3.2:

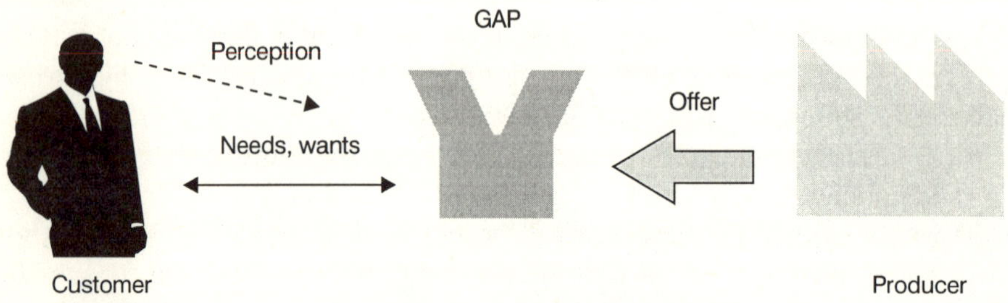

Figure 3.3 *Gap analysis*

Table 3.2

Characteristic	Market wants	Our product offers	Gap?
functionality	to show the photo clearly	a large glass area	No
price	less than £10	normally sold for £9	No
appearance	decorative	unusual, niche appeal	Yes
distribution	buy from a High Street store	mail order only	Yes
durability	to last for 20 years or more	lasts for five years	Yes
brand appeal	to boast about purchase to friends	no brand cachet	Yes
exclusivity	to own the best	anyone can make one in their garage	Yes

Our simple gap analysis shows that the photo-frame company is going to have to rethink its offer if it is to be successful. Of course, the case is not normally this clear-cut.

The key problem is that organisations often have many millions of pounds tied up in machinery and investment in infrastructure and management adopts a mind-set that says, 'We have always done it this way, why should we change?'. This type of inertia can be fatal as, no matter how you price the product, with that encumbrance, it will never be a success.

Example areas where firms have radically shaken up a market by looking critically at the product service offering would include:

Financial services where two firms, First Direct (the telephone banking arm of the Midland Bank, part of the HSBC Group) and Direct Line (the telephone-based insurance arm of the Royal Bank of Scotland Group) adopted a new method of distributing a common service using the telephone instead of 'bricks and mortar' branch networks. They reaped handsome rewards, incidentally spawning a whole host of 'wannabe' look-alikes across the industry.

Home entertainment — with the advent of the Videoplus technology, it has become much easier to tape TV programmes, and this must have contributed to an upsurge in the sale of VCRs and tapes as well. Similarly, CDs and CD-ROMS have changed the face of music, information and other forms of data transfer for ever.

Paint – some years ago, Dulux (and others) started to make paint available in tiny pots, so you could paint a patch on your wall to see if you liked the colour, an innovation in packaging and promotion that must have generated huge sales of premium priced colours that people might otherwise have been afraid to try.

On the other hand the markets for technologically based products come and go with frightening rapidity. People who specialised in games software for the Amstrad Spectrum computer had to diversify quickly or die, as did the manufacturers of monochrome TV monitors (which are virtually as redundant as wax cylinders are and as LPs soon will be).

Clearly, the secret with gap analysis is to have an excellent understanding of market wants. In practice this can only be obtained by very detailed market research, often using more than one type of research technique.

Marketers must remember that one has to mould one's offering to customer demand, and not try and adapt customers to one's products. Whilst there is always the exception that proves the rule, the fastest way to go out of business in this day and age is to be production led rather than customer led.

So, before setting a price, check your overall offer in the marketplace. If you find a good match to the CVP then you can price high, if you don't then a low price might be the only answer. Remember, they couldn't even give the Sinclair C5 away at one point!

What to look for

Gap analysis is used to look at the following four areas:

- product quality, utility, fitness for purpose;
- consumers' perception of the supplier (manufacturer);
- service issues;
- customers' objectives from the purchase.

It is beyond the scope of this book to look at these areas in detail, but the key points are as follows:

Product quality, utility, fitness for purpose

As well as the obvious legal requirements, it is surprisingly common that people who make and sell products have an inflated idea of the importance of their own products, and take the view that because their life's work is invested in the idea, so it will be top of the consumers' agenda.

No doubt many consumers do take their purchases seriously, but it is safe to assume that most vest their purchase with less than the amount of seriousness that the manufacturer would like. A good case in point is instructions. No matter how many times we are told, most consumers simply open the box, plug the product in and fiddle around to try to get things to work.

For the business manager the key is to listen to people and find out what they actually do in practice, rather than what you would like them to do. It can be possible to save money and reduce prices in this way. For example, eliminating extra features that are never used (can you honestly say that you have used every feature of your video recorder?) or perhaps junking expensive instruction manuals, and replacing them, with a booklet and a free-phone telephone hotline.

Consumers' perception of the supplier (manufacturer)

Advertising is key in this area, although in many areas word of mouth is perhaps as important. If you are a low-quality, cheap supplier fighting to get up-market, you could make the best engineered products in the world, and no one would believe you for 20 years or so!

The subtle shift in perception that Japanese products are not cheap, flimsy or unreliable, but are high quality and keenly priced has taken decades, and other suppliers face problems with such perceptions. We have seen how in the car market Skoda is trading heavily on the quality image of Volkswagen to move up-market. Saab use its aerospace products (jet fighters, no less) in its adverts to persuade people about the technology and even French wine producers are now having to fight hard against the rise in consumer confidence in superior products from the New World.

Service issues

For many of today's consumers, service is becoming a very important issue. Supermarkets are fighting to making product checkouts easier to use (queuing is a notorious turn-off for shoppers), and many companies will now send someone out to fix a fault. When one of the author's Hewlett Packard printer broke down, a trained service engineer was round in four hours, and fixed the fault free of charge. This service was included in the price paid.

What business managers often forget is that pricing strategies can so easily be undermined by faults in internal systems. If your switchboard cannot answer calls in 10 seconds and pass callers on to the right person, the consumer is going to think twice about paying the premium price your strategy requires.

Customers' objectives from the purchase

Finally, the pricing manager should not forget that in parting with money, the consumer is making a deal with your firm. He wants some benefit in exchange for the money. If you take the example of a paint company, whilst it sells paint, customers do not really buy paint. The average householder, for example, is buying protection for his front door, or most commonly is buying a soothing colour scheme for his front room, one that his friends and family will admire.

It pays, therefore, to think how you can help the customer meet his objective. If, for example, you put added silicone into the paint, making it tougher and longer lasting, this will hardly be apparent in a front room, but if you brand the colour with the name of a famous designer, say William Morris pink, this will give them something to talk about and be proud of.

You will be able to command a premium price for the William Morris pink, even if it is the same as the regular product, simply because you are helping the consumer meet his objectives.

Summary

There are a whole host of issues to think about in product and service offerings, but primarily these centre around the consumer. Detailed market research is the starting point, but an open mind-set is vital if you are to take the relevant actions based on your findings.

It is very common to find companies spending large amounts of money on research only to dismiss the findings because they do not fit in with the management's preconceptions.

CORPORATE STRATEGY

Introduction

Whatever pricing methods are used they must be in support of the strategic objectives of the organisation. Thus *prior* to pricing any goods or services the organisation must have set and agreed its strategy; the business plans and the marketing strategy/plans to support these.

All pricing decisions should be made in this context and should allow for differential pricing between strategic business units, where appropriate. At a corporate level the following will be set out:

The **vision** of an organisation drives the overall direction over a long-term period (typically 10 to 20 years), for example:

- Body Shop was to sell environmentally friendly products.
- Sony was to provide everyone with portable personal sound.
- Wedgwood was to sell china to the common man.
- Coca-Cola wanted US GIs serviceman to be able to enjoy its product anywhere in the world.

The *mission statement* then articulates the simple vision and lays down the overall policies that will guide the organisation in its operations.

The *strategy* will then set out how to achieve the mission. These are much more detailed documents and will be set for each division, operating unit or *strategic business unit* (SBU).

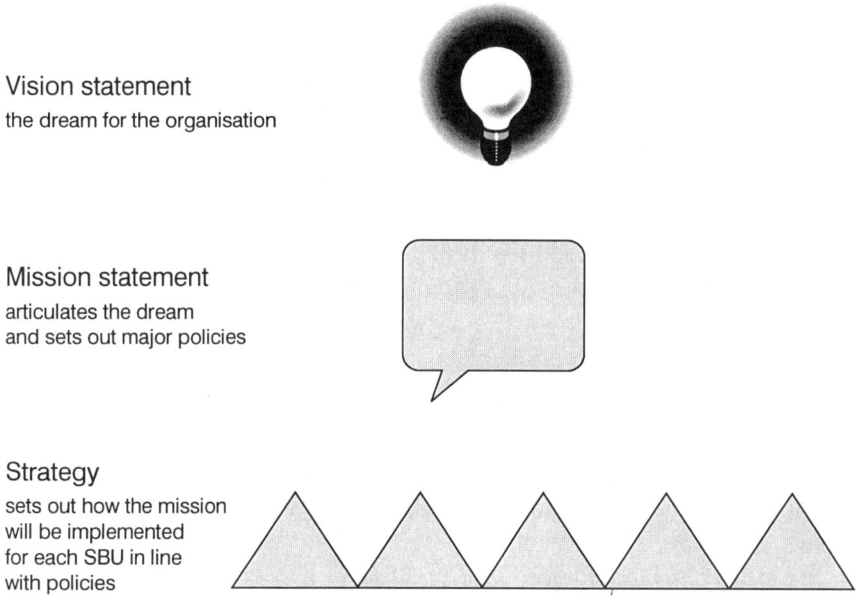

Figure 3.4 *Vision*

A key feature of a strategy is that it will contain measurable objectives (eg 20 per cent market share in two years, 30 per cent return on investment by April) as well as softer (qualitative) ones.

Note also that it is appropriate for an organisation to have sub-strategies. Typically these should be 'nested', that is the ones for smaller parts should fit into the larger ones, and the strategies themselves may be broken down into commonest parts (a financial strategy, a marketing strategy, an acquisition strategy).

Adopting a coherent approach to strategy development

Prior to pricing products, an organisation must make a number of strategic decisions which will set the framework for pricing. For larger firms there will be different strategies for different products and markets and these will need to cascade down, for example:

- a corporate strategy;
- a divisional strategy;
- an operating unit strategy;
- a brand group strategy;

- a product strategy.

Strategy is usually set in a much wider context than simply deciding what an organisation wishes to achieve for a particular product. The strategy of a company is about overall goals over long periods of time. In many cases it is about the aspirations of the set of stakeholders, management, owners and staff. A small business will normally be run to provide a reasonable standard of living for its proprietor, whereas a large multinational will have totally different goals and objectives probably expressed in terms of position in several markets and needing to provide dividends for owners, pay off debts etc.

As the strategy is progressively decomposed into national, divisional and product group strategies, and thence to product strategies, the data becomes 'harder', more factual and increasingly relevant to pricing decisions.

Once the detailed strategy has been articulated then a plan of action for pricing can be drawn up which will cover:

- *pricing policies* to provide the framework for pricing;
- the *pricing strategies* that you will use;
- the *marketing mix* which gives relative weightings to price as a marketing tool;
- *pricing tactics*.

These are considered in more detail in the next chapter.

STRATEGIC CONSIDERATIONS

Some key considerations that managers must take into account when considering strategy include:

- distribution;
- risk (those that are acceptable and the price);
- time horizons;
- value chain.

Distribution

Most organisations sell through more than one type of outlet (distribution channel) and this causes the pricing dynamics to change. This is because pricing must also reflect the needs of intermediaries as well as end-users. Take the example of a financial services company selling mortgages.

It may sell them through a variety of techniques, and the following list shows some of the considerations for each method:

Branch network	usually the most expensive due to the huge fixed asset investment
Direct sales force	may be commission only or be salaried or a combination of the two, and may require an infrastructure to support it
Intermediaries	usually recompensed by fees/commissions
Tied agents	usually recompensed by commission but usually at a higher rate than intermediaries as the throughput is guaranteed and will usually involve some extra support (PCs etc.)
Off-the-page advertising	requires only the cost of the adverts and the processing costs
Telesales	requires telephone costs and direct staff costs

Each channel has different cost structures, different methods of selling and different logistics needs. They will also have different 'hit rates' in different markets and with different types of products.

The particular channel or combination of channels used will influence pricing because of the different costs associated with them. Compare the difference in costs between a bank branch network and a telephone-based service, or between a sales force that visits prospective customers at home and a catalogue available over the Internet.

This, in turn, can lead into differential pricing which can mean that complex management procedures need to be developed to ensure that your intermediaries do not cross-compete with one another and thus lose you margin (eg where intermediaries in the beer off-sales market undercut direct sales to other outlets due to the greater discounts they can sometimes obtain from bulk-buying) or may be illegal (some financial services).

The organisation must weigh up the relative pros and cons of each type of channel and decide which it will use, and in which combination. This offer is decided at the strategic level and cascaded down to operating units.

Because of the high capital cost and long time-scales for developing distribution, it is usually a major consideration in setting the pricing strategy for a product.

Risk

Risk is inherent in everything, from crossing the road to setting your prices. This is especially true where the firm operates across borders in many markets. When setting a price, therefore, it is important that the price reflects the inherent risk(s) in the transaction.

Typical risks that must be confronted and some possible remedies (which almost always involve extra cost – hence the need to get the analysis right) are shown in Table 3.3, below:

Table 3.3

Type of risk	Suggested remedy
Currency exposure	Forward contract or bill in home currency
Cross-border trading	Insurance or letter of credit
Credit	Credit checks, bank guarantees, invoice factoring
Supplier	Partnership/vertical integration
Political	Insurance (ECGD/HERMES/NCM)
Timing	Get payment in advance, sell through intermediaries
Finance	Borrowing, treasury management
Liability	Get legal advice

The level of risk varies depending on the type of transaction involved with, say, basic retailing at one end and complex long-term projects at the other. The secret is to try to estimate the *likelihood* of the types of risk and then assess the *magnitude of damage (severity of risk)* caused if it goes wrong.

You then take steps to minimise potential losses. This, of course, impacts on pricing as it usually raises the costs of doing business, eg by paying for insurance cover, subscriptions to credit agencies such as CCN; paying for forward contracts, professional fees for advisers etc.

Figure 3.5 shows the different strategies that can be adopted to cover different types of risks. By contrasting the magnitude against the likelihood you can categorise your risks into bands of priority.

The bands range from those where the likelihood and severity are both high and, therefore, should be avoided; to those where the risk is so small that it can be ignored.

The numerical weighting or product (X × Y — severity × likelihood) has been used to set the example bands as follows:

where it is greater than 54	(*avoid*);
from 36 to 53	(*lay-off*);
from 17 to 35 (but including those where either axis is 9)	(*quantify*);
from 7 to 16	(*absorb*);
less than 7	(*ignore*).

You must draw your own bands for your organisation reflecting the likely risks you will encounter; and the combination of likelihood and magnitude you are willing to accept.

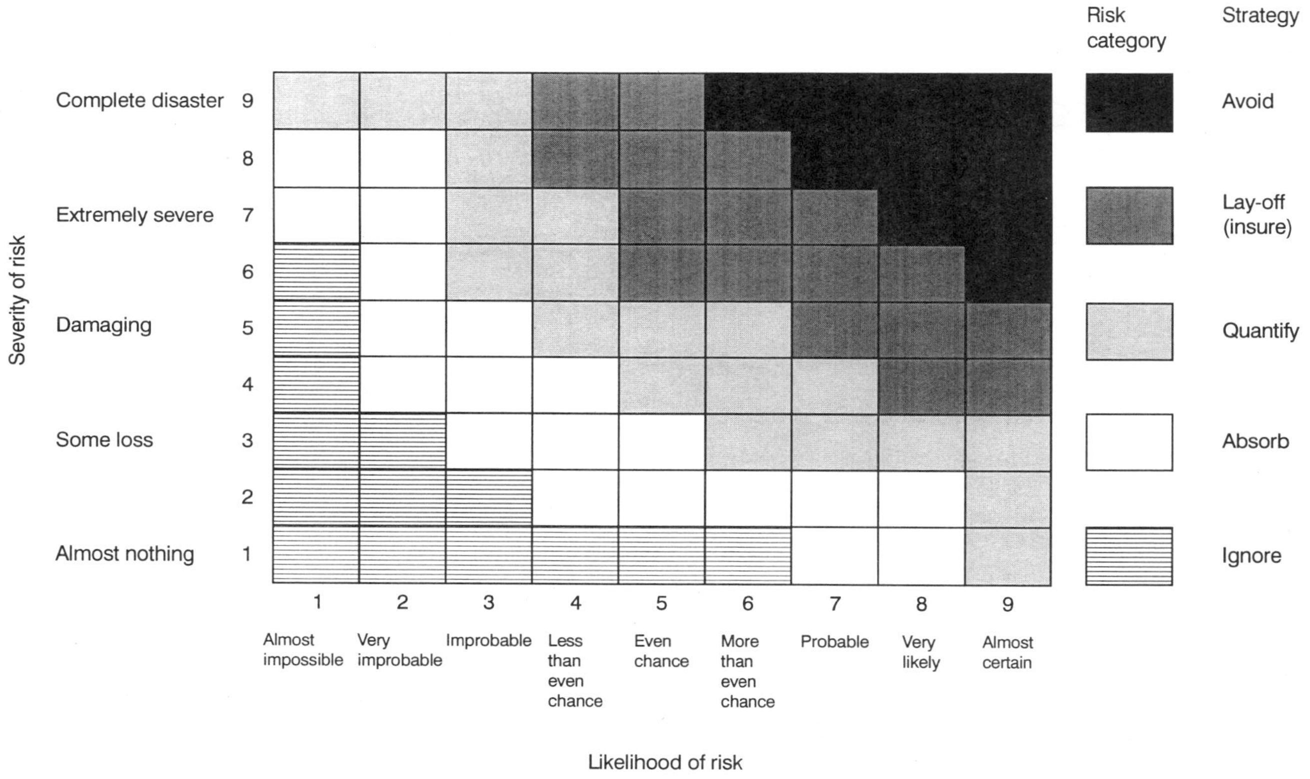

Figure 3.5 *Risk assessment matrix*

Whichever strategy you choose will impact upon your pricing, and, of course, this must be compared with the risk/return trade-off, depending on your risk profile (risk lover or risk averse). As a general rule reward is frequently *overestimated,* whilst the risk is often either *underestimated* or insufficiently analysed. As a result there is a tendency to drift down the risk reward 'curve' from 'A' towards 'B' (see Figure 3.6). This results in much greater exposure to risk (or the same exposure to a greater level of risk) for less reward than anticipated. As a result the price turns out to be insufficient.

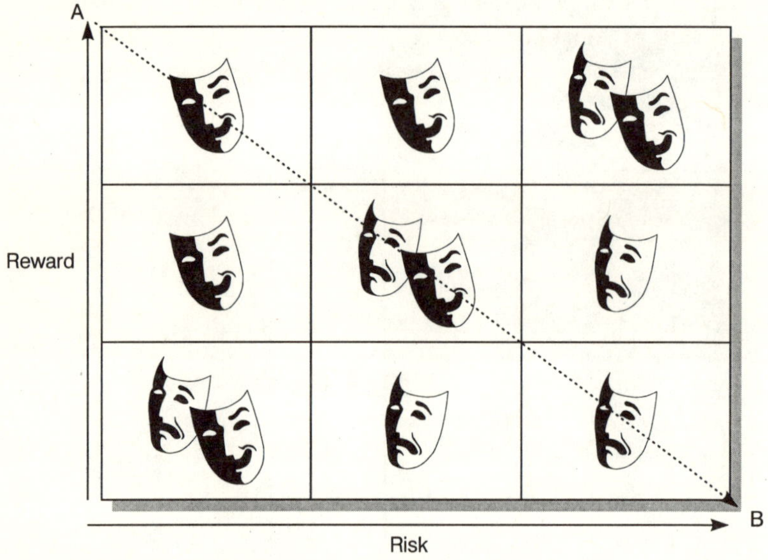

Most things start at 'A' and drift to 'B'

Figure 3.6 *Risk/reward trade-off*

Different organisations and indeed different individuals within these will have different risk profiles, and be prepared, therefore, to take different risks (gambles).

A general precept is that the higher the risk the higher the reward *but* this is not always the case and the risk of failure grows incrementally as you move up the risk reward curve. It is a fact that most risks are insufficiently analysed in pricing terms and, therefore, lower returns are received than the risk would seem to warrant.

Risk evaluation

The effort that goes into the analysis will reflect the type of product or service offered. Where consumer goods such as beans are sold, the risk decision is taken at a higher level as part of the overall strategy; for a bank loan or a life assurance policy, however, there is usually a risk decision in each case. In the case of a loan the risk of non-repayment is examined and depending on this it may be rejected out of hand or will be priced to reflect the risk as perceived. For a life policy the risk of mortality is analysed and premiums weighted accordingly.

In both cases much of the process is 'mechanical' or routine through credit scoring or mortality tables but some decisions require more input. The figure shows the increasing complexity of decision making versus uncertainty (risk).

Complexity of problems/ uncertainty of environment	Appropriate mode of decision-making
Low	Routine
	Consultational
Medium	Experience
	Judgmental
High ↓	Inspirational

Figure 3.7 *Pricing styles and the environment*

Currency risk (sometimes called Kenyon's Exposure)

With the growth in international trade it is worth looking at one type of risk in a little more detail. For many organisations transactions take place wholly within one market and, therefore, with no currency exposure. Where, however, an organisation either trades across borders or sources outside its own country then an element of foreign currency exposure is present.

Whilst this book will not address foreign exchange dealing etc, currency fluctuations have a direct impact on pricing. For example, the price so carefully set to give you a couple of pence advantage could be eroded by currency movements or even render your price wholly uncompetitive, eg where the currency in your target country is devalued. Similarly, where parts are sourced from another country(ies) fluctuations in exchange rates may affect the price of your product disproportionately, depending on the value of the contribution to the value chain.

As an example the UK pound/US dollar rate has fluctuated between $2.4 and parity over the last 10 years or so and against the yen the pound has depreciated in relative terms by 50 per cent since 1984.

When setting prices it is necessary, therefore, to factor possible currency movements into your analysis and thinking. This may require repricing or, for example, taking out forward contracts to hedge the exposure thus ensuring a stable price. Failure to do this can have far-reaching consequences. Allied-Lyons and Jaguar, amongst others in the early 1990s, suffered from a change in the UK pound/US dollar rates which impacted their prices, making their products uncompetitive thereby losing sales. Many German, French and Japanese companies are currently experiencing similar problems.

Adverse currency movements can also hurt a company by reducing the value of overseas investments when translated into the home currency. Tate & Lyle (a UK food company) reported in its 1993 review that only 24 per cent of its assets were in sterling. The rest were in foreign currencies (US dollars 28 per cent, Australian dollars 11 per cent, other EU currencies 29 per cent, others 8 per cent) and it has a sophisticated treasury operation to manage this to minimise problems.

Alfred Kenyon set out a theory that stated that you have to consider exposure to currency right at the beginning of the process, ie by hedging when you send out your catalogues *not* when you subsequently receive orders. Most large companies now have well-established treasuries to deal with this whilst others can use their banks for help.

Time horizons

For each product or service offered, the time horizon must be considered properly. Is the pricing decision being made in as a part of a strategy that is short term, eg to shift stock, or to act as a loss leader thereby encouraging purchases of other goods etc, or is it part of a longer-term strategy which must be followed through over possibly several time periods? Such a strategy might be to reduce prices down to well below the competition to gain volume/market share which will in the future allow economies of scale thereby reducing input costs.

At the time of writing the UK brewing industry is a classic example where the market is declining and the major players are jostling to maintain or increase market share. It has been estimated that any two have the capacity between them to satisfy the whole market share but no one has more than 20 per cent. Were one to follow a strategy of underpricing then it could conceivably take market share and achieve long-term dominance at the expense of the others. This would require an up-front investment in terms of absorbing short-term losses until the greater capacity came on stream thereby depressing unit costs. It is, however, not without risk and would require a long-term time horizon to keep to the strategy in the face of competitors' responses which are likely to be aggressive and rapid. Another response is for industry rationalisation via mergers to occur, and this seems to be happening.

Japanese and other Asian organisations are known for being much better at taking long-term views of the market, and acting and pricing accordingly. In many Western companies, however, where short-termist stock markets often exercise a high degree of influence, it takes secure management with a strong nerve to take such a similar long-term view. The benefits from this view can, however, be substantial where market share is consistently gained incrementally through clever pricing.

The longer a period that costs can be spread over (amortised/depreciated) the lower the break-even cost per year will be. Similarly, whenever costs can be deferred it will have a beneficial effect on short-term prices. This is particularly useful when considering some of the market/product approaches above (new start-up, attain cost leadership).

If you purchase a mainframe computer costing $2,000,000 and write it off in one year it will have a huge impact in that year. If it is written off over, say, five years, then $400,000 will count as costs each year and if over 10 years then only $200,000 per year (over the writing-off period).

Clearly this will impact the break-even costs by requiring a greater volume for a shorter 'life' to absorb costs. There are certain accounting conventions that mitigate against this but there are also ways around the problem.

At the opposite end of the spectrum heavy investment can not only raise costs but, providing it delivers benefits, will also raise barriers to entry thus (hopefully) scaring off potential competitors. A good example of this might be giving new releases of software away to enough users such that it becomes the *de facto* standard.

In the world of the Internet, the Netscape Web Browser Software has gone from nowhere to holding around 90 per cent of the market. The company is now valued in US$ billions and has a very good brand to build on.

The phasing out of CFCs (which damage the ozone layer) in the mid-1990s is another very good example. The initial investment in new production facilities for aerosols using *liquid petroleum gas* (LPG) instead of CFCs was huge; however, as LPG was much cheaper than CFCs those companies taking the longer-term view and making the investment reaped the reward in terms of increased market share coupled with lower production costs! By taking the long view, companies were amply rewarded.

Value chain

The value chain is an analysis of the components and activities which combine to make and put a product onto the market. Figure 3.8 shows a typical example (the PC industry):

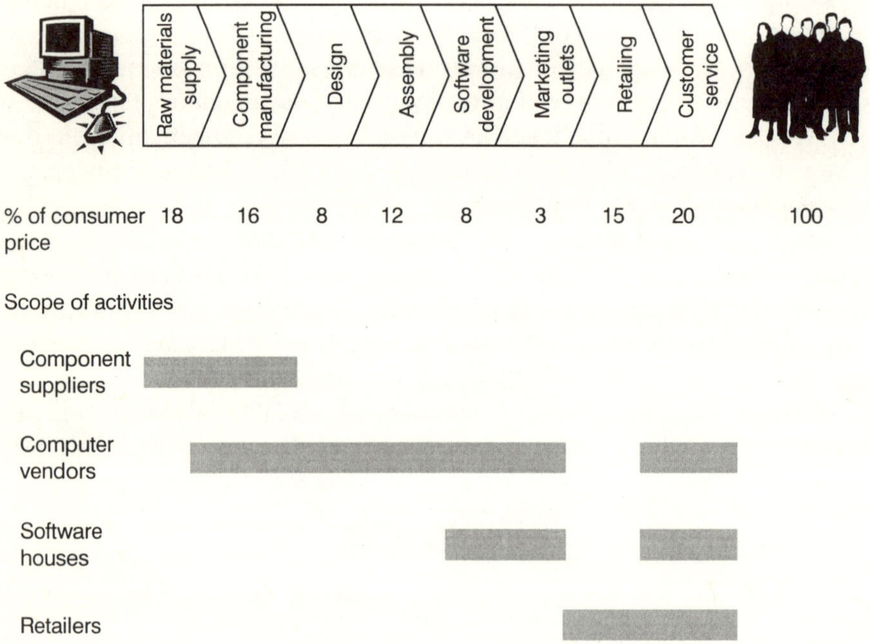

Figure 3.8 *Value chain*

This traces the chain from the initial input (raw materials) through to the delivery to the ultimate consumer of the product or service, the value added at each stage (defined as percentage of final output price) and the roles of the key players often in different (though related) industries.

The critical areas for pricing are the percentage of each step in the value chain and the relative importance it has to the inputs of a price. Clearly a change in one of these components will affect the final price and, depending on the magnitude of the component, may limit flexibility with pricing or cause a fundamental rethink.

The length, scope and dynamics of each part of the value chain are a key component in the pricing strategy. It is obvious that changes at the start of the chain (eg raw material prices going up) can have a huge 'knock-on' effect on pricing at the end of the chain, as each person adds their percentage to a greater percentage.

In the case where raw material costs are a high proportion of the final cost of the product (eg coffee), the final vendors will have to take steps to ensure they are not locked into contracts that they cannot fulfil at a profit. Examples of precautionary methods might include back-to-back contracts with suppliers, hedging or speculating on commodity futures' markets, and short contracts with buyers (so you can change your prices overnight). Companies who fail to observe these precautions can get locked into potentially disastrous long-term deals where every unit sold loses them money.

In setting the strategy, the manager should be well aware that flexibility costs money and should build in the the cost of contracts, hedging, insurance etc at an early stage.

Some companies go so far as to try to take all the value chain under their own roof, from mining the raw material to manning the retail shop (called vertical integration). This is not free from problems either, as the costs can be huge and the expertise may not necessarily be there.

Summary

This section has touched on three key areas:

- the need to understand markets;
- making sure your products and services match customers' needs;
- working within the constraints of an overall strategy.

These are critical points, and can be likened to gaining an understanding of the 'big picture'. Where managers do not understand the overall aims and objectives of a business then by definition they are more likely to make decisions that are in conflict with, instead of supporting, the organisation. This conflict very often does not show itself initially, but typically only manifests itself later, and may affect the ability to sell or even deliver output.

Consider how many times you have heard someone on the sales or marketing side of an organisation say, 'I could have closed that deal, but my boss just wouldn't go the extra inch'. They can't understand it in the context of one sale, but it might clearly be understandable in the corporate context.

In the next chapter the full methodology for pricing is described. Have the bigger picture in mind as you read this.

4

THE PRICING METHODOLOGY

INTRODUCTION

In Chapter 3 the pricing infrastructure inputs were considered; that is, the thought processes and decisions which have taken place at the corporate level to provide a general framework for operations and for pricing decisions.

This chapter examines the methodology for value pricing; that is the theoretical steps to be followed once all the inputs are in place. This is shown diagrammatically below. You will note that it is represented as a circle as it is a continuous process reviewed in the light of feedback.

The methodology

The methodology sets out the steps to be followed:

- the *marketing mix* is the first item to be agreed on, as this sets out the general approach (in which price is only one element);
- this then leads into how the *pricing policy* sets the framework within which pricing decisions will be made;

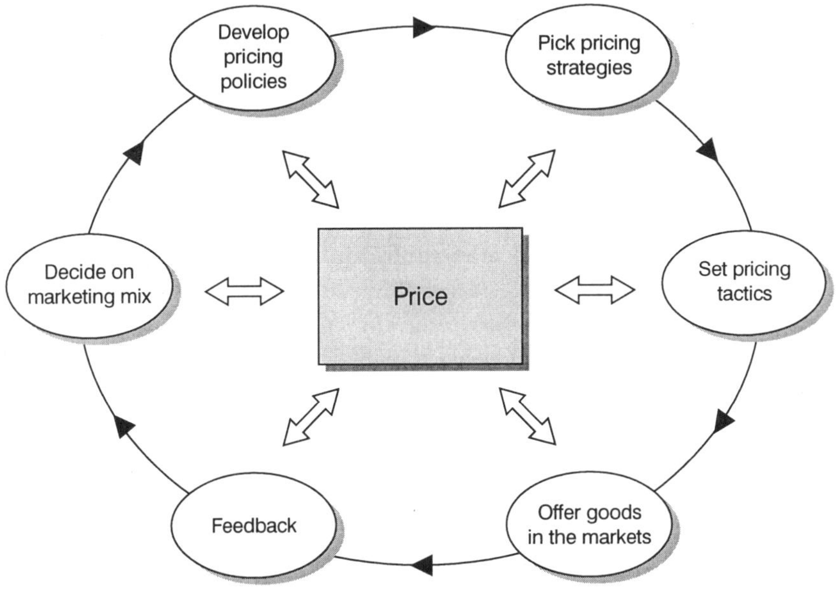

Figure 4.1 *Pricing methodology*

- the *pricing strategy* sets out how these policies will be implemented and forms the operating background to tactical pricing. This is a subset of the overall corporate strategy which is normally set at board level;
- the *pricing tactics* can then be agreed on which will drive the day-to-day operation of pricing in the organisation (this will be addressed in Chapter 5).

Following this the goods are offered in the market and consumer feedback is used to provide fresh inputs to the process.

POLICIES, STRATEGIES AND TACTICS

Before examining the steps in the pricing methodology it is worth explaining what is meant by the terms *policy*, *strategy and tactics* in this context as there is often some confusion in people's minds as to the difference.

The corporate strategy:

- sets the context for decisions to be made;
- provides information and understanding to the pricing process;
- establishes a mechanism for validation of decisions;
- sets delegated limits for decisions; and
- provides a clear communication of whether the emphasis is on profit, volume market share etc for each key divisional or strategic business unit.

It will detail the type of broad strategy the organisation is pursuing — focus; cost leadership, differentiation or whether it will wallow in the middle ground (see Figure 4.2). It will contain not only the strategic objectives and the strategy for achieving them, but also often policy statements – the general rules, regulations, mechanisms and processes that govern the overall operations at a corporate level. The strategy of a company will not deal with prices as that would be at far too detailed a level; however, it will consider profit which is, of course, related to pricing. One of these policies will, however, deal with marketing, and would contain details of the *marketing mix* and assess whether to use single products, product ranges, product bundles etc.

A subset of the marketing policy is the *pricing policy*. This policy would clarify such things as minimum prices for products and services; range of delegated authority for discounting; special deals, the image; what the basic offer should be; and price positioning generally.

This general policy framework would then be used to validate the *pricing strategy* which would develop specific prices for each situation to support the

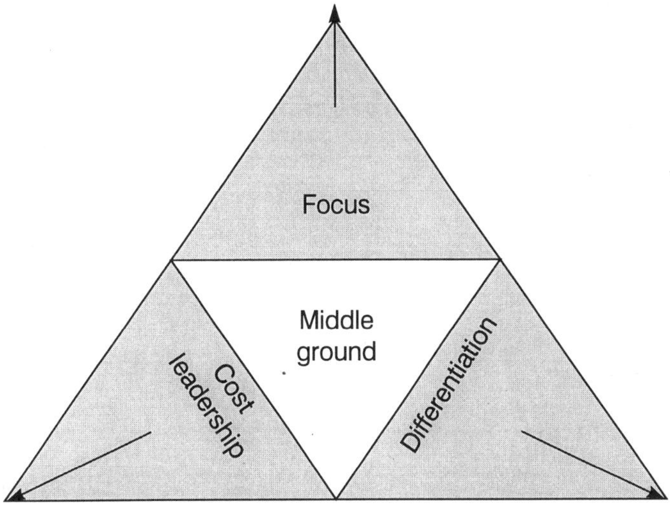

Figure 4.2 *Broad strategy*

marketing strategy for that product/market. These are normally set at product level.

Once the strategy has been agreed then the managers can develop the *pricing tactics* to carry out the strategy on a day-to-day basis, ie how they will achieve their targets, whether they be expressed in profit, market share or in revenue terms. Figure 4.3 shows how these factors are linked.

The methodology represents the steps to be followed to price successfully within a strategic framework.

MARKETING MIX

What is the mix?

Pricing policy is critically linked to the *marketing mix*. This is defined as the set of tools or options available to the firm to use in support of its marketing objectives.

The marketing mix is usually expressed as the four Ps:

- what you are selling (*product*);
- how it is distributed and sold (*place*);
- how the offer is communicated (*promotion*);
- what to charge for it (*price*).

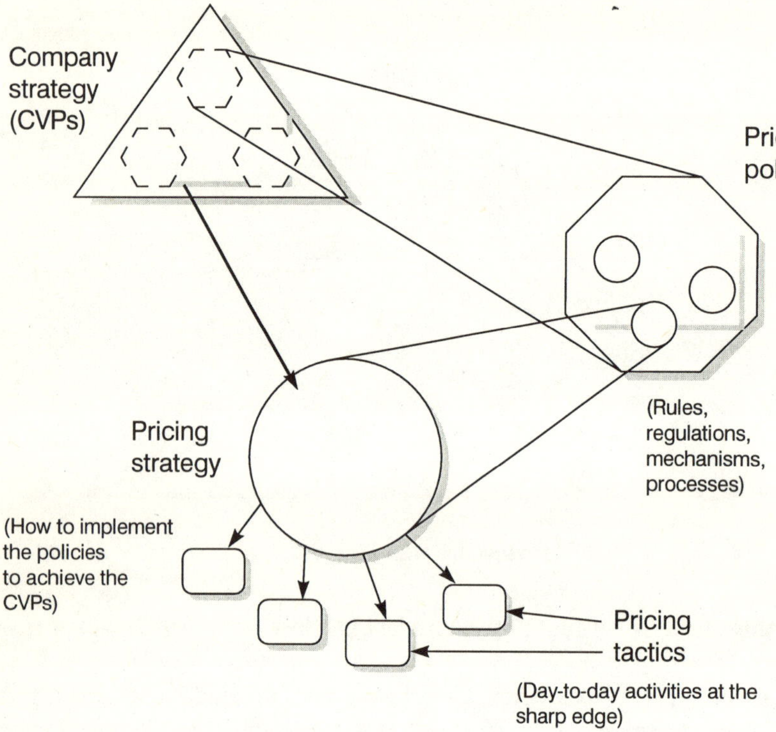

Figure 4.3 *Where pricing policy and strategy fit*

In practice the marketing mix is more complex than the four Ps suggest. The marketing and sales management in a company will have an idea of the techniques and routes they will want to use to sell any given product (maybe determined from what competitors do, what the market likes, or maybe even on what the firm is good at). It will pick a subset of tools to use and will then apply a weighting to each technique to produce the mix. Whatever they do, the price must be chosen to ensure that it supports the use of each technique. The equation becomes even more complex when you consider that each supply route may require an alteration to the mix.

To illustrate this, the typical elements in each of the parts of the marketing mix (excluding price, of course) are considered.

Museums: charging for admission?

For companies, the question is normally 'How much should we charge for a given product?' However, in the public sector this is not always the question, sometimes it is 'Should we charge at all?'

Policy on charging for admission to museums varies across the world. Some major collections, eg the Louvre, the Uffizi, the Prado and the Metropolitan Museum in New York all charge. However the Smithsonian in Washington DC, the German National Gallery and many others don't.

In the UK, several of the larger museums sponsored by the Department of National Heritage charge for admission (eg Natural History, Imperial War Museum, Tate Gallery in St Ives). The Victoria and Albert Museum operates a voluntary donation scheme.

In deciding whether or not to introduce admission charges to a museum and what charge to set, what factors do the Trustees consider?

To begin with the museums have to bear in mind their broad aims: preservation, conservation and presentation of collections. It is often argued that charging, whilst providing extra income that can be used towards preservation and conservation, deters people from visiting and thus detracts from the purpose of making the country's history and artefacts easily available to everyone.

A number of studies have been carried out on the effects of charging and quite clearly an admission charge does reduce visitor numbers (upwards of a third in some cases) but this fall is not spread evenly over all attendees. Thus, for example, women and tourists are less likely to be put off by an entry charge. Cultural aspects also play a part, for example in France paying an entry fee is seen as a means of showing respect for works of art.

The situation is complex, however, as a long-term study of visits to the Long Room at Trinity College in Ireland showed that large increases in admission charges were accompanied by large increases in visitor numbers: in 1984 with an adult charge of 50p, 159,000 people attended. In 1992 the charge had gone up to £2.50 and the numbers visiting to 229,000. This was explained partly by the fact that income from admission charges funded improvements in the service offered and also by the inelasticity of demand for such unique exhibits.

There are arguments for and against charging and the final outcome can be as much a political decision as a commercial one. This is a key point to bear in mind: the objectives and aims of an organisation or institution are as relevant as the market in some cases and no amount of study can accurately predict outcomes.

Product

This is the *actual offering to the customer* (whether consumer, business or governmental) and could consist of physical goods (cars, coal, tractors, chocolate, soft drinks, beer), or services rendered (air flights, hotel accommodation, advice, consultancy, loan of money). It is essentially what the purchaser pays for.

Key elements for consideration include:

- quality;
- variety;
- packaging;
- branding;
- linkages with other products;
- features;
- design;
- range of sizes;
- guarantees;
- instructions.

The different blends of these elements combine to yield the offering. An organisation can (and usually does) use many variations for different markets, segments and customers. Each variation affects the marketing mix.

Place

This covers *making the offering available to the purchasers* and includes:

- supply routes;
- stock (inventory);
- delivery units;
- distribution channels;
- geographical coverage;
- delivery times;
- transportation;
- support to channels.

Whichever blend is chosen (for each offering) will affect not only the cost but the manner of delivery (availability).

Promotion

This is *getting the message across*, ie telling customers and potential customers what your offering is, where it can be obtained, how to buy it etc. The methods of carrying this out include:

- literature;
- advertising;
- sales force;
- public relations;
- direct marketing;
- sales campaigns.

Modern marketers call this aspect of the marketing mix 'MarComms' (marketing communications). It is a major subject in its own right.

Customer's perspective of the four Ps

The four Ps look at the concept from the *seller's* viewpoint. A customer, however, has different ideas and perceptions, probably with different emphases. Robert Lauterborn (a US marketing guru) suggests that the Ps should also be viewed as the four Cs, to put the customer in perspective:

Four Ps	*Four Cs*
Product	Customer needs and wants
Promotion	Communication
Place	Convenience
Price	Cost to the customer

Thus success comes from:

Communicating an offer that meets the customer's needs, at a price that he considers acceptable, conveniently.

In fact, when viewed from this perspective, it becomes the *customer value proposition*, the CVP.

Managing the marketing mix

Because marketers tend to have fixed budgets, they will allocate their budgets across each element, in the hope of maximising the sales return from the overall mix.

This is clearly a very complex procedure, and although some techniques like mathematical weighting procedures and decision trees can help, in real life many managers do it mainly by intuition, backed by a little hard data.

John Wanamaker, a well-known US marketing guru, said, 'Of all the money that I spend on advertising, I know that half of it is wasted; the trouble is I don't know which half.' It is virtually impossible to work out if £5,000 spent on PR will give better sales than £5,000 on telesales, for example. If you spend a lot of money presenting your product in a bubble packet with fancy graphics, will this sell more than developing a smaller size, but selling both in plainer packaging?

It all depends on the industry and the consumers, and this again highlights the need to understand your customers in detail.

The role of pricing in the marketing mix is crucial, as you might expect. Whatever you do make sure your price supports all your other activities, and, for example, make sure you don't package your product in the most up-market packaging you can find, but sell it at a discount or through a market stall. This type of mixed message just goes to confuse everyone. Figure 4.4 below shows the interaction between the four Ps with three example mixes.

A is heavily biased towards price and therefore the message would be concentrated on this aspect of the mix. An example would be off-the-page investments where the key factor is the return (interest rate) or any 'cheap' or discount products.

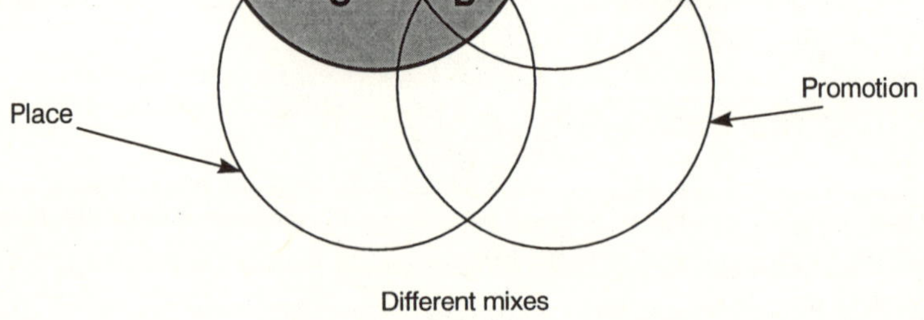

Figure 4.4 *Marketing mix*

B equal consideration for all parts. An example here would be a leaflet for, say, a fast food delivery service which will contain details of the product (menu), the price, how to order, and delivery times.
C largely product- and place-based, and the promotion will major on these and not the price aspect. A good example might be the sale of a very expensive house where the promotion will give details of where it is and the excellent features but not the price. The medium of communication is also important and an up-market magazine will be chosen. The subliminal message here would be: if you have to ask the price then you probably cannot afford it.

Summary
The marketing mix is a key driver for pricing and the mix will place the relevant emphasis on price as an element. The pricing process will build on the mix in setting the price.

PRICING POLICIES

Introduction

Pricing policies are needed to provide an overall framework within which deals may be carried out, but not to the detriment of the mission statement and within the constraints of both the corporate strategy and the marketing strategy.

Many companies do not set these properly, if at all. In some cases they may be part of the general culture without being formalised in a document.

Where they are set they should address some key factors:

- customers;
- image;
- segmental differences;
- flexibility;
- competition.

and these are addressed in turn:

Customers

The price of a product or service should be set within a range that is acceptable for its category, as laid down within the CVP. It will take account of 'barrier' prices, above or below which it is difficult to operate and may need to refer to key price points which serve as benchmarks or reference points for customers. It is commonly believed, for example, that the price of a certain soft-top car was always set at the price which a wealthy man would allow his spouse to spend on a car.

Handbags are also a good example of this. The average woman would pay somewhere around £100 for a good quality, smallish handbag and it is around this level that most are positioned. A brief glance at Harrods' 1995 Christmas catalogue reveals a Hermes handbag priced at £5,000. This price is way above that benchmark price but is clearly not aimed at the same market. The price/benefit/value equation has been equalised as follows:

- to reflect the handmade factor;
- to reflect the type of leather (crocodile);
- to reflect the expectations that shoppers in Harrods would have;
- to reflect the Hermes brand which is based on a very exclusive image (ie not for the *hoi polloi*).

In this case the price has been set well above the normal price benchmark (50 times it in fact) but in line with the higher expectations of its targeted clientele.

The policy will cover both single goods and combinations of products. The policy for Hermes will almost certainly cover all goods and would never allow a dilution of the price, except in certain controlled 'sales' perhaps, as this would reduce the exclusivity which is what the customers wish to purchase.

Image

Pricing should reflect and reinforce the image that the product intends to convey (which should be in line with the perception of customers). Do not be afraid to price to reflect the CVP. A customer is much more likely to pay a premium price for a product which 'justifies' it than if the price is out of line with their perceptions.

In a UK hypermarket (excellent places for retail pricing research for analysis), therefore, you will find umpteen different types/brands of butter:

- own brand;
- EU made (blended);
- Irish;
- New Zealand;
- French;
- Welsh;
- Cornish;
- UK branded;
- Danish.

all of which will be priced at a specific price within a range but reflecting the image the manufacturer believes they portray. The EU blend is usually cheapest as it reflects the popular perception of surplus from the butter mountain mixed up to be sold cheaply (thereby reducing the subsidies for unwanted production); then some down-market brands, the own label reflecting reasonable quality at reasonable prices; with regional, national, and quality brands at the top giving the impression of being more creamy, from free-range cows, quality, etc and people expect to pay more (and do) for these types at the top of the range. Nobody prices its butter at £16 a packet, however, and the differences are of the order of magnitude of about 20 per cent.

Wine, however, is a totally different item. You can pay anything from 99p to around £30 a bottle, even in supermarkets, and at specialist shops you might pay over £100 for a bottle of 1992 Chateau Haut Brion (first growth), £150 for a bottle of 1989 Chateau D'Yquiem and still more for others. Yet they are all different brands/marques of what is essentially fermented grape juice with an alcohol content of around 15 per cent.

The price differential is down in part to actual quality over perception and image; however, in practice it becomes difficult to quantify this, and much may be due to rarity and the supply–demand equation.

British Leyland launched the Jaguar XJ12 in 1972 and totally misinterpreted the market. The upshot was that within a few months second-hand cars were fetching a premium over new cars such was the demand and its inability to match it.

It didn't take into account the effect that its image would have on demand and as a result lost out in a big way. Key questions here are: did it price at the wrong level or did it wrongly predict the demand at that price level?

Segmental differences

Where a product is aimed at more than one target group or segment, this must also be reflected in the policy thus allowing a producer to alter and maximise the mix of price, product offer, promotion and place of sale.

This can be illustrated with a wholly fictitious example of a new perfume (see Table 4.1), where we could postulate a matrix that looks like the following:

Table 4.1

Place	Product	Promotion	Price
Department stores	standard, up-market packaging	celebrity endorsement	£40
Chemists	standard	designer type label	£25
Supermarkets	standard	own label	£15
Market stalls	standard, no packaging	none	£5

link between Price and distribution

The price will not be the same where the product is sold through an up-market retailer, a boutique or a discount operation.

The policy will set out the general range of prices that is to be used for each segment (or group of segments). The CVP will contain a lot of this information so as to arrive at the proposition:

- the target markets must have been analysed;
- split into relevant segments (ie the chosen segments; the rest ignored);
- the products tailored appropriately;
- a pricing image identified.

This final pricing image will differ for each type of segment.

Segments can be delineated by a number of means (ACORN, age, lifestyle, geography, language, demographic etc) but a segment must be:

- measurable/quantifiable;
- economical to serve;
- reachable;
- homogeneous with respect to the product offering and propensity to buy.

There are three main types of segmented pricing:

- no segments at all and all goods priced the same — this is a 'shotgun or scatter gun' approach which is very easy to price but may be difficult to manage in practice, and may possibly result in lower returns than more focused approaches;
- total segmentation with different prices for each — the objective is to gain a share of all markets and requires greater costs than no segments at all, thereby eroding margin;
- selected segments with selected offerings. This is actually targeting a large share of a small market — niche pricing.

connection with product mix.

You should remember that, as the product moves along the life cycle, it will be necessary to revisit the pricing segmentation and possibly alter it to reflect subsequent stages.

The men's clothing market demonstrates this well: the market is split up as follows:

- *Small menswear shops* in small towns and large villages, usually catering to older men. Priced above most 'city shops' because you are paying for convenience and service etc;
- *Small fashion boutiques* catering to the young and fashion conscious (not expensive but not cheap either);
- *Retail chains*, often themselves segmented to match different segments, eg Burton has 'Top Man' and 'Burton's' aimed at younger buyers and more sophisticated buyers respectively. Many items will be the same in both but not necessarily priced the same nor labelled as such. Usually fairly cheap reflecting quality and target market;
- *Department stores* usually selling a range of menswear from jeans through sportswear to suits and formal wear and usually priced in the middle;
- *Up-market gentlemen's outfitters*, eg Hacketts, aimed at the top end of the market; not premium but expensive — more for more;
- *Very fashionable chains*, eg Paul Smith, aimed at upper end of fashionable market. Premium priced for a 'name' (also Armani, Gucci etc);
- *Bespoke tailoring* — at the very top with each item individually made and fitted. Premium priced (eg a suit from a Savile Row tailor would probably be £1,000).

Flexibility

Scope for flexibility must be built in to reflect the need for 'good deals'. Many markets and many purchasers expect to 'do deals'. If a company does not respond to these types of requirement then it will suffer. This is an especial feature of business in the USA and is increasingly seen in Europe.

The pricing policy will lay down parameters on price but will also allow negotiators latitude with other items. One of the authors went to buy a second-hand car and when the price negotiation became stuck a range of (relatively) useless items such as umbrellas were offered to try to clinch the deal. The sale was lost as the 'freebies' didn't compensate for the sticking point — a car warranty. Policy in this case stated that a price had to be paid for a warranty (small) but as a result lost the sale of the substantial item (the car).

The moral here is that you must ensure that your policies reflect your customers' concerns (look back at the four Cs in Chapter 3).

Whilst central control of pricing is clearly important, it is also necessary to allow discretion to some parts of the sales chain to encourage flexibility in negotiations. This also allows volume to be played off against lower prices in the right circumstances to derive the benefits therefrom. This flexibility must, however, be controlled and within clearly defined parameters to ensure that overall targets and objectives with respect to profit/cost contribution etc are not prejudiced.

Some organisations choose to do extensive research and then publish complicated payment schedules, where the operatives who are actually selling have little or no control over deal. For example, airlines offer a vast range of prices. A simple example is that of theatres, where price is based on:

- status of individuals (student, OAP);
- time of performance (matinée, first, second show);
- location in the theatre (front row, stalls, boxes, restricted view).

Other organisations take a more relaxed view, based on the skill of their front line operatives, on their market and on the nature of their services. Thus, if you get a builder to quote for a extension, he will be happy to vary his price on the labour content quite dramatically, especially if he started at a high price, but will not be able to negotiate over the cost of the bought-in items (remember the value chain!).

Variable pricing

There are many instances where the policy set out by a company allows for considerable variance in pricing but without discretion. This is where the local flexibility is either of no value or impracticable to monitor etc.

A good example of this is a rail trip. If you wish to go to one city from another the standard price will be, say, £25 return. There will be many variances on this, however, such as:

- first class;
- single or ordinary return;
- awayday;
- period return;
- season ticket;
- OAP;
- young person's fare;
- group discount;
- saver fare;
- restricted time of travel,

etc but the variance will be fixed and published.

What the company has done is to analyse the market in terms of its competition (buses, cars and planes), the likely demands at peak periods, and the different values of passengers. The range of fares is an attempt to encourage people not to travel during peak times thereby smoothing the flow, and to generate extra marginal business during slack times.

In this case there is no discretion at all at a local level to allow variations to close a deal. This is largely as it is a quasi monopoly (although regulated and subject to competition from other substitute forms of transport — cars, buses, aeroplanes) and also because the spread of variable prices represent pre-emptive strikes on deals and so clerks merely take money for whichever deal is suitable. There is an onus on them to offer the most suitable deal to customers, which can throw up some surprisingly favourable deals.

Competition

It is vital that managers never forget that they are not pricing into a vacuum. Competitors' responses can be swift and sometimes brutal. None of us possess a crystal ball, but it is vital that the competitive structure of the market be understood. If there is a market leader and your CVP is similar, you will find it difficult to be much out of line with its prices. If, however, the CVP is different then the competition will serve as a benchmark against which to price, above or below depending on the CVP. The CVP will reflect your perceived (relative) strengths against them and will enable you to carry out your positioning through your pricing to equalise the price/benefit/value equation.

Summary

Specifically, the policy must indicate:

- the target customer groupings;
- what image is being reinforced;
- what specific segments are being addressed;
- how flexibility is built in;
- room for manoeuvre, or how competitive response is allowed for.

A policy should offer guidance and, therefore, would be couched in terms of how to interpret situations and how local management should develop local rules and procedures that reflect their situation.

Shelf life?

An interesting fact is that whereas if a tin of baked beans is unsold at the end of the day it can be sold on subsequent days, with some services this is not the case. For example, if an aeroplane has empty seats on a flight they are gone for ever, similarly for a hotel room lying empty for a day.

This, therefore, makes it important to maximise occupancy wherever possible; usually using discounts etc, as this extra revenue is mainly profit. Consequently this has a direct bearing on the pricing policies, strategies and, ultimately, tactics of companies in these fields of operations.

The absence of a pricing policy can cause serious difficulties — managers will have to 'invent' their own on the spot and many variations will develop separately across different locations without the benefit of a framework offering a cohesive approach. At the extreme it may be possible to arbitrage the same goods against different locations due to variations in discounts.

It is the pricing policy that also serves as the overall framework within which to formulate the pricing strategy and without it this becomes more difficult.

Pricing strategy

Once the policies have been set then you are in a position to formulate your strategies. It is clear that where a policy of say 'more for more' has been set then a 'pile it high and sell it cheap' approach is not going to be in line with the policy statement.

Similarly, where volume is the objective then very high prices and niche playing are not going to yield the desired results. The pricing strategy, therefore, must be set in such a way that it supports the corporate strategy, is within the pricing policy and is flexible enough to respond to the market.

Sainsburys, the UK retailer, introduced its own in-house cola in 1995, priced below well-known brands, which proved so successful that it garnered an estimated 30 per cent of its in-store cola sales; equivalent to 6 per cent of national market share. This strategy was to position its cola below the price of leading brands but to give the impression of equal quality. Being the owner of the distribution it could give whatever prominence it liked to the new line which its competitors could not and, therefore, it placed its cola in all the prominent positions using many introductory offers to tempt customers away, knowing that once they changed they were unlikely to go back — especially given the price difference.

Its CVP was of the 'more for less' brand. This particular market is very price sensitive but also brand aware and global cola wars are being fought between Pepsi and Coke as well as local players. In the UK, for example, as well as 'own brands' taking market share, Virgin (Richard Branson's rapidly diversifying company) launched its own cola which has also taken significant share.

Pricing strategies are usually set against these parameters:

- the product or service;
- the market;
- the desired CVP.

In practice firms usually manipulate two key variables to meet the desired targets:

- growth (ie market share);
- profit.

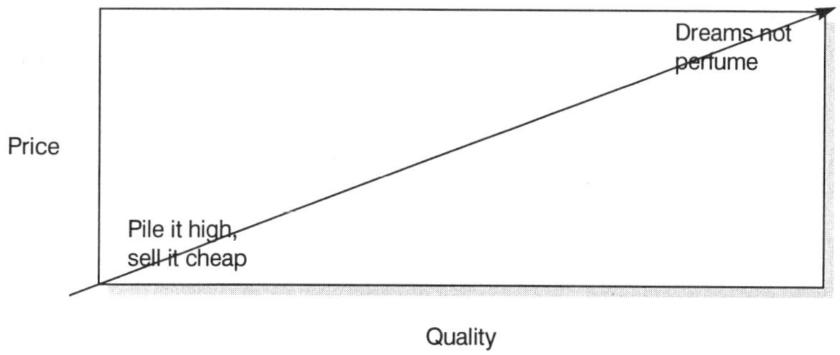

Figure 4.5 *Quality v. Price*

Where profit is the overall requirement then the highest margin that can be obtained will be looked for. On the other hand, where market share is the goal then prices will be reduced in line with expected buying behaviour to gain volume. The strategy will reflect this policy and implement it. It is usually very difficult to achieve both strong growth (market share) and good profits, although not impossible. The one usually mitigates against the other (it is normal to reduce prices to gain volume). These are not mutually exclusive, of course, as high sales can bring economies of scale, thus resulting in greater margins if prices can be held.

Figure 4.6 shows how five competitors have been doing over the last three years comparing growth in market share and profit. The largest circle represents the market leader (100) and the rest are shown in relative proportions of this size. The arrows indicate the direction of the company over that period, compared with its position three years ago.

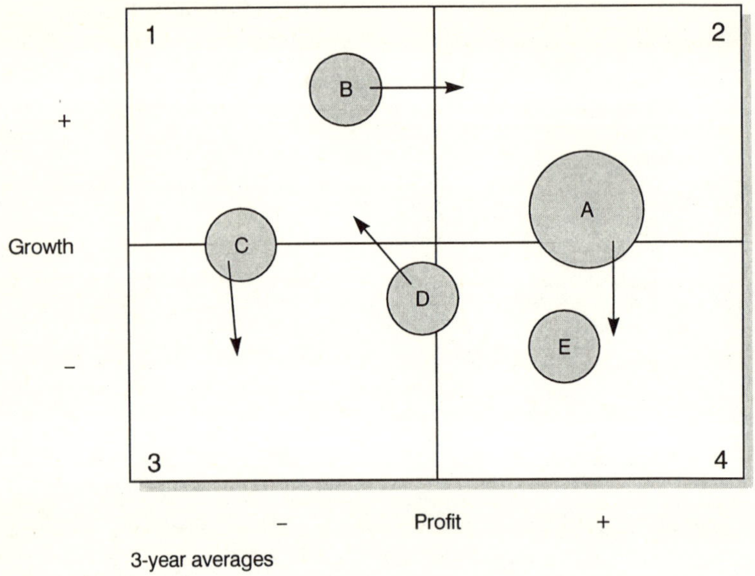

Figure 4.6 *Profit v. Growth*

Company A, whilst clearly the leader, has been losing market share but increasing its margin. This could reflect its strategy of gaining share and then increasing the quality of its sales.

Company B has steady growth and improving profit indicating that it is probably following a more-for-more strategy to which the market is receptive.

Company C has lost market share and has a poor profit performance.

Company D is clearly going for growth at the expense of its profit possibly to gain economies of scale at a later date.

Company E is losing market but enjoys good profit, although how long this can continue is an open question. This might reflect its positioning within a niche which is disappearing.

If we assume that the market is finite then this becomes a zero sum game and the gainers do so at the expense of the others. The losers have clearly failed to react correctly to their competitors' strategies.

Quality for price strategies

Figure 4.7 indicates the respective strategies available, depending on which combination of price and quality you are seeking. There are three quality levels and two types of pricing, giving six different general pricing strategy segments although, of course, a product could be positioned across the borders as in example 3. Some marketing experts use three price levels but this only results in an 'average' set of positions in the middle.

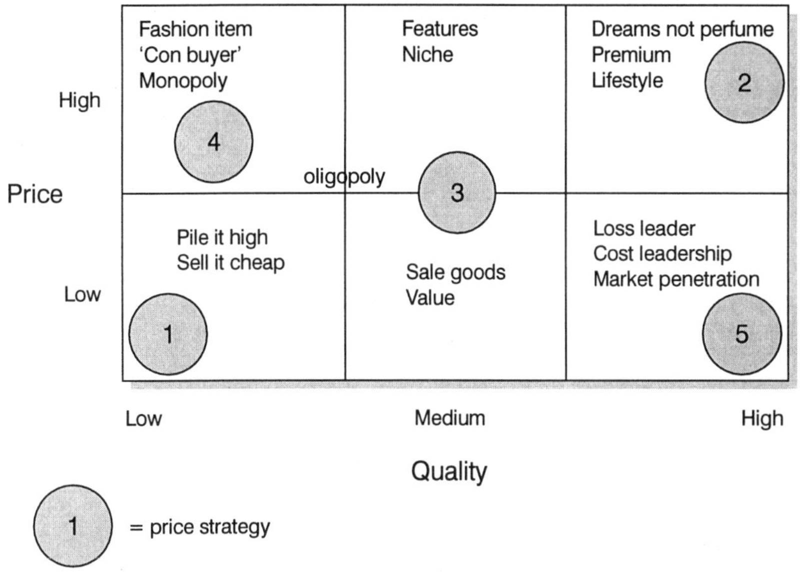

Figure 4.7 *Pricing strategies*

Five hypothetical examples are explored below:

1. This is the bottom end of the market — 'pile it high and sell it cheap'. There is no attempt to offer quality (although there will be some base standard), merely to sell at low prices.
2. This product is positioned at the very top of the market and seeks to offer the best quality (as perceived by the buyer) for the very highest price. Coutts & Co (the royal bankers), offer a service where your personal banker (in frock-coat) comes to you at your convenience to discuss your banking and you receive very nice leather wallets and cheque-book holders. The fees and charges reflect this however.
3. At this level the offer is middle-of-the-road, offering reasonable value for medium price.
4. Anyone buying this product is being 'ripped off', ie they are paying over the odds for something; however, they are prepared to pay for it so the company will sell it. This could be 'skimming' or more likely a fashion item that will appeal to those initial trend setters who want to have it first, until the prices tumble and it becomes 'commoditised' (portable telephones were a good example of this) and everyone gets it.

5. Here the buyer is getting a very good bargain indeed. For a firm to sell in this way (assuming the proprietor is not mad) there has to be a sound logic behind it. This would normally be a drive for economies of scale; a radical change to costs of production (down); a loss leader to pull in customers; dumping; stock clearance or an aggressive price war (unsustainable for very long).

Case studies
UK Food Retailing 1994–1995

In the early 1990s there was a perceived threat to the food retailing *status quo* posed by a selection of cut-price stores who were set to attack the UK food market. These companies included American-style warehouse clubs such as Cargo Club and Costco; continental discounters such as Aldi, Lidl and Netto; and British stores offering low-price formats such as Argyll and Shoprite. The traditional chains (Sainsburys, Tesco, Safeways etc) introduced new ranges of low-price goods within their store which were usually labelled 'Basics' or 'Right Price' or 'Value' to combat the threat of discount stores. This proved very successful and, coupled with the end of the recession, resulted in the competitive threat receding.

Cars

A good example of quality for price strategy may be seen from the introduction of the Japanese car into the UK market (and others) over the last 20 years. Initially Japanese car makers priced their cars at the lower end of the car market. However, in order to counter market resistance (and anti-Japanese feelings) they also offered better features than the competition as standard (eg radios). They were able to do so due to the long-term vision and the greater efficiency (thereby reducing relative costs) that they enjoyed. They gradually worked their way up-market, each time changing the price/benefit/value equation to equalise it.

Their success can be measured by their market share and to a lesser extent by the moves by EU national car manufacturers to try to stop or limit sales. Some of them have now set up plants within the EU (notably in the UK) and their cars ironically contain more nationally sourced parts than some other manufacturers who are regarded as national. Many more car manufacturers are now trying to break into these markets (notably from Korea and Malaysia) with India and China also looking this way. Given the maturity of the market it will be interesting to see whether the approach adopted, of offering competitively priced cars through 'no-hassle' direct outlets in packages that include money-back guarantees, will yield similar results.

Profit/volume

One of the key elements of the pricing framework is the profit/volume ratio. Profit is a function of the volume sold multiplied by the margin gained; ie gross profit, also called contribution. We can consider this by looking at an example:

For a company with four products, the gross profit may be £1m on sales of £5m, a margin of 20 per cent. However, if we look more deeply and analyse this by product (see Table 4.2) then the following may be found:

Table 4.2

Product	Sales	Profit	Margin
A	£1,000,000	£100,000	10%
B	£2,000,000	£600,000	30%
C	£1,500,000	£112,500	7.5%
D	£500,000	£200,000	40%

The differences are obvious and, in an ideal world, all resources would be transferred to those products generating the maximum return, ie D then B, whilst C would certainly be dropped. This may not be possible, however, as B and D may be dependent on sales of A and C. What should certainly happen is that the CVP of A and C should be addressed to discover whether the price could be raised, or the delivered product quality, and therefore the cost, reduced.

Other actions could be to license the lower margin product to another producer or outsource it, to increase overall margins. The strategy for doing this would have to be carried within the confines of the pricing policy as laid down.

One of the key relationships in this type of analysis is that between the components of costs, ie between fixed and variable costs. Where there is a very high fixed cost element then volume is necessary to ensure absorption of this cost and margin is made (eg a factory with expensive machinery, where it costs very little to produce extra products).

If, on the other hand, it is variable costs that are high then margin is the key factor to concentrate on, as volume will only have a minor impact on cost (eg strategy consulting where each job requires more highly paid consultants). This is shown diagrammatically in Figure 4.8.

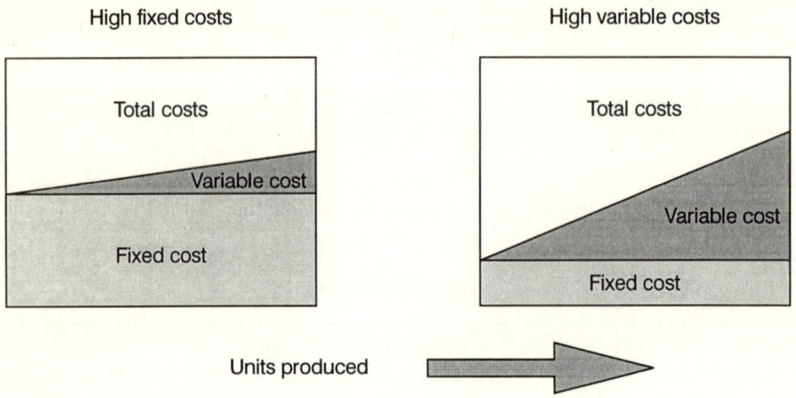

Figure 4.8 *Same price, different cost make-up*

Summary

The pricing strategy sets out the broad way ahead, but it is the intelligent application of the right tactics that will result in a good level of sales being achieved.

PRODUCT CYCLES AND PRICING

Where a product is in its life cycle will affect the price obtainable. Marketers typically describe four key phases in the life cycle:

- introduction;
- growth;
- maturity;
- decline.

Another interpretation that is commonly used is the Boston Matrix, named after the consulting firm who devised it (see Figure 4.9 overleaf). This ascribes broad characteristics to products based on market share and dynamics.

At a basic level you can take a *product approach* to pricing. By working out where a product is in its cycle, you can define a broad policy and then set tactics that capitalise on this. Remember, however, that products may be offered in more than one market and may be at different stages of the life cycle in different markets.

Table 4.3 (overleaf) shows the classic positions for products:

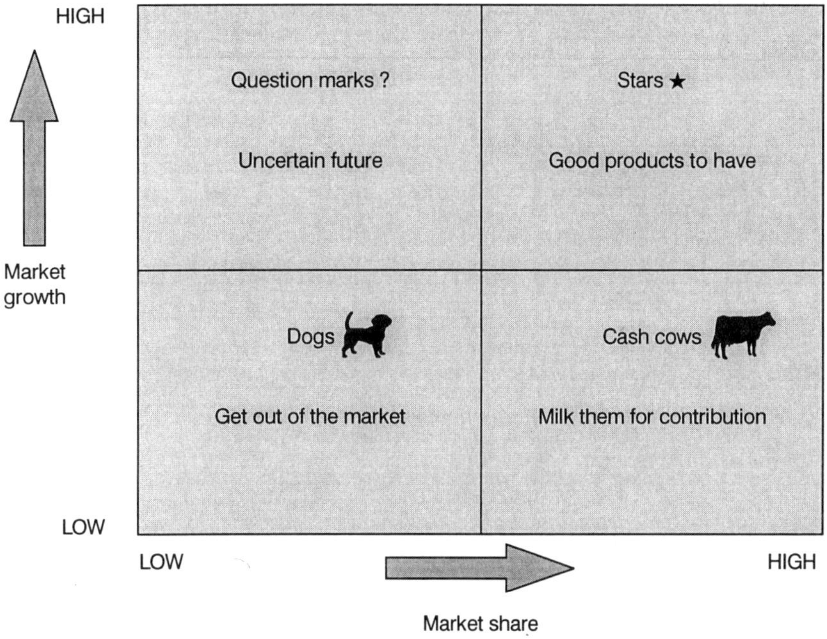

Figure 4.9 *Boston Consulting Group Matrix*

Table 4.3

Product position	Characteristics
1. Launch	A completely new product/service
2. Establish	Develop market share as fast as possible
3. Fast growth	Pursue a larger share/more dominant position
4. Price/margin	Deliver with lowest costs
5. Different	Achieve high degree of perceived product/ service difference
6. Focus	Target a segment
7. Relaunch	Restored competitiveness of a product/service
8. Expand into new markets via third parties	Convert market share or competitive position into higher returns by sharing knowledge or products with others (licensing/JVs)
9. Retrench/withdraw	Product unavailable or only by special order

Depending on where a product has been positioned it will need a different price strategy and at each of these positionings requires a different kind of tactical approach to pricing. Table 4.4 below examines these and shows a possible pricing approach in each case.

Table 4.4

Product position	Possible Pricing Approach
1. Launch	Skimming/heavy discounting
2. Establish	Maintain price equality with market
3. Fast growth	Competitive price
4. Price/margin	Lower costs to maximise margin/gain share
5. Different	Achieve high degree of perceived product/ service difference and price accordingly
6. Focus	Price for niche purchasers
7. Relaunch	Innovative pricing
8. Expand into new markets via third parties	Licensing, levy, commission, fees, franchise
9. Retrench/withdraw	Irrelevant/sell out

Innovative pricing tactics

Before we move on to pricing tactics in detail, it is worth thinking a little bit about innovation in pricing. Some businesses and customers operate in markets that have a very traditional view of pricing and use methods with a long history. This is not to say that new operators cannot break into the market and change the way things are done, and the clever manager should always be on the lookout for possibilities where pricing can make such a difference.

For example, in 1995 in the UK, Virgin launched a new type of PEP (*personal equity plan*). This was sold direct to the public (and managed on Virgin's behalf by another company). The product was sold as being free of the large management charges that often accrue with traditional PEPs and became very popular in a short time, even to the extent that more traditional operators followed the same pricing strategy. The PEP was, in fact, a simple instrument that basically followed the market, and thus was free of management charges, as the management requirement was small.

It was clearly a mixture of strong branding (the Virgin name) and innovative pricing that allowed the success of this new venture.

Even apparently established markets can differ in surprising ways. For example, if you want to buy a house in Australia, there is a very good chance it will be at a public auction. In England, however, most sales will be private, through an estate agent. This again is in contrast with Scotland where sales are commonly by means of sealed bids. Same type of market, entirely different characteristics.

Other markets have been characterised by similar innovation in recent years: in the past the only way to buy a car was by cash, a bank loan or on hire purchase. Nowadays there are many options, involving leases, buy-back, trade-ins and others.

Similarly, if you wanted to hire a management consultant, you would either pay them a fee per day or perhaps a fixed fee for the job. Nowadays, most consultants would be happy to discuss contingent fees, value based fees and other innovative types of pricing.

What these examples have in common is that the seller has looked at the buyer's requirements and decided to be more flexible in pricing so that a bargain can be struck that meets both parties' needs in a better way. This is a classic example of the development of the CVP.

The moral here is that just because something has always been done one way, don't assume that it can't be done differently. Innovative pricing can be a key to huge success, and remember also that innovative doesn't necessarily mean cheaper: it means different.

Segmental strategies

The strategy of a company must be flexible enough to respond to changes in markets, particularly new competition or aggressive pricing. Proper analysis of the possible segmentation and a measured response rather than a knee-jerk reaction will yield better benefits.

Philip Morris, the firm who produce Marlboro cigarettes, is often quoted as an example of a perceived incorrect pricing strategy. On what has come to be known as 'Marlboro Friday' the price of the leading up-market brand was reduced in response to an aggressive pricing onslaught; with devastating effects for margins. The perceived wisdom is that the introduction of a new brand at a lower price — say Marlboro 'Metro' or Marlboro 'Value' — aimed at price-sensitive smokers would have enabled it to keep the exclusivity of the original brand, and therefore its premium pricing, possibly at a reduced level of sales, and meet the attack.

Given that the merchandising of non-cigarette goods was so important and built around this image it could be thought surprising that it took the action it did. The market view, however, is that it has ultimately emerged as a winner with enhanced market share, but at what price?

If prices are merely lowered across the board with poor segmental analysis then the only result will be lower margins, unless extra compensating share is gained. Similarly, there is the future threat of further onslaughts at ever decreasing prices and price-sensitive customers are known to be the most brand disloyal. This approach could be contrasted with the following:

Smirnoff is a leading US brand of vodka. It was attacked very aggressively by a brand (Wolfschmidt) priced at US$1 below its price. Instead of matching the lower price, which would almost inevitably have resulted in a downwards price spiral, or increased promotion which would have lead to reduced margin, the producers (Heublein) took an innovative pricing approach — they increased the price by a further US$1 and positioned it as an up-market brand.

The company went further and introduced a new brand, Relska, to meet Wolfschmidt and yet another brand, Popov, priced below that one to cater for price-sensitive purchasers. This imaginative pricing approach positioned Smirnoff as a quality brand, saw off the competition and increased its profit. The real brilliance was that there was virtually no difference between the brands except labels, branding and pricing; and costs to produce were also just about the same. (Source: as reported by Kotler.)

SUMMARY AND CONCLUSION

Although the methodology sets out the steps that must be followed in setting prices it is still only the theory. The marketing mix may have been decided, the pricing policy and strategy set and the tactics agreed, but you have still got to offer the product to the market and see if, when and how it sells. The feedback from this provides vital input to the process. The methodology thus far has looked at the strategic aspect. In the last chapter in this section pricing tactics are discussed.

Innsite Hotel Services

Innsite supply computer systems to individual hotels and chains. Amongst their products is a *central reservations system* (CRS). This consists of a number of PC workstations running specialist software. This allows a hotel chain customer to phone a central number where the CRS is running. The CRS can identify room availability and pricing on all rooms in the group and make bookings for each hotel.

The are two elements to the CRS product, the PC hardware and the specialist software. As different competitors exist for each, Innsite adopt two distinct strategies. The underpinning philosophy is that the customer must feel that both elements of the package are reasonably priced.

The most obvious competitors for the PC equipment are retailers and distributors advertising in the computer press. These organisations purchase in higher volumes than Innsite and operate at lower margins. Their sales price is thus close to Innsite's purchase price. Innsite can, however, justify a modest premium (approximately 10 per cent) for the extra service they provide plus the convenience of one-stop purchasing.

The software is priced on an entirely different basis. The purpose of the CRS for a hotel chain is to increase bookings. The more hotels on the CRS and the bigger the hotel, the more likely extra business is to result. Innsite, therefore, base the price of their software on these two factors. On the basic system (there are optional enhancement modules to support direct marketing, links to international travel agents etc) Innsite charge £100 per hotel and £5 per room.

This pricing approach allows the customer to relate the price of the system to his anticipated business increase and clearly justify the required expenditure. It allows the customer to test the concept with a small investment, expanding the system to cover only hotels that will show a return. It also allows Innsite to easily accommodate groups opening or buying new hotels without the need for expensive or time-consuming renegotiation of terms.

Basing the price on the customer's increase in profits reduces the need to discount to very low levels as the profitability improvement for the client more than funds the investment.

5

CLASSIC PRICING TACTICS

INTRODUCTION

Thus far the infrastructure which sets the context for pricing policies and strategies has been examined. In this chapter pricing at the tactical level is considered.

Although two competing firms may have a similar goal in market share terms (eg both could be aiming at 9 per cent in three years' time), in practice they would probably approach this in different ways. This is because their approach to the market will reflect their different corporate objectives, strategies, policies and management outlook; will be based on the (probably different) information gathered and the slant put on the subsequent analysis; and will reflect the structure of the organisation including supplier dynamics and distribution.

There is, of course, no right or wrong way to approach pricing, only success or failure in the market, which is a harsh judge. Whichever technique or set of techniques a company adopts they will be based on a core methodology/ies and mind-set within the firm. Many can be combined and some are similar to each other to such an extent that it can make little difference which is chosen — it comes down to comfort levels and whether the results are acceptable. Some are known by a variety of names or descriptions but this book uses the more commonly known names. The name is, of course, irrelevant; it is how the techniques match your needs and objectives that counts.

The only successful approach, therefore, is that which offers the right combination of benefits for price — *value* to your customers in your market.

The main approaches

There are two main methods of setting prices: that which uses the cost of production as a base:

Cost-driven pricing;

and that where prices are set with reference to the market or customer perception:

Market-driven pricing.

Quite clearly, market based pricing is the technique of the modern business, but it is not always the most appropriate and cost-driven pricing techniques should not be dismissed: they can serve a useful purpose, and are in common use by many businesses. The most successful methods combine the two key elements but will be based more on one than the other.

Finally there are some more unusual (but not necessarily uncommon) approaches which we have grouped under the title:

Alternative.

COST DRIVEN

These types of pricing methods are so called because they are driven essentially by the cost inputs to the equation. That is not to say that market is ignored but rather that an internally focused approach is used to develop the price and the market considerations are looked at later (if at all).

Cost-plus pricing

This is far and away the most common method of pricing; it has been used for centuries, probably ever since the concept of cost accounting was developed. In its most simple form the cost of production is estimated, a margin for profit added on and a price is calculated. In reality, of course, it is far more complex for a variety of reasons; principally that cost is not so easy to ascertain.

If you asked a management accountant (assuming access to relevant information) he would be able to tell you all the cost inputs to any given product and would be able to work out how much it cost you to make the product. If you asked another accountant, however, he would almost certainly give you a slightly different answer. Illogical as this may sound, this is because they will be using different methodologies/assumptions to apportion costs to the individual item. Thus, the first accountant might be using a technique known as direct costing, whilst the second might be using *activity based costing* (often known as ABC). (See Chapter 2.)

Irrespective of the method, however, they will be able to produce a figure for you in the form of a statement that says: To produce one widget costs us £3.22p.

If you take this cost and then decide how much money you want to make in a year, you can then work out (knowing the likely demand) how much you have to charge to make the return you want. This is cost-plus pricing in its most basic form and can be expressed as follows: *A widget costs me £3.22p to make, I will add 20 per cent and sell it for £3.86p.*

A simple example illustrates this in more detail:

A company making garden sheds buys in the following raw materials (it doesn't make enough sheds to attract discounts for bulk from suppliers):

Item	*Price per shed*
Wood	£50
Glass	£20
Nails	£5
Total	£75

In addition it has fixed costs of £1,000 pa and a further variable costs (labour) of £15 per shed.

If it makes 100 sheds pa, then each costs £75 plus £15 plus its share of fixed costs (£1000/100) £10, which gives a total of £100.

If it desires a margin of 50 per cent on the final price, then final price will be £200 (margin calculated as cost/selling price × 100 per cent).

Another way of looking at this is '100 per cent mark-up' or gross profit (margin/cost × 100).

Whilst this is undoubtedly the most common form of pricing in use in industry today, there are a number of fundamental drawbacks to its use:

- There is no certainty about the costs. You can hire the finest accountants and they will all come up with different answers. There is no agreed way of costing products and in complex processes, different techniques can give astoundingly different answers.
- The effect of demand is not considered. If demand falls dramatically below plan, costs are certain to change and thus the return will be nothing like expected.
- Because consumer needs and wants are not factored in you may be offering the product at entirely the wrong price (too high or too low).

For these and other reasons, more sophisticated (in marketing terms) companies tend to use cost-plus techniques merely as a starting point. However, even this limited use can lead to further problems. If costing technique discriminates against (say) low-volume high-value products, a company might decide never to move into this area. This will not be because it cannot make money (it possibly could) but because the management system is flawed.

The reason that the system remains in use today is interesting and is probably accounted for by the fact that:

- Many marketing and salespeople do not understand costing systems and accountancy, regarding it as rather an arcane science which keeps them in the dark. When the accountant says x, the figure is blindly believed.
- Companies tend to know input prices accurately (eg the cost of raw materials, labour etc) and, therefore, they feel more comfortable about basing decisions on these factors.
- If all the companies in a particular sector are using similar techniques, unsurprisingly, they all have similar costs and they all tend to alter prices at a similar time (eg when input costs vary). This again reinforces the assumption that they are selling at the right price. This is all very well until a sophisticated competitor moves into the market.

The cost-plus approach used to be very widespread in government tenders where 'cost-plus X%' was used to negotiate deals. This was partly because governments did not wish to be seen to be giving fat margins to tendering firms.

Unfortunately for the taxpayers, in practice there was little incentive to control costs and these tended to rise, with the increase being passed on by the contractor who would say, 'But I am only making X per cent'. Of course 10 per cent on £750,000 is a lot more in cash terms to a firm than 10 per cent on £500,000.

There was also a suspicion that some extra cost was actually extra margin disguised. An apocryphal story from the USA was that a loo seat for a military jet was charged at $700 when an identical one cost $15 in an ironmongers.

Target return

This type of pricing is essentially a variation on cost-plus pricing. The manufacturer looks at an area or product range and decides that he needs to make a (say) 20 per cent return on his investment and sets the price accordingly. This technique is sometimes called ROI or return on investment pricing. If the calculated return is insufficient then he will not put the money into that business.

The products are then priced so that an overall 20 per cent return is made. This differs slightly from straightforward cost-plus pricing in that the overall return is normally calculated on the basis of the costs of a product range rather than an individual product and thus within the range, margins may vary quite widely.

This type of technique is often used by the utility companies (eg water, electricity, gas) and can be controlled by regulators. That used in the UK for the gas and electricity industries is Retail Price Index (RPI) + 'x', where 'x' is a percentage set by the regulator. It is not so commonly used by private sector manufacturers these days as it is rather inflexible and ignores considerations about the market and competitor activities.

MARKET DRIVEN

Market-based pricing (sometimes called demand-led pricing or perception pricing) is the term used to describe the setting of prices by reference to a number of external factors, principally:

- the price of competing products;
- the size and elasticity of the market;
- the utility (fitness for purpose) of the product in question. This is measured through the eyes of the customer *not* the manufacturer.

A market-based price bears no fixed relation to the cost of manufacturing or supplying the product, except that the price will normally be greater than the cost of production if the supplier wishes to stay in business.

The pressures on prices are illustrated below. Those from competition force the price down whilst demand forces it up.

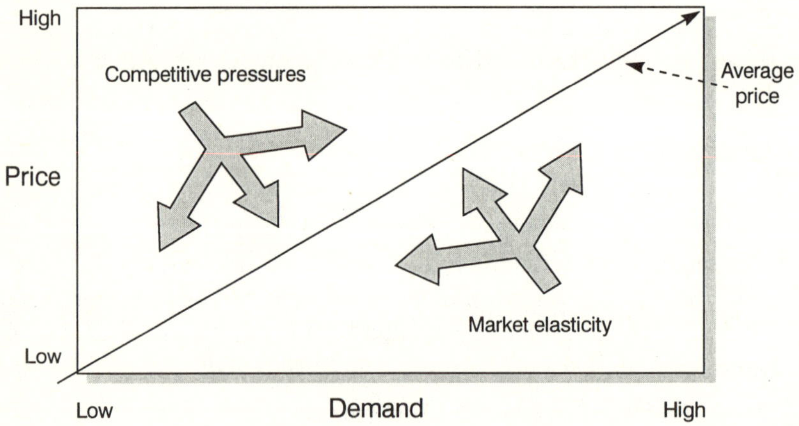

Figure 5.1 *Market pressures*

Market-based pricing

Nearly all private sector suppliers use some form of market-based pricing (whether they call it this or not) and, in general, a sophisticated private sector company will charge you the maximum amount that it can for any particular product, taking into account a variety of factors (eg will you buy the product again, will you be satisfied, their overall strategy, return on investment etc) and will seek to maximise both revenue and margin.

As the name implies, market-based pricing is based on 'what is going on the market' at any point in time. What is going on in the market can be more specifically considered as a function of the perception of the customers (buyers) at any given time.

These perceptions vary over time, and they may follow prices, or may sometimes be led by them. Before these aspects are considered in detail, it is useful to look at the forces that shape customers' perceptions.

Wants and needs

Wants and needs are at the root of perception and they are a useful way to define what the customer is looking for. Wants and needs are different, thus for example, someone who has a need for transport might say:

I need a car;
I want a Ferrari.

The expressed *want* is aspirational. The driver dreams of a Ferrari. However, as his *need* is for transport and as his wallet is probably limited, he might have to settle for something more realistic.

Most personal and business requirements can be expressed in this way, and pricing has a crucial role to play. People tend to *think in terms of wants*, but *buy in terms of need*. Thus, the closer that *wants* are aligned with *needs*, or the nearer that they are to each other, the more successful the supplier can become. Pricing is a key tool in closing the gap between these, as by supplying what someone *wants*, but pricing it to satisfy those things that compete with the basic *needs*, you will be spot on. The most popular motor bike in the UK (1995/6) is the Honda Fireblade. It sells for just £9,000 (which is an affordable price) but can accelerate up to 170 mph; thus satisfying *wants* for very fast bikes at a price that compares very favourably with other products that satisfy more basic motorcyclists' *needs* and thus beating the competition.

This difference between needs and wants is often called a perception gap, and aspects of it will be familiar to us all, both in business and personally.

Think about someone sending you a parcel. Naturally enough you want it to arrive as soon as possible, maybe the next day. However, parcel delivery services are normally priced in terms of delivery times, and thus a 'next-day' delivery might cost £20, whereas a 'three-day' delivery will only cost £5 (this is because the parcel company finds it cheaper to do it more slowly, as they have flexibility to take up slack time — a type of cost-plus approach to pricing in fact).

When you order the parcel you will be thinking clearly about how you are going to use the contents. If it is a spare part for a machine that is not working and that you need urgently to continue production then you will probably pay the high cost for next-day delivery. Your perception of the value of the contents of the parcel is high, and thus the extra delivery cost is largely immaterial by comparison.

If, on the other hand, the contents are some books for your holidays in three weeks' time, you will pay for the slower delivery. Your perception of the value of the contents is now time-dependent. Thus, although you may *want* the books to arrive tomorrow, you don't *need* them for three weeks. You will decide according to your needs, not your wants! The driving factors are the time that you need it, traded off against the incremental cost of the different methods compared with the opportunity cost of the choice.

The basis of perceptions

In the parcel example it was quite clear what the differences were between the buyers' wants and needs; however, this difference is not always so clear cut as the thought processes of people are rarely so rational. In fact, people draw on a whole host of ideas and concepts to build a mental picture of wants and needs (and often find it difficult to articulate this to, say, market researchers). This is called *perception* and it is on this that prices must be focused.

To illustrate this, consider an example with which we are all familiar: house sales. If you are selling your house the price you ask will not be based on the value of the bricks and mortar and nor will it bear any real relation to land prices. What it will be related to are other properties in the same street or in a similar locality. Thus two identical properties in the same street will sell at virtually the same price whilst a house in an area considered 'desirable' can fetch up to five or six times as much as an identical property in a less favoured location.

House prices are effectively set by the estate agent (in cooperation with the house owner). They will base their price on previous sales and will basically ask for the maximum they think they can get depending on the urgency of the sale.

The key thing that enables them to do this is information. A good estate agent will have almost perfect knowledge about a specific geographical locality and will thus be very well placed to set a market price.

They may suggest that a price is varied by a few per cent for a quick sale or if the property has some unusual features. They will also tell you whether that 'improvement' to your property has an effect on price: for example, add a garage or double glazing and you can probably ask more than a similar property which lacks these, but if you add a swimming pool or sauna you will almost certainly never recover the cost (in the UK, that is – in other countries, of course, a swimming pool may be a fundamental prerequisite for a sale.)

The reason for this is based on the idea of worth. Thus a garage is perceived as not only useful but valuable, whereas the majority of buyers will probably view a sauna room as a frippery and will not be willing to pay the extra.

How many times have you heard someone say, 'I can't sell my house — the market is dead'? This is, of course, nonsense — what they mean is that they cannot achieve the price that they want. Next time you hear someone say something along these lines tell them that they have priced it too high. They will probably disagree, and you can then say, 'I'll give you a pound for it'. They will not accept it (or at least it is highly unlikely) but it will illustrate the fact that they can sell their house, but that the price is wrong.

The correct price lies somewhere between £1 and the current price. Of course, time is a factor — if they are in no hurry they may feel that they can hold out for longer to get a higher price (usually, of course, the opposite occurs and prices are dropped after a while to move it).

Market perception

In the previous example of a house sale the buyers and sellers were private. In fact, any market is just a collection of buyers; and sellers can treat them in much the same way by collectivising them and maybe segmenting them into groups who share the same perceptions. One of the most common, early forms of segmenting was by socio-economic groupings (AB, C1, C2, DE) which is based on the view that the more wealthy or the further up the 'class line' that one is the more likely one's *needs* are to change. This is largely untrue, of course, as people are much more complicated than this; however, the *wants* both change and get closer to becoming reality.

As marketing developed the shortcomings of such a crude segmentation were increasingly challenged and new, different methods developed. These include *a classification of residential neighbourhoods* (ACORN) and of course postcodes which refine groups down to perhaps 20 or 30 houses which tend to be of similar construction, price etc. (In London and other urban areas this often falls down where some of those houses have been converted into flats and the inhabitants are often not, therefore, as homogeneous as might have been expected.)

Some more sophisticated techniques use 'life-style' indicators to give indications of perceptions and, therefore, buying tendencies.

The same types of consideration apply in pricing business and consumer products. Whilst marketing professionals know that some people will happily pay a premium for vegetables if they are labelled as organically grown or 'free range' eggs as opposed to ordinary ones, they also know that it is unlikely that you could sell many small chocolate bars for £10, even if they were made of the finest chocolate with ingredients flown in from around the world.

Thus, the market rules, or to put it another way, it is not the cost of making the product, nor is it the amount of profit you want to make, it is simply the customers' perception of the worth of the goods which ultimately determines the price. This perception can be measured and then banded for suitable target consumer groupings as shown below (relative group sizes are shown by circle size).

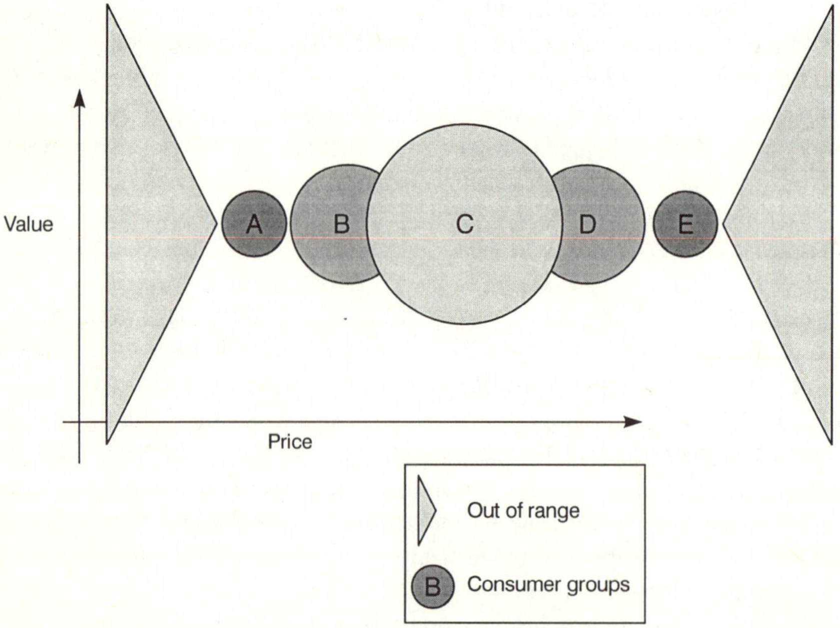

Figure 5.2 *Perception banding*

Unfortunately, in the area of perception of value, facts are largely irrelevant as this is a subjective opinion. Pricing is, therefore, neither as easy nor as scientific as it theoretically could be. Good market research, therefore, is vital to setting a market-led price.

Types of market-based pricing

There are numerous tactics and techniques used in developing market-based prices and we have classified them in Table 5.1:

Table 5.1

Classification	*Techniques*
Basic techniques	Going rate
	Perception
	Lump sum
	Piece rate
Specialised techniques	Psychological
	Contingent
	Line
Industry specific	Geographic or zone
Specific objectives	Loss leaders
	Slot/gap
	Impact assessment
	Skimming
	Penetration
	Premium
Trade pricing	Intermediary
	Dual or multiple

We also discuss alternative forms of pricing at the end of this section.

Classification	*Techniques*
Tendering	Sealed bid
Other	Auctions
	Barter
	Haggling

BASIC TECHNIQUES

Going rate pricing

This is perhaps the simplest form of market-based pricing. This name is given to the technique whereby an organisation simply looks at competitors' prices and prices its own products slightly under or above in any given area to achieve a specific market objective (eg share, distortion of supply channels etc). It is often adopted by smaller firms, ones that have difficulty in measuring costs' inputs or those in commodity or mature markets.

It assumes a kind of perfect competition (ie that there are no distortions, for example, caused by loss leader pricing) in each area and it further assumes that competitors know what they are doing.

In essence, all the manufacturer or retailer does is to look at the price everyone else charges and then simply adds or subtracts a very small amount. This differential against this reference price is then maintained come what may. The basic assumption here is that the bigger players in the market have done all the necessary economic assessments to decide the 'best price' so it is not necessary to reinvent the wheel. Essentially other players are using the major player(s) as a benchmark against which to price.

As an example, one smaller property developer in the North of England who was building and selling houses very similar to those produced by the major home builders, simply offered his properties at £1,000 less than the identical properties on a nearby site. His prices tracked what his larger competitors did, and as they changed property prices he did the same, always maintaining the differential. He was accordingly very successful.

The reason for the popularity of this technique is easy to see: as long as your price outstrips your costs you can feel you are doing as well as possible. The technique does, however, lack sophistication and techniques like charging for brand value and getting value from enhanced customer perception are not factored in.

Other examples commonly found include retailers who may mimic supermarket prices, but add a small premium for convenience. In this case there is an obvious advantage as pricing simply becomes a matter of walking round your local Sainsburys once a month with a notepad then adding a few pence onto each product in your shop!

The following example is a very simple illustration of this type of pricing:

Let us say that you have small factory that produces furniture. As an offshoot you also produce a small quantity of wooden table lamps, which are not your main business. You simply go into a few department stores and look in some catalogues to see what these types of product sell for at retail and ask the stores what kind of margin they make from the sales. You then set your price around the level of competing products.

Pros and cons

Good points

- the information collection requirement is low;

- you are certain to be in the right area;
- you can better spend your time on other areas of business (marketing, gaining new customers).

Bad points

- your product might actually be significantly better (or worse) than the competition and hence your differentiation might be incorrect;
- you are not optimising your return;
- you are operating in ignorance of the true cost of production.

Perception pricing

This term describes a particular form of market-based pricing, based entirely on the consumers' view of the value of the goods on offer rather than on specific market conditions. The determination of customers' perceptions is a difficult area to explore and, without doubt, many proponents of these techniques are doing nothing more than overlaying a certain value on top of a market price to amend their original idea of price.

Perception pricing tends to involve three main areas:

- where the customer is offered '*more for more*';
- where the customer is offered '*more for less*';
- where the customer is offered '*less for less*'.

Would-be pricing managers should note that the situation where the customer is offered '*less for more*' is not a workable one!

The customer perception is measured by using sophisticated market research and psychological techniques (for example, a process known as conjoint analysis is often used). Would-be buyers are asked to trade off certain features, so that the manufacturer can determine the relative worth of each feature. When researching the price of a new car, therefore, and trying to determine what to offer as extras, the manufacturer might ask a series of questions like the following:

- Would you prefer a CD player or central locking?
- Would you prefer a passenger air bag or sun roof?
- Would you prefer a CD player or leather seats plus an extra payment of £50?
- Would you prefer central locking or a sun roof?
  etc.

When properly constituted, the answers can be fed into a computer programme to determine the relative perception of worth of each item. The results will help in determining the scope of the product that must be offered at the price.

As an example we have categorised a selection of people's perceptions of cars into the following groups. You might disagree (and so might the manufacturers) but after all perceptions are simply opinions:

- more for more — Ferraris, Aston Martins, Jaguars, Mercedes, Range Rovers;
- more for less — Rovers, many Japanese cars;
- less for less — Skoda, Seat, Ladas, Reliant Robins.

More for more

This is sometimes called luxury or cachet pricing and normally involves high-profile brand names. For example, you can buy a very adequate wrist-watch for under £20 in the UK, and one made with a steel case and strap for around £100, but a Rolex will cost upwards of £1,500 or a Tag Heuer £500. In essence the Rolex and Tag are made from similar materials, to a broadly similar design to other watches. Of course the hand labour and finishing that go into the product contribute to a higher cost price, but the margin made by Rolex and Tag is undoubtedly higher than that made by Acme Watches of Scunthorpe.

The reason that Rolex can obtain such a high price is that the perception of being the owner of the world's best watch is one that some people are prepared to pay for, and this is nothing to do with the physical item itself. Whilst the watch has a certain utility for telling the time and date, possibly accurate to a second a day or better, it has a greater function as a fashion accessory or statement of wealth, which accordingly increases the price it is possible to charge.

Note, however, that Rolex will not look to sell anything like as many watches as Acme (and, of course, would not wish to do so, as if it did the social cachet would be lost). This type of pricing has proved to be particularly successful in Japan where there is a significant social emphasis on giving expensive luxury goods as gifts.

More for less

In this area the company positions a product up against much more expensive alternatives and suggests to the consumer that although they are paying less they are getting the same. Directly comparative advertising is neither effective nor socially acceptable in the UK so we do not see so many examples of this, but in the USA examples are legion. Thus a typical promotion in this area might read: 'Buy our product for only $20. It has all the features of the top brand name item which sells for $40'.

In order to be a successful seller the company has to overcome a number of obstacles: if the quality is the same, then the company's return will be much lower as its cost of production is likely to be similar. It must, therefore, sell many more to make the same absolute return. In addition, those people attracted by the social cachet of owning a top brand name item will be put off the pretender as their social peers will see it as cheap copy.

Examples of companies that have been successful in this field include Toyota with its luxury Lexus car (pitched right up against the equivalent Mercedes) and Marks & Spencer, whose own brand products offer high quality at reasonable prices. (Interestingly, Marks & Spencer has been so successful at this that it is now perceived to be one of the brands against which others are compared and you often see cut-price products being advertised as being of 'leading store quality'.)

Orange

Orange is the national, digital wirefree telephone service launched in the UK in April 1994. Central to its strategic objective is to offer the best value for money.

Before its launch, the UK mobile market was cluttered and confused, with complex pricing packages. Orange researched the market to find out what potential customers sought. The answers were 'a better deal', 'better value', 'more choice', and 'fairer pricing'.

So Orange's better value strategy features three critical elements for customer acquisition and retention — competitive call charges; value added services; reassurance. Together the three offer strong cost of ownership advantages for customers.

Competitive call charges

Instead of following the other networks and charging the traditional line rental plus call charges, Orange introduced five price plans, each with a different number of inclusive minutes built into the monthly charge, So, for example, instead of paying £25 a month and getting nothing, customers can pay £25 a month and get 60 minutes' worth of calls.

Orange also included incentives for high users, so the Talk 540 plan offers nine hours of talk-time a month for £100.

A central element of the better value strategy was per second billing, rather than the 60-second minimum plus 30-second increments that had been the norm in the UK.

Value added services

Orange provided a package of value added services, such as voicemail, where the customers pay nothing for a caller to leave a message and just 7.5p a minute to retrieve a message, charged by the second.

Caller-id — the ability to see who is calling before you answer — is also inclusive as well as call divert; call barring, call hold and call waiting facility.

Reassurance

Orange wanted to reassure customers that they have made the right decision by choosing the service. Thus from launch Orange offered a unique care package:

- a 14-day money back guarantee;
- inclusive itemised billing;
- a 24-hour replacement service for lost, stolen or faulty phones.

The value strategy has enabled Orange to acquire high-value customers with a very low churn (the rate at which customers decide to disconnect from the network). Revenues per subscriber are well above the industry average and climbing while Orange churn is well below the churn experienced by all competitors.

Less for less

In this area the manufacturer unashamedly pitches the product at the lower end of the market. This is sometimes called the 'pile it high and sell it cheap' technique and was pioneered by companies like Tesco in the UK and WalMart in the USA. (Interestingly Tesco has successfully moved itself significantly up-market in recent times.) In a supermarket you may see tins of beans on offer that are half the price of the branded items. Whether or not they are as good as the top-priced brand is an individual perception, but if you are on a low wage then you may not care; they are beans after all.

Some supermarkets deliberately give such ranges of products distinctive names and packing that imply that the product is without frills and it is specifically not a reduction in quality that has resulted in a lower price but rather just plain value. Thus 'Basics' is a typical name used by one store, and at another its own product offerings of this type are in plain white packaging labelled 'Value'.

In recent years a whole wave of discounters have come into the supermarket areas (Aldi, Netto etc), who not only offer the cheapest products but also only offer limited ranges (to keep stockholding costs down) and sometimes only accept cash at the checkouts (to keep handling and administration costs down). There is no social cachet to be gained from shopping at these stores, only low prices.

The rise of the discounter in the UK

Discount retailing has developed rapidly over the past five years in the UK.

The principal players are:

- Kwik Save which with sales of £3bn in 1994 accounted for nearly two-thirds of all discounter sales operating through 1,000 stores.
- Aldi, the second biggest discount chain, had sales of £267m in 1993.
- Netto, a Danish-owned company, with over 100 stores.
- Lidl, one of the fastest growing, with plans to open at least 50 stores in 1995.

In its report 'Discounting in Retailing' Mintel's consumer research among a representative sample of 991 adults reveals the presence of brands in an offer among discounters is considered to be more important than low prices. Some 43 per cent of the sample stated that a limited range was acceptable if well-known brands were present but under a third of the sample were happy to sacrifice choice for price.

The offerings of continental discounters have a narrow appeal with only under one in five consumers claiming not to mind foreign brand names and just over one in ten trust the quality of unknown brand names.

In terms of price reductions required to use a discounter when buying a major non-food item, over 70 per cent of the sample expected a discount of 10 per cent or more but only a third expected a discount of more than 15 per cent. This suggests quite sizeable numbers of shoppers could be attracted to discount stores that offered genuine reductions against comparable prices available elsewhere.

This finding has the value of identifying what incentive is required to motivate shoppers to alter their shopping habits. The use of periodic discounts by retailers committed to a value proposition is widespread. Short, sharp bursts of genuine reduction against genuinely competitive prices provides an edge which, if used aggressively, will help develop consumer perceptions of the retailer's value. (Source: Mintel.)

Pros and cons

Good points

- You can finely tune your price if you know what your customer thinks.

- You can use pricing to reinforce your whole marketing message.

Bad points

- If you apply *your* values instead of the buyers' then you can really get it wrong.
- The information requirement can be very high and often quite difficult to get in practice.

Lump sum and piece-rate pricing

These are specialised techniques, often used by service oriented businesses .

Lump-sum pricing (sometimes called bundling)

This is where all the elements of a deal are put together and offered to the buyer under one umbrella price. If, for example, you required your house to be scaffolded out and painted, the builder might give you a lump-sum price rather than individual prices for each part, as if he broke it down into the two components this could encourage the buyer to shop around for the best deal on each.

Although this technique sounds deceptively simple it is in fact extremely sophisticated and we can look at some of these elements in more detail.

Firstly, because the price of each individual element is effectively hidden from the buyer, the seller can charge a premium for some services without the buyer knowing. To take the example of the builder; here there are three main elements: the cost of the scaffolding, the price of the paint and the labour involved. If the builder has got some very cheap paint, he can, in effect, use this cheapness to disguise the high cost of his scaffolding services. The overall price looks reasonable, but if the buyer were to break it down he would see he was paying well over the odds for the scaffolding and would not buy it from the builder.

The second key sophistication is risk. Because the job is being offered for a fixed sum the buyer knows what he is getting and the risk lies with the builder. Suppose the scaffolding takes longer than expected or the weather is bad, meaning the painters have to sit around, being paid, but drinking tea? It will be the builder who absorbs these costs and, therefore, he will have ensured that a small premium to cover these eventualities will be included in the price (effectively a statistical bet on the weather). The buyer (although he does not know this) will be paying this premium and in return receives the reassurance that the quoted price is the one he will always pay.

Pros and cons

Good point

- If you work efficiently you can make a very good profit.

Bad points

- The seller can only affect/control part of the risk.
- The price can look expensive.

Piece-rate pricing

This technique, on the other hand, devolves all the risk to the buyer. In piece-rate pricing (sometimes called day-rate or time and materials pricing) the builder offers his services for each day worked or task done. Thus he will quote a price of (say) £80 per painter day. The problem for the buyer is that he does not necessarily know how long it takes to paint his house (and thus cannot work out the likely cost) and if the builders work slowly, say due to poor weather, he could end up paying a lot more money than was reasonable. Such piece-rate contracts are normally only used when both the buyer and seller are equally sophisticated, have a history of working together (thus implying a degree of trust) or are linked by a strong contract.

Because they devolve all the risk to the buyer, many sellers like them and try to use them on clients. If you take your car to a small garage for repair you will effectively be entering into a piece-rate contract ('That'll be £25 an hour guv'nor and it took 10 hours') rather than the normal £200 lump-sum quote for a service at a main dealer. Your choice, your risk.

The basic consideration here lies in the risk. If you are a sophisticated buyer, want a low price and are prepared to take the risk yourself then opt for a piece-rate contract. If on the other hand you want the assurance of a fixed price go for a lump-sum contract.

These type of techniques are increasingly becoming the norm in performance-linked pay. In the past most 'white-collar' staff were paid a fixed salary regardless of output; in manufacturing it was far more usual for 'blue-collar' workers to be paid on time and/or piece-rate basis. There has been a paradigm shift in recent years to where most staff pay is now linked to performance. Costs can, therefore, be controlled as, if performance is low, only the (low) basic salary is paid. Where performance is good commission or bonus is added in and both parties are better off.

Pros and cons

Good point

- The risk is all on the buyers' side;

Bad point

- There is little potential to make more than your 'standard' profit.

SPECIALISED TECHNIQUES

Psychological pricing

This is really a trick rather than a technique. It works by pricing products just slightly below a round number, eg one pence or five pence less than £20, being £19.99 or £19.95.

It is often said that this technique was invented over 100 years, ago with the advent of cash registers. These made a noise when they were opened, so shopkeepers, who didn't trust their staff, priced products so some change was required. This meant that they could listen out for the ringing of the till, and feel sure that the assistant wasn't simply slipping a coin or note into his pocket.

Extensive research has been undertaken in recent years on consumers' perceptions of 'price points'. Price points are the technical name given to the point where a product goes from being perceived as cheap to (say) very cheap, or from expensive to (say) too dear to buy. Of course individuals' perceptions vary, but understanding the price points in your market can pay huge dividends.

Figure 5.3 shows a hypothetical example of the different perceptions of polo shirts from a number of sources. These different perceptions form price points where the price for that particular item passes into another category of perception and, therefore, is not bought (too expensive or the purchaser trades up to the next type — perceived as better). Conversely, where the price falls below the price band the product may then be perceived as substandard and an alternative is purchased.

In the UK in 1995 the publisher Penguin launched a series of small paperback books priced at just 60p. The usual price of a paperback is around £5 mark and the price of a quality daily newspaper was around 50p. This price reduction changed the public's perception of these items from being a book (expensive, occasional purchase) to being an impulse buy. Sales have rock-

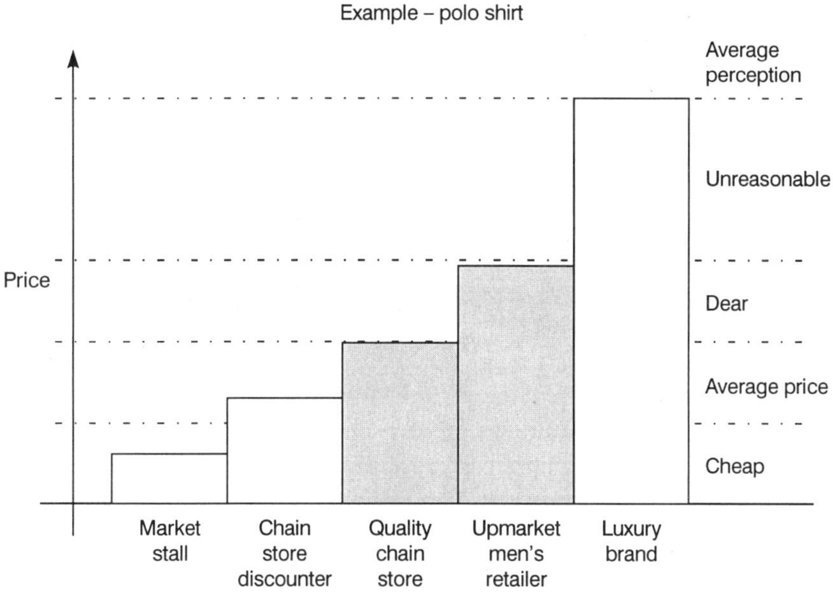

Figure 5.3 *Price points*

eted. Note that they are very small books and you will not get *War and Peace* in this series.

Prior to decimalisation in the UK, as well as the pound sterling, the guinea was in use, which was 21 shillings (105 new pence). Very often prices were quoted in guineas rather than pounds (and less guineas than the price might have been in pounds). Amongst others, professional fees and tailors' prices were often quoted in this way. There was a general perception that the price being marked in guineas was somehow synonymous with quality and that 25 guineas was better than £26 (of course it was more expensive at £26.25).

An interesting contrast may be seen in job advertisements where salaries are quoted (the price of your work). In the private sector a round figure (to the nearest thousand) is usually quoted; however, public sector adverts usually feature a scale banding (eg from £16,225 to £19,234) due to their much stricter internal rules.

Pros and cons

Good point

- Psychology is important, and it may persuade some buyers.

Bad points

- When pricing big items, it is just plain silly: who is fooled by a car costing £19,999.99?
- Don't forget to allow for the effect of VAT when pricing.

Contingent pricing

This technique relates the price of the goods or services to the eventual outcome of the use to which they are being put. Readers might be familiar with its use in the football world. Thus, for example, Lazio (an Italian soccer club) might sell its centre forward to another club — Milan. Milan will pay 100 million lire up front, and then pay a further 10 million lire for each game that the centre forward plays that season, and maybe 10 million lire for each goal he scores. The overall price paid to Lazio is thus contingent on the performance of the centre forward. For this type of contract to work well the player's remuneration should also be linked to the same things.

There are many examples of these types of contract and a few examples are given below. Such contracts can be constructed in virtually any way you want, and can even be negatively contingent where the buyer receives a refund from the seller in the event of non-performance.

Road repair in the UK has operated on a contingent type of contract for some time (called lane rental). In this the repairer quotes a price to repair (say) a mile of motorway. The repairer also agrees to 'rent' the motorway from the Transport Department for a fixed fee, per day. If the repairs are finished early, the repairer does not have to pay all of the rent and so receives a windfall bonus. If the repairer is slow or inefficient they end up paying extra rent they had not bargained for. It, therefore, gives an incentive for contractors to finish the repairs as quickly as possible which also reduces traffic hold ups. It does mean that quality inspection is necessary to prevent corner cutting.

Professional advisers. When a company is looking to buy another company it often employs the services of a firm or firms of advisers (accountants, lawyers, merchant bankers, PR agents, consultants etc). Because the takeover may or may not succeed it may wish to pay the advisers only a small percentage of the normal daily rates of its staff, but link this with a large success fee if the deal goes ahead, ie the final payment is contingent on the deal going ahead.

For this to work the adviser has to have an idea of how likely the deal is to go through. If the deal does not go ahead the advisers probably receive their costs back but make no profit, but if it does go ahead a very large payment is made — often millions of pounds for large bids.

Broking. Taken to its logical extreme the contingent fee can amount to 100 per cent of the fee. Thus if there is no deal then no money is paid. If the deal does go through a very large fee may be paid. Intermediaries who act in this way are often called brokers. They are familiar in many industries including insurance, money markets, shipping etc and contrary to popular opinion in many cases add substantial value to both parties. By using their specialised knowledge they place buyers and sellers together in a mutually beneficial way.

No win — no fee. Recently we have seen the limited introduction of the idea of 'no win — no fee' legal representation in the UK. This is common, for example, in the USA but not prevalent elsewhere. The lawyer does not get anything unless his client wins, but if he does then his fees are a proportion of the damages etc. This is not yet generally accepted in the UK, neither culturally nor philosophically.

Pros and cons

Good point

- The buyer can make huge profits if things go well.

Bad point

- Most of the risk is on the seller's side, so a big loss can result if things go wrong.

Cresswell and Company

Cresswell and Company are a small firm of solicitors in west London. Their business operates in two main areas: residential and commercial conveyancing (the sale and purchase of property) and commercial litigation and commercial advice. The company's approach to pricing is very different in each market.

Domestic conveyancing

The domestic conveyancing market, in particular, is very price sensitive and there is considerable competition from other local firms of solicitors and also licensed conveyancers. At the time of writing house sales are still somewhat sluggish and people tend to shop around for both the estate agent and the solicitor. Because the amount of work in a conveyance is generally predictable the company is able to quote a fixed fee (lump sum). Typically this is priced a little above the charges of other local firms.

This price differential is justified on the basis of a high-quality, friendly, proactive personal service by experienced solicitors.

The company does, however, recognise that these added value aspects are not important to certain types of consumer, and under these conditions will, if requested, offer a discount but will generally not meet the lowest price offered if this is below its cost base (ie nil profit). The scope for discounts is relatively small (about 12 per cent being the maximum that will be offered).

Litigation and commercial advice

In the area of providing litigation and commercial advice, the firm's approach is very different. Because the amount of work can rarely be predicted on a case-by-case basis, work is usually charged on an hourly basis (piece-work). The initial fee estimate is sometimes capped (dependent on the work, and the requirements of the client). Contingent fee pricing (ie being paid according to the outcome of the work) is only allowed by the Law Society in very specific areas.

Hourly rates are initially derived from an idea of the cost base (ie proportion of fixed overheads, plus the proportion of time and resources used on the specific case). Time and variable resources are managed by the use of time-sheets and expense accounting systems. Specific expenses are normally recharged at cost, with no extra mark-up.

After the initial fee estimate, based on an hourly charge, is calculated, this is then adjusted according to the client's perception of the value of the work, competitive quotes, the overall size of the job etc. Thus, in practice, a lower charge would be made for a large piece of work in an area requiring generic skills, compared to a short piece of high added value work that requires very specific skills on the part of the solicitor. Fee rates can vary by as much as 40 per cent to 50 per cent on this basis.

Line pricing

This is where all prices on a given 'line' or product range are set to reflect the market characteristics or expectations. If you shop in, say, C & A, BHS, or Marks & Spencer for a particular suit or dress, all sizes of the line will be priced the same. This is regardless of the actual inputs to production. A size 22 clearly requires more material than a size 6 but the price is always the same. For a large store with many branches it would clearly not be worth the administrative effort of differential pricing, not to say the probable market reaction (sizist!).

There are, however, indications of a move in some circumstances to a definition of a 'core' size (eg a 14½" – 17½" size collar for men's shirts) with a standard price, and then charging more for larger sizes. Interestingly, there does not seem to be much enthusiasm for a corresponding discount offered for smaller sizes! We call this asymmetric pricing.

With bespoke tailoring, where items are made to measure, they will all be priced individually. It is interesting to note that with food this situation almost never occurs as it is sold precisely on weight or volume.

By and large this type of pricing depends on input costs: with chain-store clothes there are high, fixed costs, and the material does not contribute too much to the final cost of the item. In bespoke tailors it is much more relevant (normally as the materials are much more expensive) and, of course, in food the raw material cost is a high proportion of the price.

Pros and cons

Good points

- administration is easier;
- swings and roundabouts in terms of margin;
- customers do not feel discriminated against, unless they are at the end of the spectrum.

Bad point

- only suitable where variable costs are relatively low.

INDUSTRY SPECIFIC

Geographical pricing

This simply involves differential pricing based (nominally) on the cost of service (eg customers in central London are charged more, or customers inside a 25-mile range of the warehouse are charged less etc).

A very common example is mobile telephone calls. On some UK analogue networks calls are charged at lower rates if made inside the M25 (the London orbital motorway). On the digital networks calls are often cheaper or even free if made in the same STD code area.

Of course, the cost of service is no different if a call is made from Oxford Street to Bond Street (100 metres) or from Wembley to Dartford (30 kilometres and both in the same STD area). However, telephone users have become conditioned to costs made across traditional networks (where the cost does change) and, therefore, this type of geographical pricing is seen by many mobile providers as an incentive.

Sometimes, of course, geographical pricing is rooted in real cost differences. It is, for example, more expensive to buy petrol in the Shetland Islands than it is next door to the Esso refinery at, say, Fawley. This is primarily because of shipping charges, but also the amount of product sold is less (and thus the overheads need to be amortised across a lower sales volume).

Thus geographical pricing can have a real basis (normally in the case of large or bulky goods, being moved from one location) or it can be just a marketing ploy.

There are a number of sub variants, as follows:

FOB origin pricing

In this case the customer is basically advised of the delivery cost, by being told the 'warehouse door' price of the product and then having to pick up all freighting charges themselves. FOB is the acronym for 'free on board', used when products were mainly carried by sea.

This has the effect of seeming not to discriminate against any buyer, irrespective of where they are. Thus the petrol company would offer its petrol to all service stations at (say) 50p a litre FOB. Because it is the buyer that is responsible for picking up the collection cost (which may come out of a different budget) the seller hopes the buyer will not feel discriminated against if they are a long way away.

However, some customers will argue that it is the company decision as to where to place warehouses or production facilities, not theirs, and so why should they be disadvantaged? This argument is, of course, fully reversible.

Just for interest it is worth knowing that international business sometimes offers a halfway house alternative: we pay for the delivery from the factory in Rome to the dockside in New York, you pay the rest. If you are going into the export or import business you need to know your acronyms!

Uniform delivered pricing (sometimes called postage-stamp pricing)

In this case a single delivery charge is levied to large, bounded areas (ie specific geographical location is not considered relevant, although transnational boundaries are considered significant).

Think of this in terms of a postage stamp. It costs the same to mail a letter anywhere in a country, no matter whether the letter is going from New York to San Diego (5000 kilometres) or New York to Boston (400 kilometres). However, if the letter is going from Detroit, MI, USA to Toronto, Ontario, Canada (also 400 kilometres) the cost could be double because it crosses an international boundary.

The problem with this technique is that it involves significant cross-subsidisation of certain customers and you, therefore, need excellent internal accounting systems to know where your costs lie.

Other common examples include car delivery charges (normally uniform across smaller countries, even though the factory could be five miles away or 500) and electricity supply into homes and offices. The electricity could come to London from any station in the UK (and, in fact, Europe) through the transmission grid, but these specific charges are not passed on to customers but amortised. How could they be worked out anyway?

Zone pricing

As the name implies, this is a cross between the two alternatives above, and may be more amenable to customers, although it is inevitably a 'fudge'. The zone is simply an artificial boundary imposed by the seller.

This system works by calculating the demographics of customers and the cost of delivery of the service. Thus, for example, it can cost an entirely different amount to travel the same distance on a bus, depending on whether you cross a zone boundary or not. Of course commuters don't know where these zone boundaries are and, therefore, the company has to supply the information. For buyers living right on the edge of a zone this can be infuriating, and if you look at the zone map of the London Underground, you will see that some stations are demarcated as being in two zones at once, depending on whether you start or finish your journey there!

Freight absorption pricing

In this technique, all delivery charges are built into the product price, and the price is therefore 'delivered' (sometimes called CIF (carriage, insurance, freight). Whilst this has advantages to customers it removes a significant area of scope from the control of the seller as the organisation cannot use changes in the delivery system to manipulate margins.

It usually results in lower prices, however, as the organisation paying the costs has usually negotiated discounts for bulk. This is common where, say, a large manufacturer is selling to a series of smaller outlets/middlemen or where a large buyer is purchasing from several sources. There are many permutations to this and the following example illustrates this:

A factory produces pattern silencers for cars (quite cheap but bulky and costly to transport). It is based in Paris.

If it sells FOB, customers in Paris will find it cheaper as delivery is less, but customers in, say, Munich or Vienna have to pay much higher transport costs (resulting in an apparently higher price). If the product is sold CIF then Parisian, German and Austrian customers all pay the same price — probably a hybrid price (higher for the Parisians, lower for the rest).

In the CIF case, if the customer in Munich orders a truck load then the delivery charges per unit will be less. The seller then has a choice: reflect this in the price by giving a discount, or keep the extra profit (supra profit) arising from the lower delivery charges.

Summary

Many organisations use some form of geographic pricing in order to maximise return (or more often, to minimise the impact of delivery charges) and the techniques are often used together.

Pros and cons

Good points

- You can make your customer feel he is getting a bargain over your competitor who may be miles away.
- You can pass on or hide some of those costs that are not in your control.

Bad points

- Some customers can feel discriminated against.
- Internal cost systems can become so complex that you lose sight of your objectives.

SPECIFIC OBJECTIVE PRICING

Loss leading (sometimes called bait pricing)

This technique is basically used to lure a customer to purchase, in the hope that they will get the habit of buying from you.

In its simplest form, if you own a shop, you can price one staple item far below anyone around (maybe even below cost). You hope that people will find you so cheap on this one item that they will make an effort to come in and buy from you, and then stay and buy other normally priced (or maybe even more expensive) items.

The big supermarket chains routinely concentrate price promotions on a limited range of popular items. It is no good offering some esoteric item, like, say Parmesan cheese at a low price. Most of us buy Parmesan only occasionally, if ever. However, we do buy milk, bread and eggs almost every day. This is a straightforward marketing ploy and is entirely above-board — the buyer wins by getting something cheap.

In more complex cases the initial offer might seem superficially very appealing, but having bought the item you then find you are paying over the odds for other necessary components of the service. The use of techniques like this is unscrupulous to say the least, if not downright illegal. It is really a trick and not recommended if you wish to command respect in the market. Here are some well-known examples:

- *Renting a photocopier*. The initial price is low or even free, but you then find the cost per copy is high and you are charged high rates for maintenance. The contract will be long and watertight.
- *A free mobile phone*. The handset may be free but the call charges will be very high, and again there is a long contract.
- *Flights to a long-haul destination for £10*. On booking you may find you are obliged by the terms of contract to stay at specific hotels (very dear) and also purchase travel insurance, even if you have it already.

The list of these scams goes on and on. Remember that there is no such thing as free lunch, and you will not go too far wrong. If it looks too good to be true, it probably is. On the other hand, if you own a shop or retail outlet, make sure that those apples you priced at 1p a kilo are not being bought from you by the chap from the greengrocer round the corner for him to resell, at a much better rate than he could get from his wholesaler!

Pros and cons

Good point

- Attractive as a marketing tool.

Bad points

- You need deep pockets to keep it up.
- Trigger a price war, and everyone could soon be making a loss.
- You have to find ways of selling on further products at a good margin to make money.

Slot/gap pricing

This is the term given to a specialised form of psychological pricing. As its name implies, it involves analysing the product-market offer and looking for a gap or slot in the current offer, then inserting your product into this, with the intention of feeding off the activities of other players and taking advantage of customer preconceptions.

The two most obvious examples are:

- *Slotting into the bottom of the market*: ie simply undercutting everyone to become the cheapest supplier.
- *Slotting in at the top*: becoming the premium player.

However, both these positionings require a certain level of work on the part of the supplier (ie lowering costs or going in for high benefits and features and maybe cachet advertising).

The real advantage of this technique is where you can slot into a really complex market somewhere in the middle. The marketing activity requirement can be quite low as you are feeding off existing perceptions.

This can be illustrated with an example from the UK book trade. A few years ago if you wanted to buy a classic book (say a Jane Austen) there were a few types of product on the market: paperbacks priced at around £5.99 (see the psychological pricing here), hardbacks with good paper and bindings at maybe £15–£20 and a slightly less expensive version available only by post from book clubs.

A new entrant to the market saw the gap and produced a hardback, albeit cheaply typeset and printed on softback quality paper, but priced very competitively at £7.99. These books simply rushed from the shelves as consumers saw the opportunity to buy what they perceived as a quality item at a lower quality price.

Of course the dynamics of this situation are more complex than we can outline here, and include the fact that many people see books as 'cultural wallpaper', nice to line the living room with, but not so good to read, and to this day, hardbacks have a cachet unmatched by the best produced softbacks.

Many other types of firm use this technique successfully, sometimes by simply rebadging an offer to push it into a different band (think of limited edition cars, basically a new paint job, as a classic example).

Pros and cons

Good point

- lets others do the work for you

Bad points

- not all markets have the potential for this;
- tends to spawn rapid competition as others seek to exploit your opening.

Impact assessment pricing

This technique involves an assessment of the likely effect that any given price is going to have on the consumers of the product, the market, suppliers, and, to an extent, competitors. To put it another way the seller firstly determines the required effect and then prices accordingly.

In order to use this technique a company has to have very good information about the market and supply channels as a whole. It also has to be able to incorporate this data into a model and thus needs to know the supply: demand relationship, stockholder objectives and market dynamics in real detail.

As an example, consider a company that has been selling a line of outdoor clothing mainly through High Street stores and speciality clothing shops. This company, if it is dissatisfied with the way business is going, could model a range of different scenarios to see 'what if' it did business another way.

Because the prices attainable though different supply chains and distribution routes (and, of course, the cost of supply) will be very different, the company will have to prepare some sophisticated models to understand the impact of significant changes.

Thus, for example, it could supply through its own mail order catalogue only (high price, but also high costs of promotion). It could choose to become an 'own label' manufacturer for a High Street chain (low price, virtually nil cost of promotion but high guaranteed volumes) or it could open its own chain of High Street outlets (large investment, high risk all round).

The company will also have to decide whether it is positioning itself as a premium supplier, or as a low price 'bargain supplier'.

Whatever the company does, its pricing policies will need to reinforce its progress towards its objectives.

Pros and cons

Good points

- The right price is a key factor in achieving specific objectives.
- The use of sophisticated techniques normally puts you well in advance of competitors.

Bad points

- Information requirements are very high, and models must reflect the practicality of the position.
- A reasonably good existing position could be heavily undermined if various channels are tried unsuccessfully or in a poorly managed manner.

Premium pricing

This describes where the price of a product is set either slightly (or in some cases massively) above the 'real' or competitive price of the product or service. This method of pricing was described in the 'more for more' section of perception pricing and an extreme example was used to illustrate the point. In practice, even the most prosaic items can be 'premium priced' if they are marketed well enough.

Typically, premium pricing is used in conjunction with heavy advertising or branding where this promotes the ideas of quality, restricted appeal, 'snob' value, shortage of supply or the perception that the product is delivering more than it actually does.

Premium pricing is very common in both the professional service sector (particularly financial markets), and in the so-called branded and quality goods' markets.

For example, consumers know that a tin of Heinz or HP beans costs a few pence more than an equivalent supermarket own brand. What is not known is whether these products have virtually identical ingredients (some do, some don't) and also the difference in margin that the two suppliers are making and whether this accounts for the difference in manufacturing and marketing costs.

You will be aware that the giant consumer goods manufacturers spend a lot of time and money telling us that their products are the best and finest. They do not tell us that many of them also use identical ingredients to make 'own label' products for others to sell; in fact they do not tell us anything about this at all — for obvious reasons.

Next time you go into Marks & Spencer in the UK, pick up one of their chocolate countlines at the counter, the one that is a long bar with a triangular pieces of chocolate containing nougat and nuts. The product is called a Mountain Bar. In the sweet shop next door you can buy a Toblerone that looks and tastes similar; the Toblerone is a lot more expensive though!

In the service sector the differences can be even more marked. Why does a senior consultant from one of the leading strategy consultants (eg McKinsey or Bains) cost around £2,500 per day, whilst a similar individual from a big six accounting firm cost half this?

We can compound this argument by suggesting that, where the consultant is being sold to a bank in the City of London, the rates may well be uplifted by a further 25 per cent compared with those offered to, eg a manufacturing firm in, say, the Midlands. The very same individual, if working for himself, might only cost £800 per day. How is this difference in charge justified?

The answer lies simply in the customers' perception of the quality of the product and, to an extent, what the buyer has become accustomed to paying, eg the market price.

It may seem normal to a Londoner to pay £25 for a taxi from Heathrow to the West End, but to a visitor from Delhi this would seem extortionate.

Taxi drivers the world over know this, and when Londoners step off the plane at Delhi and order a cab to the Taj Hotel (about the same distance) and are charged the local equivalent of £25, they don't seem surprised. It is only later when they find out that locals pay £3, they become aggrieved!

Premium pricing, if used carefully, can give a customer a very good feeling about the exclusiveness and value for money of a product or service and should be used where it can be justified.

Try the little test in Table 5.2 and don't forget it is about perception

Table 5.2

The best in each case is:

Item	**Your view**	**Another view**
Personal computer		Apple
Rain coat		Burberry
Car		Ferrari
Whisky		Talisker
Holiday resort		Disneyland
Beer		Dorchester IPA
Cigarette lighter		Dunhill
Watch		Patek Phillippe

An interesting aside to premium pricing is that there is a common finding in consumer markets that where prices are put up and up over years (especially on slow-moving or esoteric products) that sales initially go down as the price goes up and then recover as a price point is reached where consumers suddenly think, 'This must be good, it's so expensive'.

Pros and cons

Good points

- In some cases, by more than doubling a price you can quadruple sales!
- People's perceptions of the same service vary widely; you can use this technique to segment a market very effectively.

Bad point

- Brand image and quality must be closely watched, otherwise you go from being highly desired and prized to simply overpriced.

TRADE PRICING

Intermediary pricing

There are substantial differences in pricing techniques between manufacturers and trade intermediaries (eg wholesalers, suppliers etc), and it could be said that in a perfect world, if all manufacturers used appropriate pricing techniques, then all that trade intermediaries would have to do was add a suitable on-cost and everything would be fine. Sadly this is not the case and, in practice, the pricing decision for intermediaries is, if anything, more complex than for manufacturers.

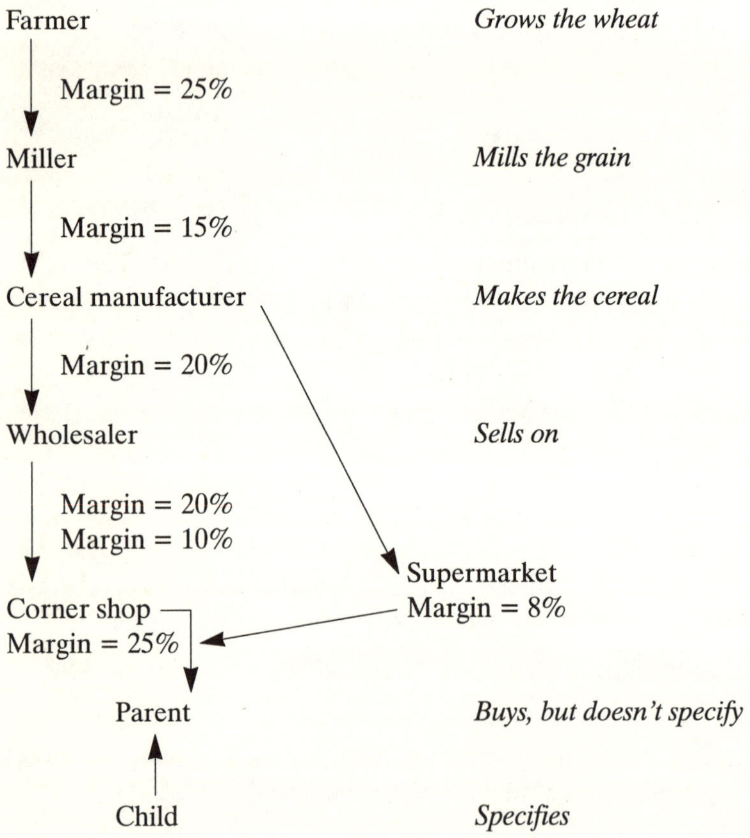

Figure 5.4 *Breakfast cereals – the selling chain*

The term intermediary pricing is used to describe the situation where a company is not selling direct to the end-user. Consider the sales and production route for a packet of breakfast cereal.

The farmer who grows the wheat has to set a price to sell to the miller. The miller in turn has to set a price to sell to the manufacturer, who then has to set several prices to sell to supermarkets (who buy directly in bulk); to wholesalers (who buy to sell on to corner shops); and possibly to others as well. In turn the retailers have to price the product to sell to the shopper.

Each party in this process will have their own ideas about pricing, about how much money they need to make to stay in business or be profitable, and about the limits to what they can charge.

In such a well-understood chain you can be sure that the farmer will know the retail price of the breakfast cereal and he will know that if he raises his prices by, say, 10 per cent this could account for a 50 per cent rise in the price in the shops, after everyone has taken their extra cut.

There is a significant skill in pricing when you are an intermediary and it requires very good information about the chain of events and a knowledge of the knock-on effect of your actions.

In practice the power is usually concentrated in one or two areas (often the supermarket and the manufacturer) and they will dictate what happens along the chain. This is often reflected in the problems faced by raw material producers in emerging countries. If their wage rates or costs go up they can often not get these back, as their customers (intermediaries) will argue that the eventual consumer will not wear the overall cost increase. This often leads to a vicious circle of debt for many poor countries as they are forced to borrow to finance imports or just the economy and are unable to recoup the costs from exports.

On occasion, however, such price rises have to be passed on. A few years ago there was terrible weather in South America which hit coffee harvests very badly and the price of coffee in the developed world rose by as much as 50 per cent overnight. This wasn't profit-taking but simply a reflection of costs being passed down the line.

William Levene Limited

William Levene Limited is a medium sized, privately owned company operating in the non-electrical housewares' market. Their range of products is large, including 250 branded items and a large number of tailor-made and own-label products for major retailers. Within this range are a number of brand leaders such as the MagiCan can opener, and the Ken Hom range of oriental cookware and accessories.

The company's strengths lie in original product development, sourcing and sales and marketing. The product range is sourced from manufacturers around the world and the company does not manufacture, although it owns tooling and exclusive rights for the largest part of its range. As a result, effective inventory management is critical, purchasing stock being the main expense of the business.

A value added range is fundamental to the company's success. It cannot operate as a lowest cost supplier. Consequently, costing and pricing are all given major importance from the very earliest stages of any new project.

The costing system calculates a gross margin based on the delivered cost of the product, plus an amortisation of tooling and development, usually over a three-year period. Also included are warehousing, distribution, financing and wastage, but not fixed overheads. To operate at an acceptable level of PBT, the company looks to earn an average 38 per cent gross margin for standard products, and 45 per cent on products which will be advertised or heavily promoted. The view is taken that for every product launched below these averages another should be launched above them, to prevent margin erosion.

Pricing operates at two levels — consumer and trade. Houseware products are retailed through a wide range of outlets: supermarkets, department stores, mail order, independent hardware and gift stores and many more. Each type of outlet has its own margin requirements, which the company needs to satisfy if it is to gain mass distribution. It, therefore, prices its product range within discount bands, for each major outlet type, reflecting their margin needs.

With most major retailers, net pricing is the subject of much negotiation, and outside pressure is always placed on the sales management team to move to the lowest price within each band. Control over pricing agreements to prevent them falling outside these bands is maintained at board level.

Retail prices do not arise from trade prices plus a fixed percentage. They are established at what the company sees as the market price for each product. This is arrived at through consumer research, normally in the form of discussion groups, and trade research, which involves price-checking competitive products in store and arriving at a value for money price to the consumer, taking full account of the perceived features and benefits of any particular item.

Wholesalers and trade intermediaries

In practice wholesalers and trade intermediaries deal with vast numbers of products, sometimes upwards of 10,000! Their pricing techniques are often

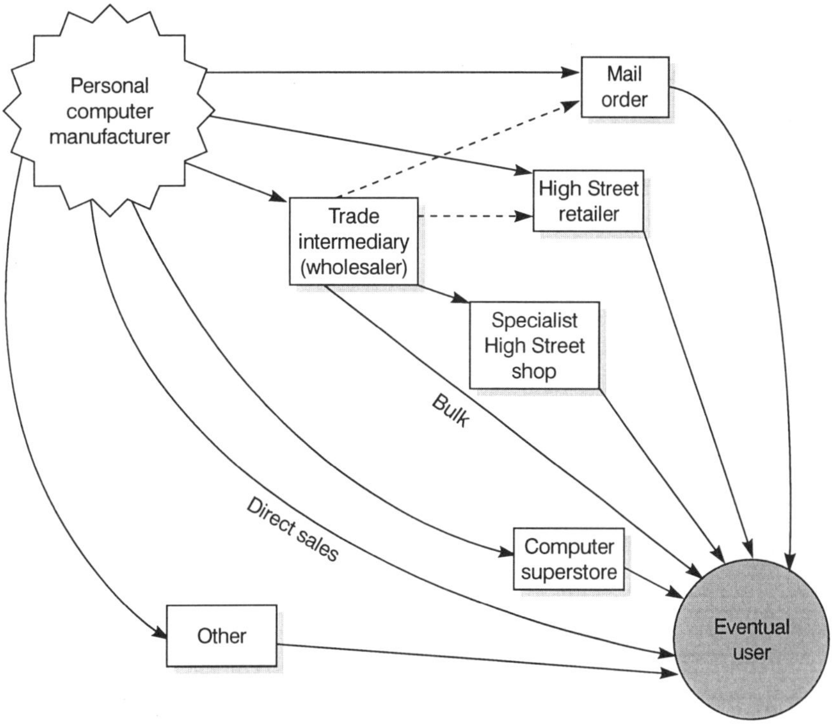

Figure 5.5 *Different supply chains*

based on the cost-plus formula — they often assume that the manufacturer has assessed the market and add on a small percentage. In fact these costs are usually quite easy to calculate, consisting of the buy-in price plus material handling, promotion and selling costs. Typically, they will work closely with the supplier with regard to promotions and discounts. It is important for them to monitor their markets closely as many products will be available through a number of channels and supply chains, and they have to be competitive with the whole market where it can impact on their operations.

Figure 5.5 shows an example of this in the PC market but it could easily apply to many goods.

In some cases the situation is even more complicated as although the manufacturer's sales force might have sold the original order, the intermediary may well supply it. An excellent example of this is prescription drugs. These are 'sold' by drug companies' salesmen to GPs; who then prescribe them for dispensing through a High Street pharmacist. It is the dispenser that actually buys the goods wholesale. Figure 5.6 shows this pictorially.

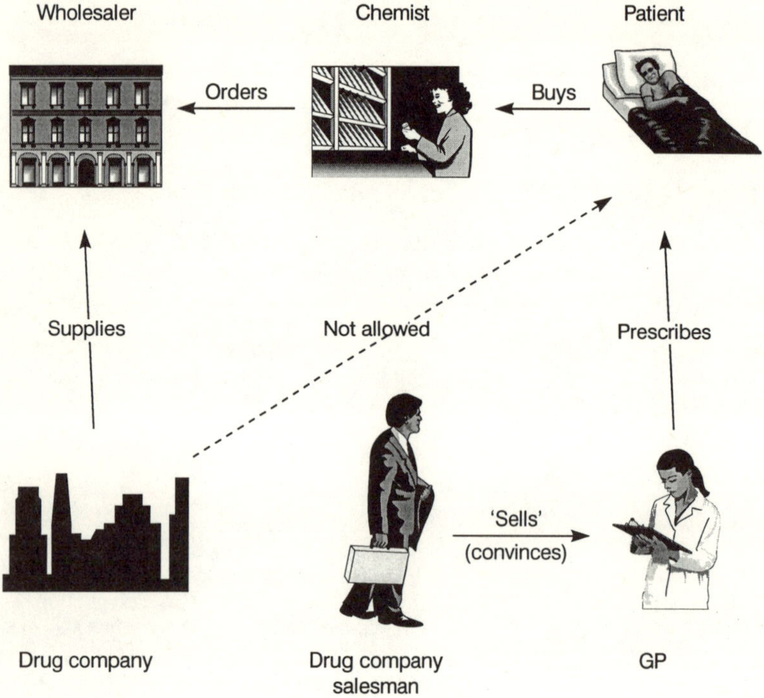

Figure 5.6 *Drug cycle*

Pros and cons

Good points

- Supply chains play a valuable role in bringing products to customer. They can make or break the CVP.
- As well as adding cost, they also add value.

Bad points

- Having other people in the supply chain invariably adds to the price, so keeping these costs under control is vital.
- Losing control over the dynamics of pricing can be a problem if manufacturers' strategy and that of intermediaries differs.

TENDERING

Neil Armstrong, the American astronaut, when asked what his thoughts were as he was waiting to take off, replied that the only thing on his mind was that every item in the rocket on top of which he was sitting had been supplied by the cheapest to tender method!

Tendering is a process used by some buyers in an attempt to ensure that they receive the best price when purchasing a product or service. It is used not only by business and government but also by individuals — those three quotes you get for your home insurance cover or a painting job represent the same process.

It has proved to have reduced prices in government contracts and also helps to ensure a free market away from cosy agreements, cartels, corruption etc by providing a system manifestly open to scrutiny and competition. In the public sector there are now complex rules governing the advertising and tendering of public sector works. This is guaranteed to add several months to any project!

Sealed bid pricing

This technique is commonly used for service contracts, but may also be used for the bulk purchase of goods (eg by Government Departments). The application of market techniques by the seller is not useful in this case and a technique known as expected profit probability is used, whereby the tenderer (if it is responding to a number of bids) assumes that it will achieve a share of contracts at any given price and thus uses a standard pricing criterion based on, for example, internal profit objectives. (This is really a form of cost-plus pricing.)

In practice it works like this:

- Bidders are invited to place their bid in a sealed envelope, to be opened at specific time and place, with the lowest bid being accepted, subject to meeting the relevant technical qualifications.
- Where the technical qualification is not straightforward (for example, bidding for a complex consultancy assignment or major engineering works) the bidder may specify that the technical and financial bids be separated so that the adjudicators can choose the best technical bid free from any preconceptions based on price.
- These are then evaluated on a matrix of technical acceptance versus price.

Tenderers may also be allowed to revise their bids at some stage in the process. This is often done by a system known as pre-qualification, whereby an original list of (say) ten tenderers is whittled down to (say) three.

For example, a firm is asked to quote for the supply of 20 electricity generators for an irrigation plant. The detailed specification is laid out by the buyer. The firm simply calculates the cost of supply and then adds a fixed sum of money that represents the profit it wishes to make.

If a firm bids for many of these projects in a year, and has developed a history of winning and losing bids, then it may be able to apply a more sophisticated system, whereby it estimates the odds of winning the contract and sets this against its profit requirement.

Pros and cons

Good points

- The supplier will have almost perfect cost information to base the price on;
- If you have a history, then you may know approximately the right area in which to price the bid;
- You are in no better nor worse position than competitors (assuming they do not have inside knowledge).

Bad points

- It is easy to be wide of the mark. If you are pricing for profit and your competitors are pricing for volume then they will probably be much cheaper than you.
- If their cost systems are different from yours, then their drivers might lead them to an entirely different starting point, and thus a different price.
- Some bids are so public that vital information can be given out (eg to competitors who can analyse your cost base).

ALTERNATIVE FORMS OF PRICING

This chapter would not be complete if we did not look at some of the more arcane systems in use and describe how these work.

Auctions

Auctions are generally fairly formal affairs and often covered by very strict laws. There is usually an auctioneer who is in charge of the sale and it follows a linear pattern with each item being called a '*lot*'. A typical auction would proceed as follows:

- A book or catalogue is published detailing the sale and provenance of items (it may contain many items or just one, for example, a house). Buyers may also view the 'lots'.

- At the start of the auction the auctioneer describes the lot which, if appropriate, is brought into view.
- He then opens the bidding with a price and if someone agrees it will then work it up. If no one accepts the opening price he will then drop to a price where the bidding starts.
- The bid is then progressively raised by the auctioneer — in large increments initially and smaller ones as he feels that final price is being approached.
- When the price is nearing what the auctioneer deems to be the maximum he will ask (usually three times) for any final bids and then bang his hammer (gavel) to signify close of bidding. This concludes a legally binding agreement between the buyer and seller.

When an item is placed in an auction it usually (but not always) has a reserve price. If this price is not reached then the item is not sold, however, the bidders are never informed of the reserve and must participate in ignorance of this. The existence of the reserve is to protect the seller against 'silly' bids and organised cartels of buyers known as 'rings' or 'circuses'.

Many types of products are sold at auction, including livestock, second-hand cars, antiques and furniture, art, surplus stocks and bankrupt stocks; and in many countries (like Australia, for example) houses.

There is also a specialised form of auction known as the Dutch auction, whereby the auctioneer starts at a very high price and then counts the price down in discrete steps. The first bidder to indicate acceptance then becomes the owner of the item. These can be very nerve-wracking for bidders!

Barter pricing

This method is often used when dealing with countries that do not have a convertible currency and may not be able to access relevant quantities of hard currency. It works by replacing the money element of the contract with goods.

For example, firm A wishes to sell an electricity generator to company B in, say, Kazakhstan that cannot pay in the currency that A wants. Company B may, however, be able to buy works of art on the local market (say, small stone statues). These statues will have a value in A's home market and were an art dealer approached, he might offer (say) £10 for each one.

If the generator were valued at £100, then firm A could accept 10 statues in lieu of cash, which it could then sell to the art dealer for £100 COD.

There is, of course, a significant management overhead in this type of transaction, not to mention shipping costs etc, and the risk that the customer for the statues may back out of the deal. Normally, therefore, the company buying the generator would have to pay well in excess of the normal price (as measured in goods rather than the price expressed in currency), to cover the extra effort, costs and risk involved. However, as it is valued in the seller's terms, not the buyer's, it may still be cheap to them. The price depends on the *relative value* of items, not the absolute value.

A surprising number of these types of transaction take place (eg the old Soviet Union used to swap oil for goods with Finland, and the Finnish government used to arbitrage the oil value and pay the supplier). In what is now the former Soviet Union it takes place every day, not only at the level of a peasant taking his goods to market to sell/swap for others but also at the intergovernmental level where, for example, Kazakhstan and Russia will swap goods with each other because the breakup of the Soviet Union has resulted in many smaller states each issuing currencies of different strengths (or weakness!) and the whole area is liable to swings of instability in both currency and liquidity terms, not to mention political terms.

A number of local schemes have been set up across the developed world to allow for moneyless transactions; however, these have only very limited usefulness in practice.

In practice, some very big deals are performed in this way (normally trading commodities for goods) and they may involve a number of consortia. In many deals the value of the goods is converted into currency (usually US$) for comparison.

Haggling

Although not strictly a form of pricing, this is a common technique in many parts of the world and reflects market forces at work in achieving a price equilibrium. Prices are deliberately set high (and are often not marked) in the knowledge that the customer will discuss the price (haggle) with the seller to achieve a bargain that suits both. You may well come across this technique on holiday when buying a souvenir. It is actually a way of maximising revenue to the seller although it takes a little longer than with marked prices.

There are no hard and fast rules, but the original price quoted by the seller is likely to be at least 50 per cent to 200 per cent above the 'real' price of the product. The normal technique is as follows:

Buyer: 'How much?'

Seller: '100 units'
Buyer: 'Ridiculous, I'll give you 20 units'
Seller: 'Maybe 90 units'
Buyer: '30 units'
etc.

This conversation will continue until the two parties are in range of one another. The final outcome depends on the sophistication of the buyer, his knowledge of the 'real price' and how close he will go to losing the purchase. This, and indeed any negotiation, can be placed on a matrix to show likely outcomes.

These negotiations always involve an end-game strategy, where the buyer will make a so-called final offer, and if it is not accepted, will then walk away. The seller normally chases the buyer and accepts. A useful tip for the buyer is to have the amount of money he wants to spend available and tucked in his back pocket. At the final moment this wad of notes can be flashed before the seller to finalise the deal! The real issue for the buyer is to know the real value of the goods — what is a two-foot high carved mask or a 5ft × 5ft tapis (carpet) from Tunisia worth?

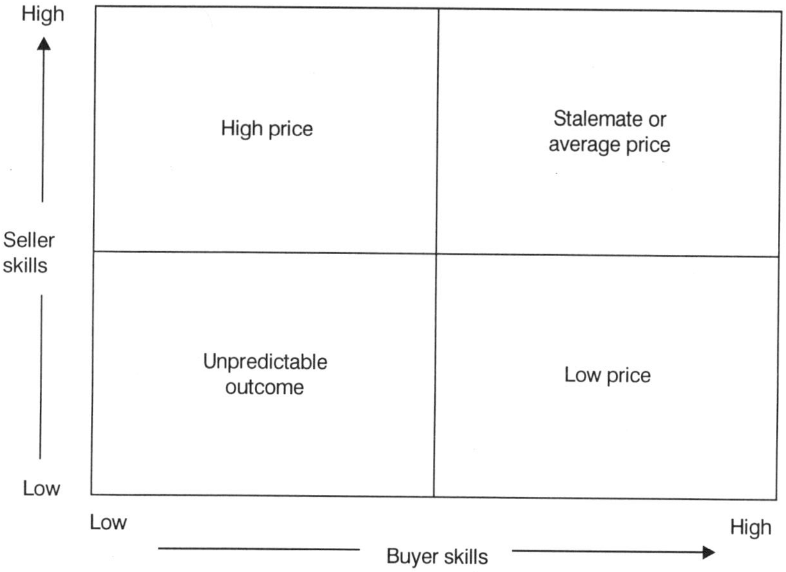

Figure 5.7 *Negotiation outcomes*

Note that a refusal to haggle will lead to difficulties as the seller will feel that he underpriced if you give the asking price without demurring and on reflection you will feel cheated.

Haggling is often used in a more refined manner such as when a sophisticated buyer knows that he can arbitrage between payment methods. For example, if Amex charges the retailer a higher transaction fee than anyone else then the customer can offer the Amex card initially, and when the retailer states that he would prefer another means of payment, the sophisticated buyer asks what discount would he get for using Visa/Access, cheque, Switch or cash instead. The quid pro quo is that if it saves the retailer money then part of this saving should be passed on to the buyer, as it makes no difference which payment method is used. This technique can often be used to obtain a discount not normally readily available.

Conclusion

The range of techniques is vast and is only governed by what is perceived to be the best fit. Many people use several methods either singly or in combination to achieve the right price as they see it. Flexibility is a key point and if one set of techniques is not working do not be afraid to try another (with due consideration of course). Where there is doubt then a good tip is to look closely at what your competitors are doing. If they are successful then there may be a lesson there.

This section has examined the pricing methodology — that is the theoretical process for pricing. The next section takes the contents of this and puts them into the context of the day-to-day managing of prices.

PART THREE

PRACTICAL PRICING

6

MANAGING PRICING IN PRACTICE

INTRODUCTION

The previous chapter examined different theoretical ways of setting prices; following the pricing process diagram pricing in practice is now considered. The key areas for focus are:

- understanding legislation;
- getting feedback from the market;
- the skills required by a pricing manager;
- validation against objectives;
- internal systems; and
- finally the key day-to-day price management tactic, discounting.

Before looking at these in detail, it is pertinent to say a word or two about information. Managing pricing in practice requires the manager to assimilate vast amounts of information. A range of techniques will be used (on individual products or product groups) in order to arrive at a price for each product.

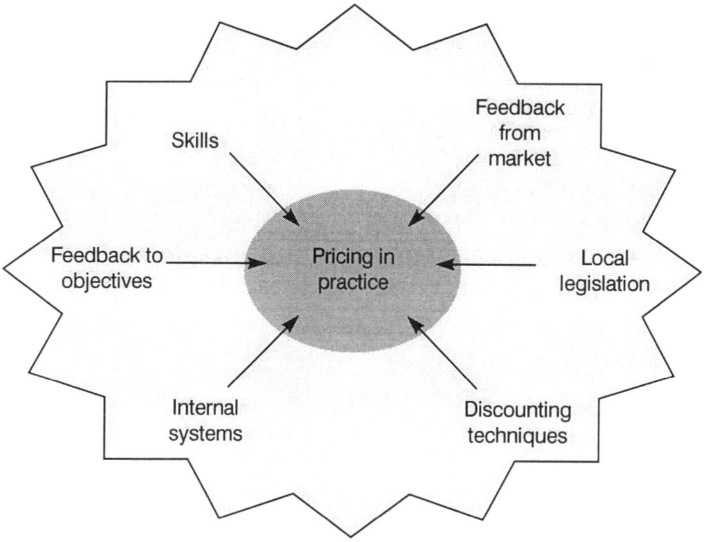

Figure 6.1 *Managing in practice*

Whilst the choice of technique should be mitigated by reference to the market and also by the potential profitability and importance of the products involved, it is often also determined by the ability of management to assimilate the information required.

The point about being able to understand and analyse information is not one that should be overlooked. The amount of information available is enormous, and its use is compounded by its reliability and your ability to process it.

For example, if you are selling apples in a street market, then there will be several other outlets also selling apples: other stallholders; the corner shop; the supermarket; and maybe even someone from a mobile truck. You will have to visit each seller, each day, to see what their prices are. Having decided on your basic price, what then happens if Mrs Smith comes up and says, 'I see the supermarket in Cross Street (the only one you didn't visit) is selling apples at 10p a kilo less than you'? Will this information be accurate, or might she be mistaken?

As if this weren't enough, one of your regular customers, Mr Brown, informs you that he wants to make some cider, and instead of his usual one kilo, he wants to buy 10 kilos. Do you offer him a discount? He might walk to the Cross Street supermarket to save a pound, decide that he likes the place and never come back to buy from you.

You may think this example somewhat simplistic, but in practice, holiday and tour operators, who can use computers to check on competitors' prices in an instant, frequently update their prices more than once a day. One well-known company took to revising its prices slightly later in the day than its competitors so its information was the last to appear on the screen, but it had a lead over everyone in competitive pricing. It could undercut every price by just a pound in three or four hundred 'lines' every day if it wanted to and it gained a fearsome reputation as the most competitive company around.

Many companies sell large ranges of products through many outlets and get information on pricing in a myriad of different forms. For most companies processing this amount of data would not only require a NASA-sized computer, but also vast human resources spent in getting, checking and analysing the information.

Most companies, therefore, adopt a rather more pragmatic approach to pricing, recognising that it would be counter-productive to spend considerable time and resources on products that sell only a few hundred pounds worth each year. Equally, time needs to spent on those products with potential.

So for the stallholder, if apples are his biggest seller, it will be worth the effort. If he mainly sells potatoes, however, that is what he should concentrate on.

Do not confuse this idea with the concept of a 'loss leader' — that is a product that is deliberately priced cheaply to lure customers in. The point here is about maximising the profit or market potential by judicious use of market and cost information.

PRICE LEGISLATION

Because governments commonly intervene to protect consumers of goods and products, it is appropriate to take a brief look at legislation surrounding prices. This will be in a general sense as each country is different.

Typical legislation

The pricing manager will need to understand and have details of all relevant legislation and trade association and industry guidelines before he starts to decide on the appropriate mechanism to use, given not only the type of business he is in, but also the development of the market and competition. Companies operating across national borders will also need to understand local regulations (either directly or through their local agents).

Typical legislation tends to cover the sale of goods to consumers rather than business-to-business transactions, however, it is still possible to fall foul of the relevant law if you are selling industrial goods.

Legislation tends to cover the following main areas:

Price fixing and cartels

This is where a group of companies get together and all decide to raise their prices by the same amount (often called a cartel). Because this works to the complete disadvantage of the consumer, who often has no alternative supply channel, it is outlawed in most developed countries although not always as well 'policed' in some as it might be.

Cartels are rarely found in consumer markets because the wide availability of products renders them difficult to manipulate in practice. They are, however, found more commonly than we might suspect, in business-to-business and more specialised areas.

To illustrate this with some completely hypothetical examples: If all the German manufacturers of (say) washing -up liquid were to get together and double the price overnight, it would only be days before some entrepreneur would drive a truck to (say) France, buy a large quantity of a competing brand, and sell it at a lower price on the German market, thus breaking the cartel.

However, in the case of a piece of highly advanced scientific equipment, which only three companies in the whole world can produce, there is no alternative and if they all decide to jack up their prices by 20 per cent overnight what can their customers do?

To protect the consumers governments usually look out for the development of cartels through periodic investigations of suspect markets and enact regulations through monopolies or anti-trust commissions (eg in the UK the Monopolies and Mergers Commission; in Germany the Bundeskartellamt, and in some cases the EU also carries out this function).

Coincidence or collusion?

Airlines are resorting to high technology and cosy arrangements to fix fares at identical rates on some of the most 'competitive' routes, according to new studies of key business flights.

The 1980's promise that air fares would fall because of increased competition has failed to materialise on European and long-haul flights, as the airlines match fares pound for pound and leave consumers little or no choice.

A CAA report shows that despite predictions of a 'European fares revolution', after the easing of government restrictions, most continental routes are still dominated by inefficient and expensive state-owned carriers. Using high-speed computer reservation systems, airlines can learn of fare changes among rivals within hours and alter their own rates to match them exactly. This happens with price rises as well as cuts.

In mid-1995, British Airways (BA) changed fares between London and Paris nine times: some were copied immediately and almost identically by Air France and Air UK.

Analysis by the Reed Travel Group shows that the situation is little better on many long-haul routes. Here, prices are fixed by government treaty rather than computer.

The standard economy fare between London and Sydney is £3,154 return on BA, Gulf Air and EVA, three of the four biggest carriers on the 'kangaroo route'. The other, Qantas, which is quarter-owned by BA, has just (1996) been given permission by the Australian government to pool services with BA.

These prices are fixed through IATA's fare scheduling committee in Geneva. It was thought to be a spent regulatory force, but the recession has restored its powers as airline profits have tumbled.

London–Singapore economy return	
Finnair	£2,156
British Airways	£2,156
EVA (Taiwan)	£2,156

Gulf Air	£2,156
Air Seychelles	£2,156
Air Lanka	£2,156

(Source: CAA/Reed Travel Group, *Times* article)

Discriminatory pricing

If a manufacturer prefers to sell its products through up-market retailers rather than High Street discounters then it may either refuse to supply products to the latter or it may simply ask a much higher price for the same trade terms. This is generally an outlawed practice.

This is difficult to prove as the manufacturer may argue that its costs are different in dealing with different types of outlet (which would be a reasonable and allowable argument). Fundamentally, however, the onus will be on the manufacturer to prove this and a dim view is taken of price discrimination unless it is justifiable.

There have been some recent, highly publicised cases in this area in recent years, including designer perfumes being offered through discount High Street supermarkets and chemists as opposed to the more traditional 'classy' sales through department stores.

It is often difficult to prove where the market is very competitive and where information is transparent. Any firm which understood its market would respond very quickly to changes in the prices of its competitors' products and quite rightly. This type of price fixing is more likely to be occurring where prices do not move very much — why should they? — there is a cartel in operation.

The banking industry is one where the charge of a cartel is frequently levied, particularly by interested parties wishing to score points from an easy target. However, it is not only unlikely that banks will remain out of step for very long, it is downright foolish as they would go out of business. The following (very simple) example illustrates this:

Scenario I: All banks offer funds for loans at base rate (10 per cent) plus 3 per cent; all banks pay base rate on deposits.

There is no reason to choose any bank over any other as all pay the same and charge the same.

Scenario II: Bank A reduces its deposit rate to base minus 1 per cent but reduces its loan rate to base plus 2 per cent (to maintain its spread); the other banks do not charge.

Borrowers will borrow from bank A, as it is cheaper, but its depositors will put their money in the other banks and no new money will be attracted. This will reduce the amount of money bank A has to lend and it will either have to pay the same rate as others to attract the money or take the loss in its margin to maintain the spread. In practice it would be unable to sustain the reduction for very long and would be forced to respond to the market forces and increase its deposit rate to correct the imbalance in its funds versus loans.

Scenario III: All banks follow bank A except for bank G which keeps its rates the same.

It will, therefore, have a surplus of cash as money flows into its vaults to gain the higher rates, but will be unable to lend as all other banks will be undercutting it. There will, therefore, be an imbalance in funds as those banks wishing to lend will have insufficient funds to do so and bank G will be unable to get the return to pay the higher rate on its deposits. Those willing to pay the higher rates will usually be much higher risk and this would disrupt its risk return profile. The market will, therefore, adjust to rectify this imbalance either by bank G falling into line or the others moving back.

This example is very simple and ignores many facets of the market but illustrates the simple point that it is very difficult to maintain a differential price unless you have a different cost base or a defined strategy in which the costs of the changes are known, quantified and accepted.

The following table (Table 6.1) shows how hard it is to be much out of line in a competitive market. It shows the base rates of 30 British-based banks at the time of writing. Note that there is very little difference (0.25 per cent which is largely insignificant and does not reflect the rates that large customers would enjoy).

Table 6.1

BASE LENDING RATES

Bank	**%**	**Bank**	**%**	**Bank**	**%**
Adam & Co.	6.50	Co-operative	6.75	Leopold Joseph	6.50
AIB	6.75	Coutts & Co.	6.50	Lloyds	6.50
Henry Ansbacher	6.50	Duncan Lawrie	6.50	Midland	6.50
Bank of Ireland	6.75	Robert Fleming	6.50	NatWest	6.50
Bank of Scotland	6.50	Girobank	6.75	RBS	6.75
Barclays	6.75	Guinness Mahon	6.50	Rea Brothers	6.75
BBME	6.50	Hambros	6.50	Singer & Friedlander	6.75
Brown Shipley	6.50	Hill Samuel	6.75	Smith & Williamson	6.50
Citibank	6.50	C Hoare	6.50	TSB	6.75
Clydesdale	6.50	HSBC	6.50	Yorkshire	6.50

(Source: *Financial Times,* December 1995)

Deception

The need to protect consumers from false 'price cuts' is a key tenet of most countries' consumer legislation and one that we are all familiar with at sale time. Generally speaking, an organisation cannot say that the price of a product has been reduced unless it can prove that, within the recent past, the average consumer could actually have purchased the same product at that higher price.

Consumer legislation usually states that a certain wording has to be placed on point of sale materials to ensure the consumer knows what they are getting. In the case of services and complex products it may not be so easy to determine what is actually being sold in the 'sale' and this can again lead to deception, especially where the sale of one item is linked with another, for example, the offer of half-price holiday insurance with each holiday booked would only be 'fair' if the insurance was being offered for sale at some time in the past at the higher price and if it could have actually been bought by the consumer.

The use of expressions like 'sale', 'wholesale prices' and 'lower than recommended retail price' etc are generally to be avoided unless each statement is qualified.

Predatory pricing

This expression can be used in two senses. In the absolute sense, where the price of product is lowered by a large amount (and especially below the cost of production — 'dumping') with the express intent of driving competing firms out of business, then it is usually not allowed by law. Proving this is very difficult and is commonly asserted by home firms defending their prices against a foreign competitor. A good example of this is in the EU where home firms are constantly alleging that non-EU firms offering similar goods are 'dumping'. The EU investigates but few cases are found to be true and the real reason is often that home firms are just less competitive (perhaps from intrinsically higher costs from too high or poorly focused investment or maybe from labour rigidities imposed by the Social Chapter or similar legislation). Sometimes dumping is found to have occurred and steps taken to redress this, but it is a long and difficult process.

Marketing people often use it in a less stringent sense to describe the period where a company is going for market share (rather than taking over a market completely). In this sense it is an acceptable business practice.

A recent example of cutting prices for market share in the UK has been the price war between the broadsheet 'quality' newspapers. *The Times* cut its cover price to 20p to gain market share (with the intention of thereby attracting more advertising revenue) leading to a response from its competition, both in terms of matching price reductions but also adverts stressing the quality and value of the higher priced papers (ie reminding readers of the benefits – price = value equation). It is not clear whether readers of quality papers, the prices of which are very low in relative terms (25p or 30p is an insignificant sum to almost anyone), really change 'brand' because of price and it is interesting to note that at the end of 1995, *The Times* raised its prices again.

This type of activity is not in any way against the law, although the company may well have been asked to justify its actions.

Resale price maintenance

Older readers will no doubt remember when the price of a product was stamped on the wrapping by the manufacturer and the product was sold at this price by the retailer (eg pre-1971 a Mars Bar used to be 6d (2.5p) in the UK).

By and large this type of resale price maintenance has gone off the statute books and generally manufacturers are not now allowed to specify the price at which the retailer sells. A producer, can of course, still suggest a retail price, but they cannot enforce it (*recommended retail price* (RRP)).

There was, until 1995, only one well-known remnant (excluding drugs) of this legislation still operating in the UK, the Net Book Agreement (NBA), a device that meant that publishers still printed the price on the back of a book and the retailer had to sell at that price. The NBA had come in for a lot of attack in preceding years and eventually it was ignored by booksellers, particularly the big retailing chains. Interestingly enough the publicity given to this type of price fixing provoked another type of price maintenance to come under scrutiny — that of 'over-the-counter' drugs sold through chemists and pharmacies. It is likely that this agreement will also disappear.

The arguments advanced for maintaining these types of price agreements (which result in higher prices for consumers) were that it allowed more (smaller) shops to keep going (as they had low sales and didn't benefit from bulk discounts) thereby resulting in better choice for customers. This argument is now discredited in almost all areas of business but is still an emotive argument advanced in many countries and cases, and often exists informally as well as formally. The results have usually been the same choice for consumers but changes in buying patterns; and as a side consequence demographic patterns. (Witness the progressive demise of, *inter alia*, butchers, greengrocers, bakers and paper shops in the UK, under pressure from the big retailing chains. This will almost certainly lead to the same result in book shops and chemists.)

The story is similar in other countries, especially where they have centralised planning regimes. It can be argued that fixing a currency exchange rate is a form of price maintenance. When the controls are released and the currency floats, it normally falls to rock bottom before returning to a market, rather than an artificial level. The Russian rouble went through astronomical inflation in the early 1990s: as at mid-1995 it was 6,500 to the pound, whereas in 1990 it was fixed at parity with the pound!

These changes can have a disastrous effect on the population as well, as it is still common for many countries to regulate the price of staple foods: thus bread might be offered at a fixed price per kilo, meat similarly. In times of rampant inflation there is no incentive whatsoever for producers to meet demand at these prices, and huge queues and even famine result.

In some countries the prices of staple items like bread and flour are often subsidised to such an extent that it is impossible to ease the prices without disastrous effects and history books are littered with examples of food riots.

GETTING FEEDBACK FROM THE MARKET

You might like to think of typical sources of price information in your own business, but here is a general list:

- from market research (some people even go round local stores to check display prices). For example, this is used by the John Lewis Partnership (JLP), a UK department store chain, which checks competitors to ensure that their CVP 'never knowingly undersold' is maintained;
- from competitors' price-lists (but are these really what they are selling at?);
- from friendly customers, who tell you what they paid for something from your competitor (JLP offers to refund the difference between its price and that of the same good bought from a competitor for less — within a certain radius. This gets them accurate and frequent feedback on prices);
- from published sources (eg magazine adverts, shopping guides);
- reports from your own sales force;
- feedback from lost orders ('I am sorry Mr Smith, but you were 8 per cent more expensive than the cheapest bidder');
- trade journals;
- general press;
- debriefing new salesmen who join you from other companies;
- for government, para-statal bodies and others such as the EU, tendering is often public and results are available for study.

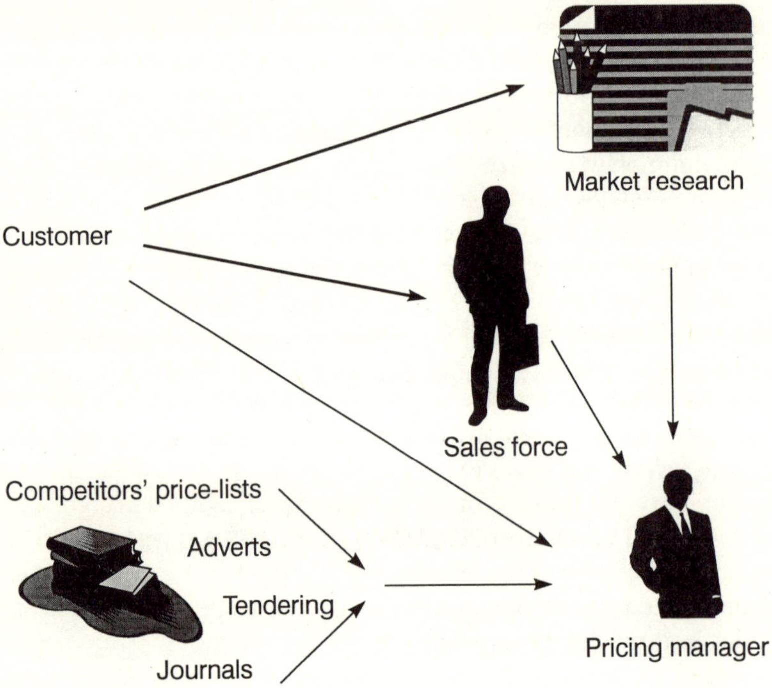

Figure 6.2 *Sources of market information*

This kind of information comes into your firm in different types (both qualitative and quantitative) and different forms (on paper, by telephone, on computer disks) and at different times (some regularly, some occasionally). For example, you never know when you are going to bump into one of your sales staff by the coffee machine and he will casually tell you that he was having lunch with a representative from your largest competitor and they are planning a 15 per cent price hike next week.

The secret of assimilating this data is not a formal system as such, but simply understanding how information flows into your company and what is the best and most appropriate way to collect the data.

For example, always ensure that a section on competitor pricing goes on the agenda at any sales meeting. Similarly, subscribe to relevant journals and trade magazines and be sure you remember to look specifically for price information each time.

There are companies who collect and analyse such information for you, if you pay them enough. They will go round stores and check displayed prices and will religiously write off for price lists and other data. But remember, at this stage it is only data: it is of no help in arriving at a pricing decision until you have analysed what it means.

It virtually goes without saying that a competent pricing manager will maintain a small database of information on a PC and that he will be competent in the use of spreadsheets and presenting information in an understandable way. This means using graphs, charts and other visual aids. If you cannot use these then go on a course right away.

It was once said that during a budget debate in the USA, one side was for cutting the military budget, the other for raising it. Those for cutting it spoke for 45 minutes and produced tables of data, graphs and other visual devices to persuade the President of their (unarguable) case. Their opponents, however, had only one picture: that of a Russian tank. The presenter simply asked if the President wanted to see this vehicle trundling across the White House lawn. The result of this was the huge military spending on the Star Wars programme. This goes to prove you can have all the data you want, but if you can't present it in a form that the manager can understand and make sense of, he will never come to the best decision! (It is perhaps also a comment on the credulity of the audience.)

It is very useful to understand how competitors think, their strategies and their decision-making processes. Many companies choose to accomplish this by buying in the services of consultants or even employees from competitors. In many cases the ability to second-guess or react fast to competitors provides the key competitive edge.

This is especially true in wholesaling where product inventories are measured in thousands, if not tens of thousands of items. Imagine being asked to go round your local supermarket and note down the price of every pack and size of product. By the time you had finished, it would be time to start again and if you then had to go back to your own supermarket and compare every one of your products with every one of theirs it could take you weeks.

The secret here is to undertake this kind of detailed research only once in a while, and in the meantime use your knowledge of competitors to guess what they are going to do. If you understand their strategies then you can follow them and even take the lead without too much effort.

WalMart, a leading retailing chain in the USA, has perfected this. Each week it gathers information from all its outlets and management and uses this to produce a new tactical strategy for the following week. Its internal systems are so well-tuned that it starts each new week as virtually a new company to respond to the challenges it feels it will be facing over the next seven days.

Technology

Sophisticated users of these processes use complex computer models to provide them with an automatic method of incorporating changes. With the advent of bar coding, prices across the board can be changed in an instant, simply by altering the central computer database and changing just one sign on display. Models that think for themselves (neural networks) exist that even take most of the hard work out of the process. However, it is still up to the human manager to add the final touches.

As computers and automated data capture become increasingly a feature of life, it becomes possible to build ever more complex and reliable time-line models of what has happened in the past and to second-guess what will happen in the future.

If you are the stallholder selling apples this must all seem very far-fetched to you, but the principles are the same: understanding and getting feedback from the market is crucial.

Be your own customer

On a final point, don't ever forget to become your own customer once in a while. Take a look at your organisation or get a friend or colleague to act as a customer. See how well the real customer feels you are doing in understanding their needs. This relates directly back to the concept of the CVP.

To find out whether you really are offering the right CVP you must talk to your customers — what Lanning and Philips call spending a 'day in the life' of your customer. One of the authors has worked a lot with banks, in many parts of the world, and the first thing he does is to go and try to cash a cheque, send money or transact foreign exchange. By doing this you then experience the actual frustrations of the customer notwithstanding what the staff will tell you they are. Many organisations do this often by way of 'phantom' shoppers and customers or by incognito inspection visits. The results are usually revealing and often disturbing for organisations. Where just a few customers represent a large proportion of your output — often the case in business-to-business — then a visit by management to the client will yield dividends, both in terms of getting to see things from your customer's viewpoint but also in building the relationship with him.

The key point here is to act to change any 'wrong' items in your offering to ensure that you really are offering your CVP. This may mean working closely with your customer to give him what he wants so that you are both better off and you end up with a stronger relationship than before.

PRICING SKILLS

The breadth and depth of skills required to carry out pricing depends on the level of sophistication of operation, the market in which you are operating and the product width/depth. A market stallholder will typically undertake only cursory analysis and it will all be carried out by the person running the stall. The larger and more complex the operation the more difficult it becomes to do this. Having the *right skills* in the *right areas* and with the *right knowledge* is essential.

It is difficult to list all the competencies and skills required for the introduction of market-based pricing, but the following list provides some guidance:

- numeracy, and the ability to make decisions based on financial assessments;
- good selling and communicating skills;
- a developed strategic view (senior staff);
- a working internal liaison system, that can make decisions fast;
- agreement to, and observance of, a set of planning and operational guidelines;
- regular access to, and proactive advice from qualified accountants;
- ability to use complex spreadsheets;
- product or product range champions with internal influence;
- customer champions;
- market research skills.

The easiest way of deciding what skills and competencies will be needed is to think through all the roles that will be needed to price correctly. Roles do not necessarily mean a separate person — roles can be shared across several people and conversely people can play more than one role depending on the exact nature of the position and the size of the roles.

Roles require a mixture of the following:

Knowledge: what the person will need to know or to have access to information about (services; products; processes; systems);
Skills: what learned ability is required to apply the knowledge (sales; negotiation; keyboard skills);
Characteristics: what sort of person is best suited to fit the role (extrovert; meticulous attention to detail; communicator; go-getter).

Depending on the nature of the position and the responsibilities some examples would be:

Sales

Knowledge	market, competition, product, customers
Skills	selling, closing, interviewing techniques, interpersonal
Characteristics	appearance, enthusiasm, loyalty, self-expression, punctuality, motivation

Pricing

Knowledge	product, costs, market dynamics, competition
Skills	numeracy, economics analysis, teamwork
Characteristics	solidity, flexibility, orderliness

Management accounting

Knowledge	accounting principles, product, suppliers, inputs
Skills	numeracy, organisation, analytical
Characteristics	accuracy, timeliness, methodological

etc.

Some firms choose to let small teams work on these areas, others leave it to individuals. If you think you are weak in even one of these areas then address the problem as soon as possible. Investment in a few days' training will be far outweighed by the benefit you will receive.

Some people would argue that good pricing managers are born, not made, and that pricing is an art, not a science. However, the skilful manger will combine an analytical approach with the lightest of touches, plus a dash of inspiration. Knowing how to play the odds is a totally different matter to playing a hunch. Remember that bookmakers set their prices scientifically and that punters bet with their hearts. You see many poor punters, but not many poor bookmakers.

VALIDATION AGAINST OBJECTIVES

Most companies have a number of formal documents that set out their objectives, whether they be straightforward commercial ones, or, in not-for-profit organisations, more complex ones.

Typically these will be stated in:

- the business plan;
- the marketing or corporate strategy;
- the mission statement;
- the annual report to shareholders.

Make sure you are completely at ease with these formal statements and that you and your colleagues are in agreement that pricing can help you in your goals.

We can illustrate this by example. If your objective is to maximise profit in any one year, there is little point in going all out for bulk or volume orders. You should instead be trying to clinch high margin sales, perhaps by concentrating on specific sectors.

If, on the other hand, you need to develop market share (or even develop a market) then you need to achieve volume so that your name and product become well known. In this case, low margin sales may be appropriate to shift the bulk volume you need.

Many companies will have a mixture of objectives, depending primarily on the product or service and the market sector. Within each product/market sector the possibility of managing returns depends on a number of further factors. Each must be considered in detail.

If there are no formal objectives or you are not in agreement, then it will be wise to write up a specific pricing plan for the given area, and circulate this widely so that the organisation can see the reasons behind the pricing decision.

It is also worthwhile considering that many parts of an organisation will have differing objectives, and these may not fit easily with each other. It is common practice, for example, that sales departments, and their staff, are motivated and incentivised by volume of goods sold, rather than by margin targets. Most salespeople will tell you that they get the greatest satisfaction out of selling large quantities or striking large deals than they do by making the most return. The pricing manager has to be careful that this type of motivation does not undermine the overall strategy.

Similarly, in firms without correct regular reporting (and this is very common towards the financial year end), production departments may develop an urge to increase output, to ensure that their costs per unit produced go down and they will make a good recovery. This is simply a function of internal accounting procedures, which never seem fully to match up to the practicalities of maximising margin.

It is possible that the factory will go straight to the sales director and tell him that if he can shift 10,000 units, they can get them ready in a very short time. Beware this alliance! The key to controlling this is to ensure that you have correct internal systems in place for validating actions on a regular timely basis against the overall objectives, the agreed strategy and the plan for the period.

INTERNAL SYSTEMS

The importance of good internal systems cannot be overestimated. When one of the authors first started out in business all pricing modelling was done on a mainframe computer. Staff laboriously filled in every projected sale and every price and the machine calculated it for us overnight. If the answers didn't match up, it was done again. This process could take weeks and people usually ended up using a calculator, because it was quicker.

Nowadays things have changed. The advent of the high-speed desktop computer and sophisticated spreadsheets and relational databases means that information can be accessed and processed in seconds from the desktop rather than going through IT departments.

However, this does not mean that the results are going to be any more accurate than our steam-age mainframe. In fact, they may be even less so, as whilst we were waiting for the computer to do its stuff, we often used to sit around and discuss what the meaning of our assumptions were. This led to many insights, and we liked to think our pricing decisions were pretty much spot on.

Good internal systems are those where the management processes are in order and the data fed into these processes is adequate for the task. Only then will the output be meaningful.

The data

To be useful, any piece of data must have the source, a date and an idea of its accuracy attached. This is important as figures often attain an integrity all of their own and, if they are wrong, this can lead to seriously compounded errors.

If I was to tell you that the price of company A's widget was £30, you would need to ask me where I got this data. If I said it was a written quote from company A, sent to customer B on 30 August, then you could be pretty sure it was right. If, on the other hand, I told you that I had met a representative from company C, who was chatting to a receptionist from company A in the pub, then the data integrity is reduced and acceptance is more subjective.

This attitude to accuracy can be very telling, and is often a problem in market research. If you stop someone in the street and ask them how much their last gas bill was, they may say around £50. If you mail them a questionnaire and they bother to fill it in, they will say £52.43, because they have bothered to go and look it up.

Data needs to be assembled, categorised and sorted to be useful. Many managers choose to prepare a small database, and as this is used over the years, so a good picture of the history of prices (both yours and the competitors) builds up. This can be a valuable resource.

The process

Pricing is normally conceived of as an iterative process. Someone, somewhere, comes up with an idea for the price and this is then discussed until a final solution is achieved. The originator of the price may be as diverse as the chairman's wife, through to the actual pricing manager themselves. The key point is what is known and can be related to test the pricing hypothesis. Figure 6.3 indicates this by contrasting new or old products against new or old markets and charting the inherent riskiness, which will affect pricing.

The situation is more complex when new products are being launched, as there is often not much market-related information to go on. In the case of established products there is usually a history to provide clues. Launching a new product in a new market can be a recipe for disaster as all variables are unknown. The more work that can be done to quantify the unknowns — and, therefore, reduce the potential risk — the better.

	Existing products	New products
Existing markets	1 Market penetration *Low risk*	2 Product development *Higher risk*
New markets	3 Market development *Medium risk*	4 Diversification *Highest risk*

Type of action	Where the company is looking to increase sales by:
1 Market penetration	increasing current product/service sales in current markets by better marketing
2 Product development	developing new products/services for its current markets
3 Market development	taking its current products/services to new markets
4 Diversification	developing new products/services for new markets

Figure 6.3 *Product/market expansion grid*

Where an important pricing decision has to be made, it is normally appropriate to call a meeting of interested parties to discuss the main issues. The pricing manager should prepare a short report prior to this meeting setting out the basic data used for the original price and any other information that might be useful. This document would also include the objectives of the pricing.

Pricing forum

Except in the very smallest of companies (in fact, one person operations!) it is appropriate that managers should get together to make pricing decisions. Although it depends on the company, at the very least representatives of the following functions should attend:

- marketing;
- sales;
- commercial;
- production;
- finance.

This is to ensure that all relevant points of view are considered and the price has been evaluated in context rather than in isolation.

Steps to be followed include:

- When the issue has been discussed, there will still be various unanswered questions and suggestions for further research. At this point the pricing manager, accompanied by a member of the sales team, should go out and visit some customers to find out their perception of the value of the product and their view as to the price. Customers will, of course, normally say that they like the product but it is too expensive. However, careful analysis of information from structured interviews can usually arrive at a more accurate picture.
- When the price has gone round as many loops of the iteration as required, it is also appropriate to carry out some financial modelling exercises to determine the scope and scale of margin expected.
- At this point, the pricing manager should also prepare a set of templates or guidelines on discounting and volume orders. Almost as soon as the price is announced there will be a flurry of calls from both customers and sales staff enquiring about the change.
- Although it is not within the scope of this book to discuss in detail, it is normally appropriate to prepare what marketers call a *cost benefit analysis* (CBA), especially if the rise is significant or the product is new.

The CBA is, in reality, a qualitative and quantitative analysis of the CVP proving its benefit to the company and also to potential customers. That is to say that the CBA starts by defining the customers need, explains the benefit of the product or service in terms the customer is empathetic with and then finally goes on to quote and justify the price in these terms.

You typically see phrases like:

'. . .and saving you over £300 per year in costs, product X is only £600.'
'. . .the payback period can be as short as three months.'

- Linked into this will be a template, addressing likely queries and/or negative responses from customers, stressing which benefits to promote in response to specific points. This underlines the CVP assumptions and will reinforce these in the customers' and the sales forces' mind.
- After the initial pilot of the price a feedback session should be held to assess progress to date and, if necessary, alter the price.

When this process has been followed you should be on course for a successful price introduction.

DISCOUNTING

This is a complex area, as there are many different types of discount, and they give very different messages to customers.

The first question to ask is, 'Why are we discounting this product?' This is to ask why we want to suggest that our first offer (list price) is not what we expect to close the deal with. Note that this is at odds with our behaviour as consumers, where we rarely bargain or barter in shops for our goods, although it happens all the time in business.

Some industries have traditional discounting cycles, for example, the holiday industry cycle is shown in Figure 6.4 overleaf.

Discounting can be explained as a human need to negotiate over the detail of contracts, but many people forget that there are many other issues that can be negotiated as well as price (eg delivery, quality, pack size, service considerations etc).

General principles

Discounting is a factor of business relationships and will always be required. The ability to authorise a discount is seen by customers as a good pointer to staff seniority (and thus power) within the supplier, and thus the ability to authorise at least some level of discount must be available to all sales staff.

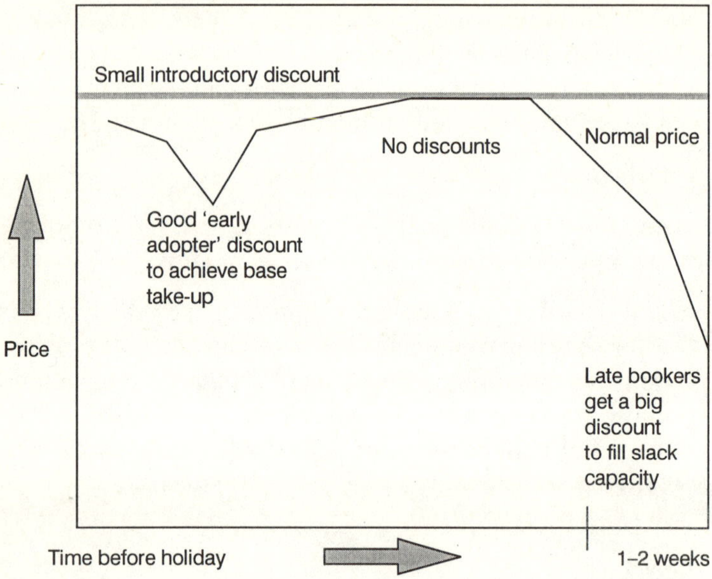

Figure 6.4 *Discounting example – holiday bookings*

Discounting is sometimes a useful technique to close a sale as the ability to provide an on-the-spot discount can usually (although not always) provide the final impetus.

Discounting must, however, be tightly controlled to avoid junior or less experienced staff giving unnecessarily large discounts, and is usually arranged in a tiered manner (eg up to 2.5 per cent, 2.5 per cent to 5 per cent etc). Special or one-off discounts may also be authorised in advance, so that even relatively junior staff can strike deals during customer meetings.

Discounting is only one of a number of ways of offering something extra to customers (ie a negotiating point) and it should not necessarily be the first thing tried.

On the assumption that some discounting will be required, this can be categorised into four main areas:

- trade discounts;
- quantity discounts;
- promotional discounts;
- cash discounts.

These are provided for different reasons and give different messages as follows:

Trade discounts

This is the area where trade intermediaries (eg wholesalers or agents) make their profit. They are given discounts by manufacturers in recognition of the intermediaries' cost of servicing the supply channel, and the fact that the manufacturer does not have to supply customers direct. Note, however, that the manufacturer will still look after advertising, some selling etc. The extent to which manufacturers discount to intermediaries depends on the importance of the sales and distribution channel supplied by the intermediary.

To illustrate with an example:

- Manufacturer A sells to retailers at a price of £100 for a unit, but will not sell less than 20 units in any one order.
- Wholesaler B, who buys a hundred units at a time, gets a discount of 20 per cent from the manufacturer, and sells to retailers at £110, but only if they take more than five units a time.
- Wholesaler C, who buys 50 units at a time, gets a discount of only 10 per cent. They sell individual units to retailers at £120.

Retailer D (a large retailer) buys 10 units at a time. He goes to wholesaler B, paying £110 and sells to the public for £140. Retailer E, who is very small, has to buy from wholesaler C at £120. Because of market competition he has to sell to compete with retailer D, but prices the product at £145, banking on the fact that his personal service is worth the extra.

The spanner in the works, however, is Superstore X. Because they can buy 500 units at a time, they get an even better price than Wholesaler B, agreeing a discount of 25 per cent with the manufacturer.

However, even if they choose to undercut Retailer D, they still do not necessarily make as much profit, because they have all the costs of shipping, distribution etc, which the wholesalers normally incur.

Some industries have seen major changes in this area in recent years, no more so than the supply of personal computers.

For example, in the UK personal computer market:

- some manufacturers choose to go direct from the start (eg Gateway 2000);
- some choose a dual route (eg Dell, who supply direct and though some superstores);
- some only supply direct to large firms or through what they call value added resellers (essentially high volume retailers), for example, Compaq and Toshiba; and

- one company, Amstrad, recently changed from supplying through the main chain of High Street stores in the UK, Dixons, to selling directly to the public by mail order.

In many ways trade discounts are a type of quantity discount, and really only differ in that they are labelled as such. This is a recognition of how business has developed over the years, and it has brought into everyday currency the phrase 'I bought it at trade', meaning that as a consumer you got a big discount. In some parts of the UK you will also hear the phrase 'factory price', which is much the same thing.

Quantity discounts

These are provided in recognition of the fact that the customer is buying in bulk and thus reducing the cost of supplying them with the goods, eg no matter how large the order there is one invoice to process, and you may get bulk reductions in carriage etc. There is a clear balance between the amount of discount given and the perceived saving to the customer. It is very easy to misjudge this type of discount and end up with a lower margin than the sale of a smaller quantity might provide.

Quantity discounts can be given in a number of ways:

- as a percentage reduction in price (eg 2 per cent off);
- as free goods (eg buy 50 packs, get one free);
- at the time of purchase (eg discount off invoice) or retrospectively (eg 2 per cent off at the year end if targets are met).

The retrospective discount encourages customer loyalty, whereas the off-invoice discount has a more immediate effect, eg to close a sale.

Quantity discounts are normally offered in a progressive manner, and usually on a logarithmic scale, for example:

Units	*Discount*
0–10	Nil
10–100	2.5%
100–1000	5.0%
1,000–10,000	10.0%
10,000 plus	Maximum (12.5%)

The discount amounts are normally calculated on the overall margin and the marginal cost of the extra production.

Promotional discounts

These are used for the purpose of pushing or promoting particular product(s). Thus, where a reduction in old stock may be required or a push for market share, it may be appropriate to offer a (limited period) discount on a product or product range.

Promotional discounts can take many forms including:

- period discounts (eg 10 per cent off this month);
- deferred payment (eg buy now, pay later);
- free product (eg buy this product, get a related product free);
- timing discounts (eg out of season sales);
- allowance discounts (eg buying back old stock for resale etc).

The most obvious example is the so-called 'January sales', which now seem to extend from December through to Easter! In the USA, sales are almost a permanent feature of the retailing landscape, and companies will think of almost any excuse to offer a limited sale (eg Easter Bunny sale, National Book Week sale).

Many restaurants in the USA also offer the 'dish of the day' at a reduced rate. This is called the 'Blue Plate Special' (for no very obvious reason) and, of course, the idea of happy hour (eg half-price drinks between five pm and six pm) is common across the world. The dish of the day is, of course, at a good price because the restaurant has estimated that it will sell a large number and buys the food accordingly. It is also easier and cheaper to make lots of one dish than 20 à la carte dishes. The happy hour is to attract people into a bar when maybe they would not normally go but the lower price might tempt them to pop in on their way home and, of course, the bar-keeper hopes, stay on longer.

Price promotions

The price of a product encapsulates all the values that the consumer attributes to that product. As the customer hands over money for a product they are, therefore, striking a bargain with the supplier, with the money representing the total of a complex equation.

It is possible to reduce (and increase!) the price of products in order to reinforce customer perception of the value they are receiving from the deal and various techniques for this are discussed briefly below, together with a generalised description of the message that is passed. These usually involve a mixture of techniques and are usually a temporary time-limited change in pricing. This allows for very innovative approaches to pricing, for example:

- better and better discounts as a sale goes on culminating in a 'half-price' day;
- huge discounts on a few well-publicised items for a short time (*vide* the queues outside Harrods on the first day of the sales);
- purchase (up-front) of a discount voucher for use in a local restaurant that enables one to enjoy different types of discount (one person eats free with the holder; four meals for half price; free bottle of wine with every £40 spent etc), to tie you in to frequent visits;
- special 'tie-ins' with coupons or other retailers, eg you can use the loyalty card from your regular retailer in a DIY store and gain points etc (buying garden furniture could get you a 'free' box of tea-bags).

Cash discounts

All discounts can be given in a number of ways (extra products, vouchers off next purchases etc), however the transmission of actual money has a special place in the hearts of businesspeople everywhere.

Cash discounts often relate to the provision of a rebate for early payment of an invoice. Examples include:

- 2 per cent off the bill if payment is received in 15 days or less;
- A 1 per cent discount for cash, rather than a credit card payment (reflecting the cost to the retailer of processing the card payment and waiting for the money).

These types of discount are valuable for generating cashflow and many manufacturers will offer them if asked.

However, this type of discounting can be easily abused and we will outline how this works:

- Manufacturer A sells goods worth £1,000 to Company B.
- In a letter to Mr Smith of Company B, the seller (A) offers a 5 per cent discount for payment in 15 days.
- Mr Smith authorises payment rapidly, but does not tell his accounts department of the discount, and they thus pay £1,000 to manufacturer A.
- Manufacturer A then raises a refund cheque for £50 and sends this back to Mr Smith.

There are two possible outcomes:

- If Mr Smith is in collusion with the manufacturer this cheque might be made out to Mr Smith himself (or would more likely be in cash). This is, of course, fraudulent and corrupt.

- If Mr Smith is merely devious rather than corrupt he will receive the cheque for £50 made out to his firm and ask his accounts department to credit it to a different budget code. Thus, he may use this money to take his staff on an outing or to pay for a brochure. Whilst not necessarily fraudulent, this is at best a clear breach of financial responsibility.

One of the authors was involved in a major promotion some years ago, where vouchers, exchangeable at a major UK off licence chain, were used to incentivise purchasers to buy extra goods. Great care had to be taken to ensure that these vouchers (which are, in effect, money) were not passed directly to employees but were received by the management of the purchasing company at a corporate level. The sales promotion company handling this matter was very careful to adhere both to the letter of the law and also to the guidelines of its professional body.

Messages

Before offering any kind of a discount it is appropriate to think of the message that it gives to the customer. A number of positive and negative examples are shown below:

Positive

- You are a valued customer and we demonstrate this by reducing your purchase price.
- We are prepared to accept a lower margin now to develop a long-term relationship.
- We are aggressive and going for market share.
- We are becoming even more efficient.
- (Premium pricing/negative discount) This is a 'hot' product and demand may soon exceed supply.

A practical example of the first of these positive messages is the John Lewis Partnership (a UK department chain) whose slogan is 'Never Knowingly Undersold'. The company offers a refund if you paid more in one of its shops than you would pay for the product elsewhere in a given radius (and can prove the veracity of your claim). This shows consumers that the company values their custom and is in line with its CVP of offering quality at the best price.

Another example is the introduction by BT (a UK telecommunications company) of discounts for 'Friends & Family' numbers. This allows you to nominate a set number of telephone numbers for which you will be billed at discounted rates. Naturally, people usually pick those numbers which they call frequently but which are furthest away. The objective here is probably twofold: (a) to ensure that you do not switch to another provider, eg Mercury which also offers discounts on long-distance calls and (b) to tempt you into calling them more often (thus partly mitigating the discount by higher volume).

However, as well as a positive side (closing the sale), discounting has its negative aspects:

Negative

- This is old stock/redundant and we must sell it.
- Our business is not doing well and we need the sales at all costs.
- The item is faulty or substandard.
- Quality is being reduced.
- The item will be replaced shortly by a better model.
- The item was overpriced to start with.

Good examples of this are signs saying: 'bankrupt stock sales — everything must go' (which tends to beg the question, why did the original seller go bankrupt?) or 'designer clothes at trade prices', which again raises the issue of why these clothes aren't being sold in Bond Street at high prices. The answer is normally either that they are fake (which is, of course, illegal) or that they are last year's models, and thus not what the fashion conscious might wish to wear. Frequently they have been bought cheap from a liquidator and this explains the low prices.

To an extent the message depends on how it is delivered and the tone applied. Remember that a last minute big discount is nearly always seen as a sign of desperation.

Discounts, however, often play a crucial part in price negotiation. Whilst a final, well-judged 1 per cent can make the difference between a sale or no sale, an ill-judged 10 per cent early on can erode any hope of profit on a deal. Understanding how to use this 'tool' is the key.

Price negotiation

This book does not seek to deal with negotiating behaviour in any detail. There are a large number of excellent works (and training courses) on this subject. Nonetheless, discounting is such a key tool in a price negotiation it is perhaps appropriate to discuss it a little.

Discounting will usually rear its head somewhere well into the sales process. The customer will need to be basically satisfied about the durability and suitability of the goods in question and will then simply be seeking to drive the price down.

Considering the price (and the price alone) what will happen is that the buyer will have an upper limit of what he will pay in his mind and the seller a lower limit. These are often referred to as negotiating bands. From Table 6.2, we can postulate a number of scenarios, as follows:

Table 6.2

Seller band	Buyer band	Result
100–90	85–95	Agreement between 90–95
100–90	80–85	No agreement
100–90	110–100	Immediate agreement with no negotiation

This is, of course, a stylised example and in practice it is nothing like so simple.

We can, however, consider what the dynamics of this meeting might look like.

In the first case, there will be a lively discussion and the seller will inch down (100, all right then, 98 etc), whilst the buyer inches up (85 is all I'll pay, OK then I'll go to 87 etc). Depending on how skilled the parties are, and in what increments they move, they will agree somewhere where their bands overlap.

There are a number of techniques to beware of here, especially the offer to 'split the difference' to finish a negotiation. If you have been moving down faster than they have been moving up, this will disadvantage you even further.

In the second case, the meeting is likely to be unproductive as it is clear that no agreement can be reached. The buyer will perceive the seller as 'unreasonable' and the seller will consider the buyer 'tight-fisted'. Either way this not a healthy state of affairs for a long-term relationship. The way out of this issue is for the seller to try to convince the buyer that other, non-price, features, make the price reasonable. In effect this shifts the buyer's band up so that there is some overlap. This is using the CVP argument in effect to make the buyer feel that he is equalising the price/benefits/value equation.

In the final case, the meeting is over in an instant, but both parties will be feeling rather bemused. The seller will know that he has set his price too low, and thus missed out on valuable extra margin. The buyer, on the other hand, will either think the seller an idiot for not negotiating hard enough, or, more likely, will start to feel there is something wrong that he has missed (for example, is the quality really OK? Will they deliver on time? etc). In either case, this is not a healthy situation.

Managing discounting in practice

Managing discounting in practice can be problematic: if sales staff are given too much leeway then there is potential for large amounts of margin to be given away unnecessarily, and if they are not given enough scope they will be unable to close deals.

The traditional solution, that of providing the sales force with some small measure of scope and then inviting them to get separate authorisation for larger levels, simply does not work well in practice.

Similarly, a procedure often used in large contracts, where junior staff start off the negotiation, making way for more and more senior staff (and bigger and bigger discounts) again does not work. No one is empowered by these processes.

Whilst there have to be rules and procedures, the best approach is that of education and training, combined with an incentive or motivation system, that focuses the minds of the sales staff on what is important, be it market share, volume orders or maximising margin. These are notoriously difficult to set up and manage in practice, because of the large number of 'drivers' that have to be considered, and the variety of situations that occur in practice. Consider the situations in a firm of management consultants, with three levels of staff:

- directors — who can give any discount they like but, of course, are answerable via their profit and loss statement;
- managers — who can discount up to 20%; and
- consultants — who can discount up to 10%.

If we assume that the staff are all well-paid and motivated, what type of incentive system can be put in place to ensure that only the minimum discounts are given?

A system based on sales turnover would be insufficient because this would drive staff to sell the largest amount of work they could, without thought of how much money it would make. In practice, you would often find the larger consulting firms selling jobs worth millions of pounds, at low or no profit at all, simply by quoting the rationale that 'it contributes to our overhead cost'.

If, instead, staff are motivated by margin, then they may well turn away highly discounted work, and then the utilisation of the firm will fall dramatically. This in turn will drive up the overhead, thus erasing part of the margin.

Individual motivation must also be considered. If the manager is incentivised by (say) utilisation (eg how many man-days he can put on the job) he will go all out to sell volume (this is often a key driver in professional service firms). This will present the director with a dilemma: he will get the credit for the utilisation but not the profit.

The situation is further complicated by teams: if one person is out doing the selling, but the other is a technical expert, how do you ensure they are both equally incentivised?

What happens in practice is normally a 'dog's dinner' of different schemes and complicated rules books of instructions on what and how to do it. The alternate approach, that of simply rewarding people based on how well the firm is doing again doesn't work very well, as people often cannot see how giving a specific customer an extra 5 per cent discount will affect the final profit and dividend.

These complex schemes generally serve neither to incentivise nor promote responsible discounting and often leads to excessive administration involvement. The staff must clearly understand the scheme and it must have some impact in practice. Above all it must be realistic.

Many times you hear stories of how, when firms have had a good year, they refuse to pay a bonus because 'next year is looking bleak, and we need to reinvest', and when they have had a bad year 'they can't afford it'. This type of behaviour does no one any favours.

The optimum type of scheme is one which uses a simple algorithm which takes as inputs, sales, margin and utilisation, making due allowance for the type of role an individual plays in the firm by setting appropriate targets at individual, group and firm levels. This recognises all key factors and allocates commensurate rewards in turn.

For discounting to be effective, the reduced price should result in more sales. Whilst these sales generate increased revenue, this is not important. It is the absolute *contribution* that is vital. A 2 per cent reduction in price can result in a 20 per cent reduction in contribution if margins are thin. The following worked example shows this:

A manufacturer makes a product for £8 and sells it for £10. A 'normal' sale to customer A is 100 units. However, by offering discounts, the customer will buy more, as follows:

- A discount of 5 per cent will generate sales of 130 units.
- A discount of 10 per cent will generate 210 units.
- A discount of 18 per cent will generate 500 units.

Which is the best sale?

We calculate the answer, not by looking at the revenue (which is obviously largest in the case of the high discount), but the contribution.

The normal sale generates a contribution of £200 (100 units by £2 per unit). A discount of 5 per cent results in a contribution of £1.50 per unit, being a total contribution of £195.

The 10 per cent discount generates a contribution of £1, being a total contribution of £210.
The 18 per cent discount generates a contribution of only 20p, giving a total contribution of only £100.

Thus, in this case, 10 per cent is the right figure to go for.

In the real world, the sales force must be able to get an instant response to a question about discounting, and this must be again based on facts and information rather than prejudice. In addition, everyone who deals with discounting should be able to do the type of calculation above, in their head, as you often only have a few seconds in front of the customer to make the decision!

Stories abound of organisations where one sales manager is known to be a softer touch than another, and when a salesman needs an extra discount to close a sale, he will ring up George for the OK, rather than Fred, who would give him a hard time and ask questions.

Of course, from the company's point of view, Fred is the right person to take the call, because his questions will be the right ones. It pays, therefore, to ensure that your organisation is full of Freds, not Georges.

Conclusion

Managing pricing in practice is notoriously difficult. Different departments in companies will have different agendas and drivers, and within each part managers will have their own agendas. In order to avoid dysfunctional operations there have to be rules, but these should be short, practical and above all else should empower managers and staff by engendering responsibility for decisions related to remuneration and reward where it matters.

To summarise managing discounting in practice it includes:

- regular training and refresher course for sales staff;
- clear and unambiguous guidelines on behaviour;
- an incentive system that gives the right message and results in the right behaviour;
- regular information about the aims and objectives of the organisation or even the particular promotion;

and above all make sure that senior managers sing the same song. It may not matter which song, but they should all be in tune.

The final chapter provides a brief review of the book, and offers some key tips and techniques to bear in mind.

7

TIPS AND TECHNIQUES: PRICING TO WIN

KEYS TO SUCCESS IN PRICING

There is no single key to getting pricing right, but getting the process right certainly helps to avoid errors. The first stage is, quite clearly, to put yourself in the mind of the consumer. Ask what he wants, what he values, what he needs, and you have the first key elements of the *customer value proposition.*

The customer value proposition is central to all pricing. Remember that a sale is simply a bargain between two parties. Customers give you money, you give them a product or service. Both sides must be happy if a long-term relationship is to result (what negotiators call a win : win situation).

The fundamental business objective is to make sure that your price encapsulates all the benefits that the customer is getting from the product. Many of us have a tendency to undersell ourselves and our products: a kind of natural modesty. Don't let this get in the way of maximising your return from a sale. The title of the book says it all — price for the VALUE part of the CVP.

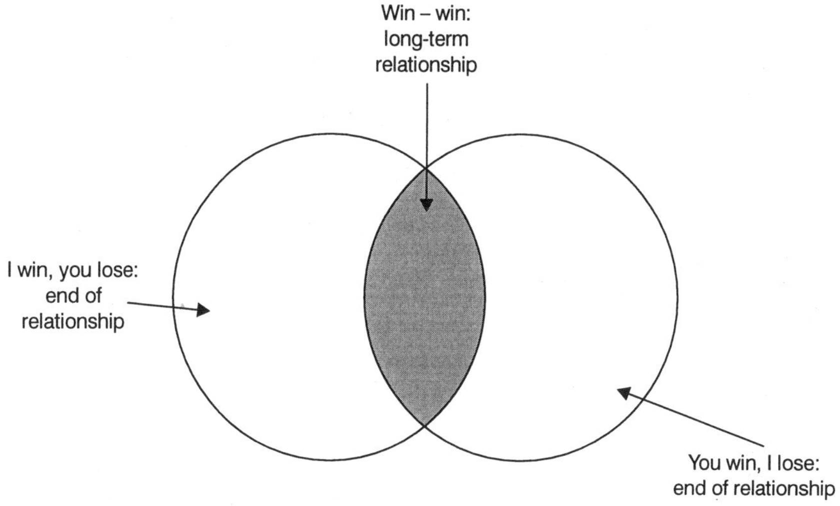

Figure 7.1 *Customer value proposition*

Vary price with benefits
Always listen to customer criticism and act on it
Live a day in the life of your customer
Understand what your customer needs
Equalise the price/benefit trade off

Remember as well that there are certain situations where you do not want a long-term relationship with the customer; these are one-off situations such as when you are selling your house or your car. In this case just go for the highest price you possibly can, and don't worry too much if they are upset or feel hard done by as long as you get that sale — there is no trade-off between relationship and price here.

In business, however, generally the opposite is true. The authors and Kogan Page believe that this book represents a good value proposition. We want you to think that you got value for this book. The price has been set to equalise the perceived price/benefit to potential readers and to meet internal expectations. We are satisfied with the price you paid: we hope that you are; and we want you to come and buy our other books and recommend them to others etc.

And finally don't forget that the customer perception of value may be different from yours. In the low-cost jewellery market the famous remark, made by the firm's chief executive, comparing the value of his firm's jewellery unfavourably to that of a prawn sandwich, caused an enormous furore resulting in his resignation. Maybe customers already knew that jewellery from this firm was poor quality and not good long-term value, but chose not to believe it – but telling everyone was an error.

The perception of 'nice jewellery' to a CEO from a large public firm is going to be very different from that of someone who is, say, existing on a low wage. Thus, whilst both people might want to buy a bracelet for their wives at Christmas, the recipient is not going to be very pleased if she knows that even the manufacturer thinks they are ripping you off.

It was not the value proposition that was wrong in this case (reasonable jewellery for low prices), it was the pejorative, insulting way in which it was described that was the crucial error as it destroyed the value customers placed on the offering thereby destroying the price/value equation.

VALUE PRICING STEPS

This book recommends that you follow a distinct pricing process as shown in the diagram.

This process considers:

- the inputs to the pricing **infrastructure;**
- the pricing **methodology;** and
- managing in **practice**.

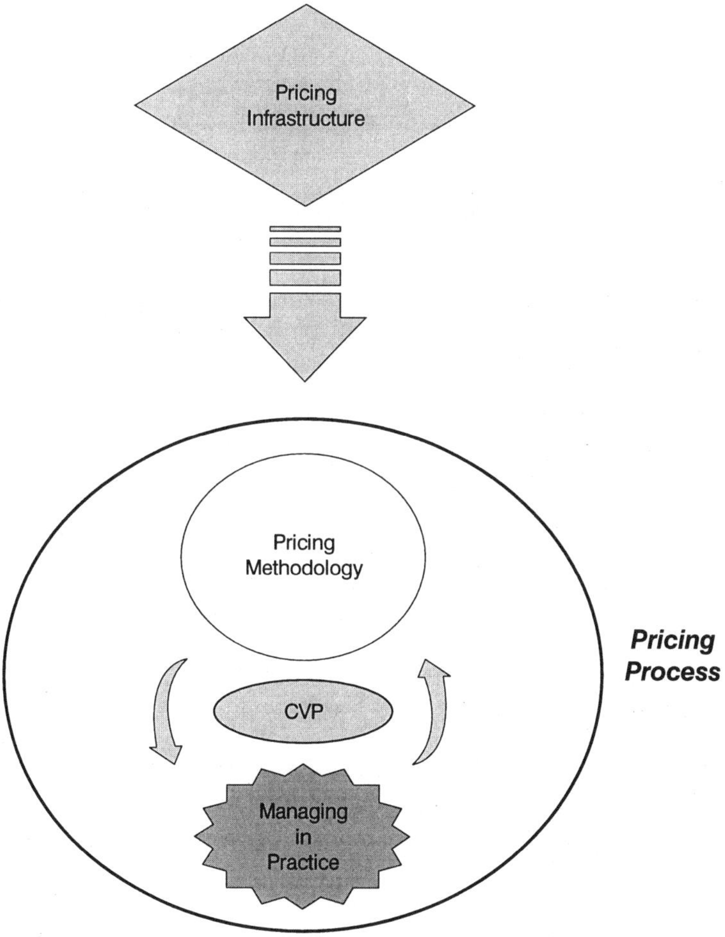

Figure 7.2

In the following paragraphs we illustrate the key points.

PRICING INFRASTRUCTURE INPUTS

For informed decisions about pricing, you require some degree of understanding about many issues, but in particular you should have a detailed overview of:

- your markets;
- your customers;
- your product offering (including costs and risks);

and set these in the context of your corporate strategy.

This forms the core of your customer value proposition(s), ie what you are going to offer; to whom; when; and how you will differentiate yourselves.

This basic research and analysis should have been done as part of the strategy process. If it has not then you must revisit your thinking.

Once you have completed this analysis it then feeds into the pricing process.

THE PRICING METHODOLOGY

The pricing process

Processes work well in organisations. Most people like to know where they stand within a framework, and what is expected of them. It also makes progress easier to track.

It is the discipline of the process that makes it so powerful, because one is in a team and there is a level of expectation, and often performance criteria; work is more likely to be delivered on time, accurately and with confidence. If you ensure that your organisation follows a formal pricing process then results should be delivered.

The pricing process must develop the following key elements:

- purpose and vision of the action;
- detailed objectives;
- clear and unambiguous policy (what and how things are to be done);
- a detailed plan (who, what, where and when); and
- a discussion of tactics and how matters are interrelated (the combination of pricing with other marketing and promotional techniques).

Policies and strategies

It is clear that pricing policies and strategies will vary widely between firms. What one thinks appropriate will have been discarded by another. Basically they will fall into well-defined areas:

- A top-down approach to control, rather old-fashioned and authoritarian, but nonetheless usually easily understandable;
- A bottom-up approach. Entrepreneurial and flexible but often difficult to control, particularly as firms grow in size and complexity.

Strategies will vary depending on the firm's goals. Table 7.1 shows both ends of the spectrum, but of course, there are a myriad of positions in between:

Table 7.1

Strategic question	Alternative 'a'	Alternative 'b'
Where to compete?	Global	Focused
How to compete?	Efficiency	Differentiation
Which direction?	Hold	Improve
How to measure?	Contribution	Market share
How to change scope?	Increase	Decrease

The combination of choices gives many different permutations and each company will choose variations to suit its goals.

And when, and only when, the methodology has been enacted it is time to put matters into practice.

CLASSIC PRICING TACTICS

The tactical level of pricing is its operation in practice at the sharp end, ie the sale. A successful business gets its sales at the right price and at the right time to maximise its return, whether long or short term depending on the strategy. Tactics are how this is achieved on a day-to-day basis and must reflect the objectives as set out in the policies and strategy.

Here is a mnemonic for pricing tactics:

T	Treat your customers with respect
A	Always look for long-term relationships
C	Cut your prices only to maximise your revenues
T	Take heed of the 'on the ground' feedback
I	Investigate complaints and act on real ones
C	Considered response to your competition
S	Spread the right message with your prices

Many organisations put a lot of effort into pricing their offerings but then lose ground daily due to poor negotiation; lack of understanding of the real cost of a discount; or losing sight of the basic objectives during a sales meeting.

Some firms have the following message placed at frequent locations in their offices, or on pocket-sized cards:

Better the loss of a sale, than a sale at a loss

to drive the message home to staff.

Table 7.2 is a summary of the features of the main pricing techniques.

Table 7.2

Features >>>>> Pricing techniques VVV	Information requirements 1	Risk to seller 2	Opportunity to capitalise on good timing 3	Management complexity 4	Mass market 5
Going rate	L	M	L	L	MM
Perception	M	M	H	L	MM
Lump sum	H	H	H	H	
Piece rate	L	L	L	L	
Psychological	L	L	M	L	MM
Contingent	H	HHH	H	H	
Line	H	M	L	L	MM
Geographic or zone	H	L	H	H	
Loss leaders	M	H	H	L	MM
Slot/gap	H	M–H	H	M	
Impact assessment	H	H	L	L	
Skimming		M	H	L	
Penetration	L	M	L	L	MM
Premium	L	H	H	L	
Intermediary	H	M	M	H	
Dual or multiple	H	M	M	H	
Sealed bid	M	L	L	M	
Auctions	L	HHH	–	L	

Key

H = High
M = Medium
L = Low

Some tips:

- Whatever you do, *don't underprice your offer,* or customers won't think it a bargain: they will suspect some flaw or fault.
- Similarly, *don't overprice your offer*: people only fall for it once or twice and they will not come back once they realise they can go somewhere else to get it cheaper; or merely decide not to buy it.

A worked example

It is very easy to read a book and think that it is all theoretical: it doesn't apply to me. The following worked example collates all the key points in the book.
Background: The authors have been pleased by the reception of this pricing book, so they decide to organise a public seminar, incorporating case studies from the book and a question and answer session. The seminar needs to be profitable, so the crucial question is:
How much should we charge?
The pricing process is illustrated as follows:

Item	Action
CVP	The first step is to consider: will this provide value to attendees? Will they part with their money for the experience and be happy at the end?
Economics	Consider the market size and what other people are doing. In this area one seminar makes so little difference it is not necessary to consider competition in any real sense.
Marketing	What are the best techniques to promote seminars? Perhaps direct mail, some flyposting, advertising in the local papers, PR (eg on the radio).
Finance	What kind of costing system to use (probably direct costing), consider cashflow (hall hire and catering will usually be paid up front)?
Target return	Is it worth doing? Only if the target return is met, and this is defined by how much money the authors want to get in return for their time.
Supply and demand	Being sole supplier position the book is unique so there is no direct competition; however, instead of parting with money to attend the seminar, people might prefer a training course, or to buy more books: all forms of indirect competition.
Price points	What kind of money is it appropriate to spend for an hour-and-a-half in our company. The cinema costs £5, West End theatre costs maybe £15, and a seat at the opera £100. A ticket to hear a world-famous business guru could also cost this.
Market research	In this particular case it is relatively easy: the intended promotional media is scanned to yield details from the 'competitors'. Conference organisers may also be asked for their views.
Strategy development	The general level of pitch to the audience must be decided: 'world-famous business gurus' v 'businessmen with a good line in tips and techniques'.
Planning	A detailed plan is needed, firstly because these things take time to organise, and secondly as risk minimisation.
Implementation	Should the marketing and organising be carried out using internal resources ourselves or should specialists be hired?
Break-even analysis	We have to calculate all our production and selling costs, and then compare these with sales projections on a market-based price to see if the conference is worth

	doing — in bald terms it comes down to how many seats we can fill at what price.
Cashflow	It is not just sales that are important: getting the money in is vital, so giving long-term credit and dealing with recalcitrant payers is an important consideration. We ask: what are the characteristics of paying in this market (normally cheque with order, so no problem)?
Consumers' perception of the supplier	The basic issue here is whether Kogan Page is seen as a purveyor of quality texts on business issues (they are) and the authors as 'experts'. The Mills and Boon book of value pricing would give a seriously mixed message to consumers!
Distribution	Again, the make-up of the market is important. In this case distribution centres on how we advise potential attendees of the conference and how we attract them. Seminars have to be local, so city centre venues seem a good idea.
Risk	The risk is that after we print leaflets, hire halls etc, there will be a very low take-up on seats and we will have to cancel. This is a difficult decision (often faced by theatres and concert promoters), as a 10 per cent full hall has no atmosphere and thus everyone comes away disappointed
Marketing mix	For conferences this is relatively simple: direct mail and some advertising. We can easily calculate the cost and return parameters.
Pricing policy	We would normally set out with an idea of the profit we want to make (eg based on the number of seminars, likely attendances and our time input in arranging the seminars). If the figures do not stack up then we need to go round an iterative loop, but we must be very careful not to alter assumptions that are factually based, just so we can project a paper profit. We care about the money in our hand. Our policy is likely to be based on good value, but still quality (a high-medium price).
Pricing strategy	Our strategy then might be to premium price our offer, especially if the book has sold well and got good reviews. If, however, the book was poorly received we might have to undercut other conferences in this area (or more likely, not go ahead).

Pricing tactics	By and large conference organisers use going rate techniques: they look at what others do and then just vary these a little. This is because it is a well-defined, niche market with well-understood characteristics.
Discounting	Should the unthinkable happen and only 50 per cent of the seats be sold, we could consider last minute discounting; however, this would give such a poor impression of us as speakers that it would probably be counterproductive. In any case there is no good mechanism for advertising this to consumers. However, at an earlier stage, if someone asked for a block discount (eg for a party of 20 people from the same firm) then we would certainly consider this.
Managing discounting in practice	At all times we would need to run a small model (probably based on a PC spreadsheet) showing costs v. revenues, with these being categorised as paid, firm, potential etc. You always need to know where you are financially.

The key tips in each area are presented as a checklist below. This list is neither exhaustive nor exclusive so careful consideration is required in use.

Issue	**Question**
Pricing infrastructure	Are all the necessary components in place? Is it communicated?
Pricing methodology	Is the process transparent to all employees?
Managing in practice	Are the correct management processes in place and working?
CVP	Is it clearly articulated and understood — is it right and unique?
Economics	Have the relevant concepts been analysed and explored?
Marketing	Have marketing and other relevant departments been involved at the right level?
Finance	Have the financial consequences been explored and understood?
Target return	What targets and measures have been set?

Supply and demand	Has the relationship (elasticity) between these two factors been assessed and have forecasts been undertaken?
Price points	Have these been understood and factored into the strategy?
Market research	Have the targeted markets been analysed and the results presented and factored into the strategy and planning?
Strategy development	Clear process, completed?
Planning	Is it displayed for all to understand and 'live' — does it have buy-in?
Implementation	Have tasks been allocated and agreed?
Break-even analysis	Is this clearly understood, for products and product groups?
Cashflow	Are outflows balanced against inflows, or provision made — are break points known?
Consumers' perception of the supplier	Is the written CVP matched with the results from market research?
Distribution	Are the dynamics understood and maximised?
Risk	Have they been analysed, understood and a contingency plan developed?
Marketing mix	Has it been set to maximise the USP for each product/service in line with pricing policy?
Discounting	Are guidelines set and understood — adequate discretionary levels matched with controls?

A logical summary

To assist in crystallising the thinking required it is helpful to think of the pricing decision as a pyramid, with increasing levels of detail as the pyramid progressively expands from the top:

Apex — *the key thought*	How much should I charge?
Second level — *supporting lines*	a — my costs are 'w' b — my competitors charge 'x' c — the market characteristics are 'y' d — my CVP is 'z'
Third level — *detail behind each second level,* eg	a i — direct costs 'p' a ii — indirect costs 'q' a iii — break-even is 'r'
Fourth level — *further detail*	

Fifth level — *supporting analysis*
The number of levels is that required to logically articulate the thinking and provide an 'audit trail' to demonstrate how the price was achieved. The detail should be no more than is necessary to provide a logical flow that 'takes the reader by the hand' and leads them to the conclusion you have reached.

It will also help you in marshalling your thoughts logically as, to present the case, you must understand the logical flow yourself.

In conclusion

The medium of business is money. The seller suggests an amount that seems to them to encapsulate all the values of the goods on offer. If the buyer thinks this fair, they hand over the money and a deal results. Psychologists call this process bargaining. Where this happens profitably for you then the CVP is right.

Remember that a bargain is where both parties feel satisfied; and satisfied customers are ones that come back.

If you are involved in pricing then it will be your job to choose the crucial number (ie price) that provides the link between buying and selling.

By using the process and the techniques contained within this book selectively, as appropriate to your business, you should be able to price your products and services accordingly.

APPENDICES

APPENDIX 1

VALUE PRICING: EXAMPLES

The following exercises are set for you to work through. The answers are shown in a separate section. The examples show the following:

- pricing a manufactured product, the Gizmo (looked at from the point of view of the manufacturer, the wholesaler and the retailer)
- pricing a service, IT consultancy as supplied by the small firm of Raymond and Partners.

The examples illustrate the following points:

Gizmo

- **Exercise A:** This shows how to maximise revenue by plotting the demand: selling price
- **Exercise B:** This shows how to maximise margin looking at the cost of production compared to selling prices and demand
- **Exercise C:** A decision-making matrix is shown to illustrate how you might compare competitive prices
- **Exercise D:** This illustrates the decision-making process with a trade intermediary, and how they might arrive at a price based on supply channel considerations
- **Exercise E:** This example illustrates target profit pricing, as applied by a retailer

Raymond and Partners

- **Exercise A:** Illustrates cost-plus pricing as applied in a small service organisation
- **Exercise B:** This shows market-related pricing in the context of competitive tendering
- **Exercise C:** This example uses a market sector focus to the show the development of pricing strategies for dissimilar areas

APPENDIX 2

Gizmo — Exercise A: pricing and revenue maximisation

This is the first exercise in a short series illustrating the pricing strategies and calculations.

The product in question is the Gizmo, a mechanical device used in building work by both professionals and do-it-yourselfers. The Gizmo is an entirely new device with no competitors or alternatives. Acme (the manufacturer) is selling these products direct to end-users (by mail order and direct response advertising)

The Gizmo is now ready for launch! You are the manufacturer, Acme, and have carried out some research that shows that the proposed selling price of the Gizmo is related to likely volumes sold in a linear fashion.

The table and graph below show the projected relationship between quantity sold and price.

Table A2.1

Quantity	Price
90	£2.00
81	£3.80
80	£4.00
70	£6.00
61	£7.80
60	£8.00
50	£10.00
41	£11.80
40	£12.00
30	£14.00
21	£15.80
20	£16.00
10	£18.00

Calculate the price at which Acme will maximise its revenues. You may need to plot a small graph on a piece of lined paper.

Gizmo — Exercise B: pricing and margin maximisation

Acme has identified that the price to maximise revenue is £10. However, the company's cost of production varies in a stepwise fashion, comprising two key costs:

- the variable cost of producing each Gizmo. This cost is £5 per Gizmo and does not alter with volume;

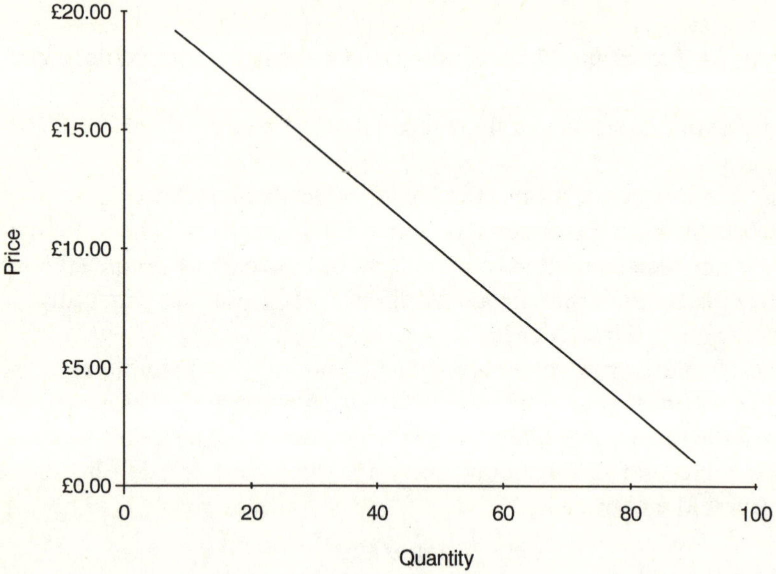

Figure A2.1 *Gizmo sales – projected demand v. price*

- the fixed cost of Gizmo machine. Each Gizmo machine costs £50 and can produce up to 20 Gizmos. To produce the twenty-first (forty-first etc) Gizmo, Acme has to buy a new machine.

(*Note:* you do not need to calculate any timing or depreciation issues etc.)

The table below shows how the cost of production varies with quantity produced

Table A2.2

Quantity	Fixed cost	Variable cost	Total cost
90	£250.00	£450.00	£700.00
81	£250.00	£405.00	£655.00
80	£200.00	£400.00	£600.00
70	£200.00	£350.00	£550.00
61	£200.00	£305.00	£505.00
60	£150.00	£300.00	£450.00
50	£150.00	£250.00	£400.00
41	£150.00	£205.00	£355.00
40	£100.00	£200.00	£300.00
30	£100.00	£150.00	£250.00
21	£100.00	£105.00	£205.00
20	£50.00	£100.00	£150.00
10	£50.00	£50.00	£100.00

Calculate at which price the margin to Acme is maximised (*note:* you will need to refer to Table A2.1). You may find it helpful to draw a rough graph.

Gizmo — Exercise C: competitive pricing

Because of competition in the market Acme has been forced to introduce a *New Improved Gizmo* (NIG). This NIG bears little resemblance to the original model, and now has an electric motor. It also has a much higher price.

Acme has been selling it for one year now, at a price of £29 per unit. All the competing companies sell their products through mail order and direct response advertising.

The market is growing very fast. This growth is partly fuelled by advertising, and also by the introduction of competition from other suppliers. ChromWidge has overtaken Acme to become a clear leader.

Acme faces competition from three other suppliers of New Improved Gizmos. The market can be characterised as follows:

Table A2.3

Manufacturer	Acme	BetaWidge	ChromWidge	Delta
Current price	£29	£37	£25	£18
Quality	Medium	High	High	Low
Advertising support	Some	None	A lot	A lot
Endorsed by a leading builder	Yes	Yes	No	No
Delivery time to retailer/wholesaler	3 days	1 day	5 days	2 days
Stated company objectives	To be the number one or two supplier of Gizmos	To be seen as the highest quality supplier	To be number one	To make money from Gizmos, which are only a part of larger line
Cost base	Known	Higher than Acme	Unknown	Lower than Acme

Notes:

Do not consider the cost of production implications. Ignore any financial calculations as to the profitability of the pricing decisions.

Table A2.3 is not meant to be exhaustive, so please use your judgement in analysing the facts.

In order to preserve your business you may have to revise the price of the Acme New Improved Gizmo. Suggest a method, a new price and give reasons why this will help Acme meet its objectives.

Gizmo — Exercise D: wholesaler pricing

Acme has revised the price to the ultimate consumer of the *New Improved Gizmo* (NIG) to £31. Its analysis of the market indicates that distribution through wholesalers would be a big improvement to selling direct. It has had discussions with the biggest wholesaler in the market, Tradeace, and now seeks to agree a price.

Acme has now stopped selling direct, but will sell direct to retailers (who are, of course, Tradeace's customers).

The scenario is as follows:

- NIGs are supplied by Acme in a case, each case containing 10 NIGs.
- Acme's suggested price to Tradeace is £185 per case (10 NIGs).
- Acme's price for direct supply to a retailer (two case minimum) is £225.00 per case of 10 NIGs (this bypasses Tradeace entirely).
- Tradeace's costs are all variable. It costs them £1.00 to unpack and display one NIG.
- Retailers are still recommended to sell a single NIG for £31, and most do.

Suggest the range of prices that Tradeace will offer NIGs to a retailer:

- if the retailer buys one NIG;
- if the retailer buys one case of 10 NIGs;
- if the retailer buys two or more cases of NIGs.

Gizmo — Exercise E: retailer pricing

The major retailer in this market, Oklahoma, has noticed that the NIGs are selling well and has decide to mount a major promotion. It has struck a special, one-off deal with Acme to buy 5000 NIGs for £19.50 each.

It expects that all the products will sell over a four-month period, and will mount a price promotion for just one month. It expects to sell twice the amount in the promoted month, compared to each normal month. The cost of the promotion is £5000. Other retailers are selling the NIGs at £25 so Oklahoma decides to sell during the non-sale period at £23.99.

Calculate the minimum price that Oklahoma can sell NIGs at during the sale month and still make an overall profit of £10,000 on the period.

APPENDIX 3

Raymond and Partners — Exercise A: cost-plus pricing

This is the first exercise in a short series illustrating the pricing strategies and calculations in a service environment.

Raymond and Partners (or RandP as they are known) have just set up a business to offer advice on computer selection and procurement. In developing their business plan they are able to set out the projected costs of their first year as follows:

Cost item	*Cost for the year*
Office space	£10,000
Telephones, mail etc.	£4,000
Stationery	£2,000
Secretaries' wages	£16,000
Travel	£6,000
Leasing equipment	£6,000
Marketing	£4,000
Other items	£4,000
Total	£52,000

In addition to the secretary there are three partners, each with equal skills and shares in the business. Each partner decides that they want to take home a monthly wage of £2,000.

Thus, the total costs of the business are £52,000 plus (3 × £24,000) ie £124,000. (These calculations ignore all taxes.)

Initially, the partners reckon they can find enough client work (ie chargeable time) for 50 per cent of their time each, being 100 person days.

Calculate the daily rate they need to charge to break even. If they decide they really need to make £15,000 profit, how does this affect the rate (see Answer A).

Almost immediately, however, and before they publish their price list, one of the partners is offered 200 days' work at £250 per day, which she decides to accept. She is thus fully employed all year.

What rate will the remaining two partners have to charge to break even, based on them each doing 100 days of chargeable work ? And what if they still wish to make £15,000 profit (see Answer B)?

Raymond and Partners — Exercise B: market-related pricing

Things are going well at RandP and the firm has taken on some new, lower grade, staff and has been invited to bid on a lump-sum contract against an informal tender. They estimate that it will require 100 partner days at £370 per day and 50 assistant days at £200 per day, being £47,000.

Last time a similar bid was put in, they know that three firms bid for the work, at £42,000, £45,000 and £50,000. The winning bidder was the firm that bid £45,000 who were chosen because of their track record and experience. The lowest bidder apparently put the client off by appearing cheap and cheerful.

Suggest a price for the RandP bid and also a phrase they might include in their bid to ensure that the client knows they could be flexible on their pricing.

Raymond and Partners — Exercise C: competitive pricing

Things have moved on at RandP and the firm has been operating successfully for two years. The published charge out rate for partners is now £400 per day and assistants are charged out at £250.

The firm notices that its main business seems to come from two areas: the financial services industry and local government. Its main competitors are two firms who seem to specialise in just one sector, and looking at their prices they notice a major difference:

Firm	*Partner rate*	*Assistant rate*
RandP (general)	£400	£250
Local government specialists	£350	£225
Financial specialists	£500	£300

This gives RandP a problem: should they develop two price lists, one for each market, should they raise its prices to the higher level and discount or should they operate as they do now?

APPENDIX 4

Gizmo Exercise A: model answer

The price at which Acme will maximise its revenues is £10.

Example graph:

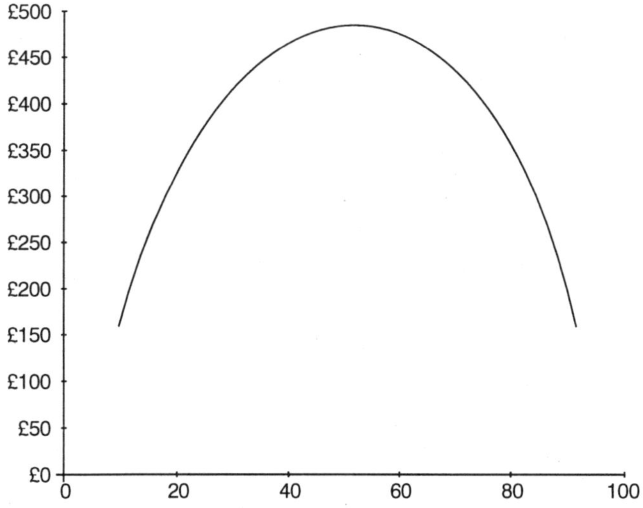

Figure A4.1 *Total revenue v. quantity*

Gizmo Exercise B: model answer

The price at which the margin to Acme is maximised is £12.

Quantity	Price	Total revenue	Fixed cost	Variable cost	Total cost	Total revenue	Margin
90	£2.00	£180.00	£250.00	£450.00	£700.00	£180.00	–£520.00
81	£3.80	£307.80	£250.00	£405.00	£655.00	£307.80	–£347.20
80	£4.00	£320.00	£200.00	£400.00	£600.00	£320.00	–£280.00
70	£6.00	£420.00	£200.00	£350.00	£550.00	£420.00	–£130.00
61	£7.80	£475.80	£200.00	£305.00	£505.00	£475.80	–£29.20
60	£8.00	£480.00	£150.00	£300.00	£450.00	£480.00	£30.00
50	£10.00	£500.00	£150.00	£250.00	£400.00	£500.00	£100.00
41	£11.80	£483.80	£150.00	£205.00	£355.00	£483.80	£128.80
40	£12.00	£480.00	£100.00	£200.00	£300.00	£480.00	£180.00
30	£14.00	£420.00	£100.00	£150.00	£250.00	£420.00	£170.00
21	£15.80	£331.80	£100.00	£105.00	£205.00	£331.80	£126.80
20	£16.00	£320.00	£50.00	£100.00	£150.00	£320.00	£170.00
10	£18.00	£180.00	£50.00	£50.00	£100.00	£180.00	£80.00

Figure A4.2 *Answers*

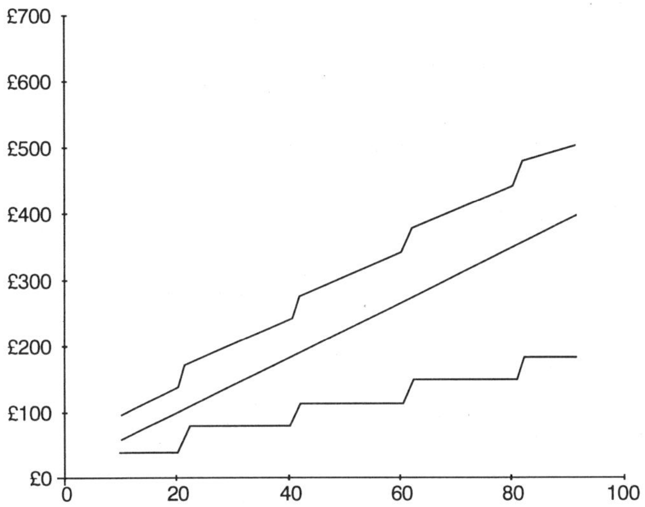

Figure A4.3 *Answers*

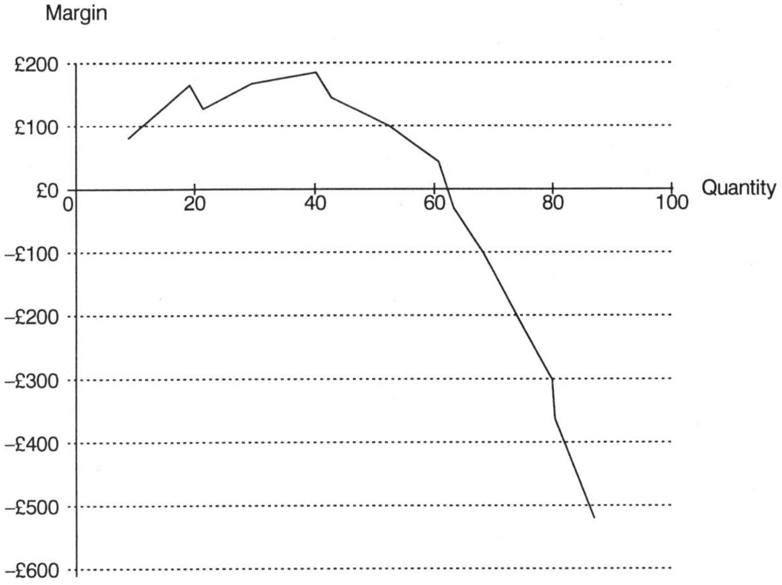

Figure A4.4 *Answers*

Gizmo Exercise C: model answer

A mathematical weighting calculation is sometimes useful to provide a numerical basis for decision making and an example is shown below. The weighting is derived from the importance factor (perhaps obtaincd through market research) multiplied by the product factor (ie how well the product performs against the competition).

The calculation of price is based on the market leader is ChromWidge, and the assumption that because they are successful their product is priced about right.

(*Note:* all ratings are between 1 = low to 5 = high)

Table A4.1

	Manufacturer	**Acme (You)**	**BetaWidge**	**ChromWidge**	**Delta**
Importance factor					
3	Quality	3	5	5	1
2	Advertising support	3	1	5	5
4	Endorsed by a leading builder	5	5	1	1
2	Delivery time	4	5	3	4
Total score		**43**	**47**	**35**	**25**

Table A4.2

	Manufacturer	**Acme (You)**	**BetaWidge**	**ChromWidge**	**Delta**
Current price	£29	£37	£25	£18	
Notes	Currently under priced	Overpriced	Standard	About right	
Suggested price, based on weighting analysis	£31	£33	£25	£18	

Note that it is very important to consider not only the absolute level of price, but also the differential.

Thus Acme could probably increase its price to gain extra margin, but may want to leave the price as it is to gain share from BetaWidge (note the objectives of each company).

Gizmo Exercise D: — model answer wholesaler pricing

If the retailer buys one NIG:

The total cost to Tradeace of selling one NIG is £18.50 plus £1 handling, ie £19.50, so the price must be above this. Any price below £31 is acceptable, although as the retailer has to make a profit then it must be less than this.

Thus, the range is £19.50 to £31. However, the retailer (if they buy in bulk) can achieve a price of £22.50 thus a small premium over this would seem to be acceptable, say £25–£26.

If the retailer buys one case of 10 NIGs:

The same arguments apply as above, except the retailer will expect a bulk discount and the price should, therefore, be somewhere between the £25-£26 for a single item and the £22.50 available for direct bulk purchase, say £24.

If the retailer buys two or more cases of NIGs:

In this case Tradeace has to beat Acme's direct price of £22.50 or the retailer will go direct. Thus a price in the range £22.49 to £19.50 is appropriate.

Gizmo Exercise E: — model answer retailer pricing

Cost of purchase of product: 5,000 × £19.50 is £97,500;
Cost of promotion £5,000.

Total costs £102,500.

Sales will be 1000 NIGs per month (for each of the three non-sale months), with 2000 sold in the sale month.

Revenue for non-sale months is therefore 3,000 × £23.99 = £71,970.

As Oklahoma wants to make £10,000 profit then the total revenue must exceed costs by this figure. Costs are £102,000, plus £10,000 required profit, being £112,000. Revenue from non-sale months will account for £71,970, thus the revenue required in the sale month (2000 NIGs) is £40,030 and the price that can be charged is, therefore, £20.01 (although Oklahoma would be wise to drop the 1p and maybe even move to £19.99 as this would psychologically move below the £20 level).

APPENDIX 5

Raymond and Partners Exercise A: — Model answer pricing and revenue maximisation

A) The daily rate charge will be £413, being the total cost divided by the number of working days. If they want to make £15,000 profit then the rate must be increased by £15,000 divided by 300 days, ie an extra £50 per day, raising the rate to £453.
B) The effect of one partner being out for 200 days at £250 per day will be to bring in £50,000 of revenue. Thus, the other two partners have to earn (£124,000 – £50,000, ie £740,000. This figure divided by 200 days gives a daily rate of £370.

If they still require to make £15,000 profit then only the two partners not on the big job can increase their rates (by £75 per day).

This answer illustrates the fact that cost plus pricing depends not only on the fixed cost base but also on variable costs.

Raymond and Partners Exercise B: — model answer market-related pricing

This is a difficult question to answer, but RandP clearly do not need to drop their price as low as £42,000 as the last time the client paid £45,000. However, they need to ensure that they are perceived to have a price advantage over the last winning firm, so they should bid below £45,000, say £44,000 or even £44,500.

The phrase they use should include the following points:

- their skill and track record in the area in question;
- their suitability for the work;
- their flexibility in pricing (ie if pushed they might consider dropping the price without reducing their input).

You should always state the benefits to the client in detail.

Raymond and Partners Exercise C: — model answer competitive pricing

This is a difficult question to answer, as it rather depends on the flow of information between markets. However, if RandP continue to offer one set of prices they will be too cheap in one market and too expensive in the other, which is, of course, uncompetitive.

If they offer a standard higher price, then their local government buyers will have to receive a very steep discount on each job, which may lead them to question how the firm does its business, and there is always the danger that this information will 'leak' to financial sector clients, thus causing them to ask for similar discounts.

If two price lists are prepared then the danger is again that information leakage can occur.

In practice, when faced with this dilemma, many service sector firms choose not to publish a price list at all and simply quote each job separately, thus minimising the chance of a client knowing the actual rate. They also sometimes charge specific people (who are known to be specialists in a certain area) out at higher prices.

References and further reading

Blight, D and Shafto, T (1989) *Microeconomics*, Hutchinson, London.
Collier, R (1995) *Profitable Product Management,* Butterworth-Heinemann, Oxford.
Hawkins, A and Turney, C (1995) *Cost Analysis,* Management Pocket Books, London.
Hawkins, A and Turney, C (1995) *The Managing Budgets Pocketbook,* Management Pocket Books, London.
Hawkins, A and Turney, C (1995) *The Balance Sheet Pocketbook,* Management Pocket Books, London.
Kotler, P (1994) *Principles of Marketing*, Prentice Hall, London.
Kotler, P (1994) *Marketing Management,* Prentice Hall, London.
Porter, M (1980) *Competitive Strategy,* Free Press, New York.
Porter, M (1985) *Competitive Advantage,* Free Press, New York.
Ruffin, R and Gregory, P (1990) *Principles of Microeconomics,* Harper Collins, USA.
Russell-Jones, N and Fletcher, A (1994) *Marketing for Success,* Kogan Page, London.
Russell-Jones, N (1995) *The Managing Change Pocketbook,* Management Pocket Books, London.
Russell-Jones, N and Fletcher, A (1996) *The Marketing Pocketbook,* Management Pocket Books, London.
Sudgen, A and Holmes, G (1996) *Interpreting Company Reports and Accounts,* Hutchinson and Dyer, London.

INDEX

References in italic indicate figures and tables.